SH

A CL

A CLEAN BREAK

A CLEAN BREAK

MY STORY

Christophe Bassons

with Benoît Hopquin

Translated by Peter Cossins

BLOOMSBURY

LONDON · NEW DELHI · NEW YORK · SYDNEY

Bloomsbury Sport
An imprint of Bloomsbury Publishing Plc

50 Bedford Square
London
WC1B 3DP
UK

1385 Broadway
New York
NY 10018
USA

www.bloomsbury.com

First published in Great Britain 2014
This paperback edition published 2015

British Library Cataloguing-in-Publication Data
A catalogue record for this book is available from the British Library.

Library of Congress Cataloguing-in-Publication data has been applied for.

ISBN: PB: 978-1-4729-1038-7
       ePub: 978-1-4729-1037-0

2 4 6 8 10 9 7 5 3 1

Printed and bound in Great Britain by CPI Group (UK) Ltd, Croydon CR0 4YY

MIX
Paper from
responsible sources
FSC® C020471

To find out more about our authors and books visit www.bloomsbury.com.
Here you will find extracts, author interviews, details of forthcoming events
and the option to sign up for our newsletters.

Contents

Prologue

I remained silent for a long time. I pedalled without saying a word. I shut myself away in the peloton and kept my counsel. For almost three years, all that came from me were sighs when the climbs got steep, my legs got tight, my rivals were pitiless and my breathing got laboured. I stoically endured all the excesses of the cycling world that I so wanted to be part of. Initially, when my nose was all but pinned to my bars because of that effort, I didn't see anything. Then I pretended I couldn't see anything. I held my words back. I needed every little bit of breath I could muster to stay with the multi-coloured convoy as it sped along the roads. I did notice it getting faster and faster, even when those policing the sport claimed that it had been slowed down.

I even felt happy to be experiencing this wild adventure. The whirr of bearings lulled my thinking. I heard chains clicking up and down the gears and thought I could detect the magical hymn of the so-called convicts of the road, of whom I was a proud member. I didn't realise that it was actually the muted murmuring of a prison, masking the cries for help emanating from the deepest of dungeons. The wind that whistled in my ears gave me the feeling of freedom. These familiar sounds hid my doubts – in those moments when I wasn't simply too exhausted to have them.

I cried a lot during those long months. I cried in pain on the bike and then with impotent rage beyond the finish line, or at least on those occasions when I didn't abandon beforehand. I reasoned that suffering gives cycling its nobility. My tears were providing sustenance for its legends, preventing them from withering away. Come on, kid! Forget the arrows that pierce your legs every time you stand on the pedals. Take a look around you! Everyone else must be going through the same torture and yet they are not letting it show. They are braver than you. Look at these impassive faces. They've not even got their mouths open, even when on the toughest gradients. They're not grimacing at all. Admire their ability to control their suffering even in adversity. How do they do it? They must be working harder than you, you slacker!

I flogged myself. I increased my training load. I sweated even more on my favourite roads in the Tarn, telling myself that the water seeping out of my pores couldn't now flow as tears from my eyes.

To be honest, it was this that really bothered me: not only were the other riders not crying on their bikes, but they weren't sweating either. They were still dry at the finish, bone dry in fact, while my jersey was drenched.

I didn't know that giving every little bit of sweat was not enough. You also needed to give blood.

I didn't say anything when I finally grasped the extent of the fraud. I had known about doping since I first started to race. As an amateur, I didn't really believe what was being said about it. It seemed abstract, overrated, nothing less than cheating. After turning professional, I discovered how effective these potions were. Above all, I learned how the corrupt use of medical products had become inextricably linked not just to achieving great success, but even to everyday riding.

Cyclists are always ready to trot out the same expression: *faire le métier* – doing the job. I thought that this principle signified a rider devoting himself entirely to his career, by training with complete commitment, following a strict diet, and maintaining a disciplined lifestyle. This was certainly how I applied myself, being what I thought was a complete professional. I thought I was doing the job correctly, but I was told I wasn't. I was mistaken about the meaning of this precept. As it stands, the phrase is a huge understatement and also quite hypocritical. It would be far more accurate if it said: 'Do anything and everything for the job.' Or, better still: 'Flog yourself into the ground for the job.'

I wasn't ready to do all that was required. I accepted the need to rein in my appetite, to berate myself for any indolence, and to lead a nomadic existence, torturing my body for half of the year on the road. But I refused to surrender my honesty, to sacrifice my health on the altar of victory. During those years of anonymity, that was where I fell short as a cyclist, but it was what made me proud as a man.

My rejection of absolutely everything the job entailed went well beyond simple concern about putting a needle in my arm and the poison that it would pump into my veins. I've never been capable of cheating in order to win. I use the word 'capable' purposely because of my complete inability in this regard. It's not simply a matter of choice. My education and upbringing – and also my bad temper, my hopeless tendency towards contradiction and my fanatical individualism – created a barrier that made me impervious to any temptations. To use a medical analogy, these characteristics created antibodies that have protected me. This in-built antidote allowed me to stick to my categorical refusal, while others, who are no worse than me as characters, simply could not hold out any longer. I'm not a hero, just someone incapable of yielding, who is constrained by certain taboos and a certain concept of victory, sport and life in general.

At that time, I didn't say anything. I didn't feel the need to. I was sure I was going to succeed without needing to resort to subterfuge. I believed I had enough ability to take me to the very top. I didn't need a chemical crutch. I was just into my twenties, an age when you feel heroic. I thought I was in one of those trashy novels where the main character overcomes heavily armed adversaries with his fists alone. Virtue always triumphs. Children rejoice, women swoon, men laud their saviour, while the hint of a smile can be seen on the face of the Herculean hero as the baddies lay scattered all around. I could see myself in exactly that role, with a healthy glint in my eye and my arms full of flowers, saying: 'I am happy to have won. I hope to do as well next time.'

But the great history of cycling is not that kind of swashbuckling tale. I had to submit to a fate that I'd thought I could brush aside as easily as I could my opponents. Without doping, I couldn't achieve anything, or at least not very much. Having initially failed to finish races, I then managed to do so, but was utterly defeated. The hardest thing to take was those races where I performed well. I came away from them full of regret. The incentive to succumb to temptation was strong and never-ending, like a huge press slowly crushing the toughest metals until they are in the required shape. Being part of such an insidious set-up made me question convictions that I thought were deeply rooted and inseparable from my being. Doping myself would have meant disowning myself. And yet I did almost betray myself. I wavered. I had injections, three or four times. I injected myself with water and glucose. On another occasion, I was tempted to take a shot of caffeine. The needle missed my vein. But what did it matter? I tried to do it, even though the jab missed its target. I saw this willingness to take supplements as a betrayal and, above all, as a potential first step on a very slippery slope, even though the products concerned were harmless.

I was on the verge of complete collapse, but love arrived just in time. I met Pascale. She became part of my struggle, and everything became easier with two of us on board. She released me from the morbid isolation into which I was sinking. She found the right words when they needed to be said. When I was demoralised, her support was a wonderful balm. She shored up my resolve, even when it was shaken to its foundations.

So I was able to hold out. I remained uncompromising but, I admit, mute. The same arrogance that enabled me to cling on to the ideal of riding clean prevented me from condemning loud and clear the little tricks and big scams within the sport. I was engaged in a personal battle.

Thanks to some heightened feeling of distress, I believed that I was the only one interested in this issue. For the public, at that time, doping was a dim shadow cast across cycling, but one which in no way tarnished the vivid colours of the riders they cheered on from the roadsides. Spectators used to say, 'Their sport is so hard,' and offered absolution along with applause. Worse still, fans would say, 'They are all doped,' which was intellectually convenient. This prejudice enabled fans to let their champions off lightly and celebrate their victories without restraint. The idea that there might be guys among the also-rans who were trying to compete despite a considerable handicap would have spoiled their fun. Forget about the outsider who refused to go with the flow: that was his problem. Don't bother us with thoughts of these wet blankets and, above all, don't do anything to undermine our childlike happiness.

Nobody wanted to see anything or know anything. At least that is what I thought then, walled in by my own resentment. I was wrong, and what happened later would prove that to me. The concern that many of those onlookers showed towards me, even as I was thinking they were as about as interested in my fate as a cow is in a passing train, leaves me feeling confused now. I am ashamed of feeling so desperate about the state of humanity simply because I no longer expected anything of those in the cycling *milieu*.

My solitude made me bitter. I thought I was nothing more than a rider who had been written off, one of the completely misunderstood athletes who end up forgotten. I let both the hypocrites and those naïve souls embellishing falsely achieved glory jabber on, without attempting to refute their nonsense. I knew that some successes had not been fairly come by, but was careful not to criticise. In spite of the peloton's other failings I respected its code of *omertà*.

I had other things to do besides pour my heart out. I was trying to survive in the peloton, or at least to stay with it. That was the only way to justify a salary which some felt I didn't have any right to at all. At our hotels each evening, my poor performances earned me reproaches, gibes, snide comments and, worst of all, the disappointment of those who still believed in me a little. I accepted what came my way, or at least I gave the impression I accepted it. In my heart of hearts, I could clearly see I was fighting a losing battle. My professional days were numbered. I would soon be ejected, having reached the end of the road and the end of my contract. My departure was imminent. My epitaph was already being prepared: 'He had the talent but he didn't do the job correctly.' Make of that what you will. My ejection from cycling would be discreet. I was going to be chased out through the sport's back door, just as others who had thought they could win without losing their soul had been chased out before me.

As you would expect in that situation, I would have tiptoed away. Losers don't go looking for publicity. All that I had to my credit was victory in a minor Breton race and some decent performances in some other second-level races; results like these are hardly going to leave a mark for posterity and certainly aren't going to enable you to thumb your nose at the sport's champions. Would my denials and accusations have been seen as anything other than the ramblings of a sore loser?

The police just managed to grab me when I was sinking without trace, like those captains in operettas who salute as they go down with their ship. They saved me or, if I am to be more precise about my thoughts at the time, they granted me a reprieve that I still savour completely and with the relish of someone who has been miraculously cured. The 1998 Tour de France became my salvation just as it was a nightmare for others. I ended up as one of the moral victors, even though I wasn't even on the list of starters in Ireland. I had even given up hope of ever playing a walk-on part in that race, which sets a seal on a career.

I was astounded to see the Tour turned upside down. In my eyes, whether you decided to use banned products or not was a question of sporting ethics and, to a greater extent, human philosophy. I didn't suspect that it was a point of law, and the guilty parties didn't either. Thanks to their feeling of impunity, these fraudsters had forgotten they were cheats and perhaps even delinquents. They shamelessly swindled the public. Justice reminded them that they had also broken the law. She blew their cover away, exposing them for what they were: the peloton had become the realm of junkies.

I was shocked by the police raids that followed the arrest of Willy Voet, the soigneur who worked for the same Festina team that employed me, and the searches, interrogations, medical examinations and subsequent imprisonments. I can bear witness to what they were like: I ended up in custody at the police station in Lille and had several samples taken in their laboratory. I didn't enjoy the experience. Some of those who went through the same thing denounced the brutality of the police's methods. But I think that kind of electric shock was necessary. The cycling *milieu* was so corrupt there was no hope of it reforming itself.

I am not happy writing these lines about how this success was achieved using strong-arm tactics. However, the insidious return of corrupt behaviour and the rather sinister normalisation of this kind of conduct, which has occurred since the Black Marias were removed from the scene, only confirms my opinion. My grandfather was a Spanish refugee, an anti-Francoist Republican, who learned all about life and its many twists and turns during the civil war that tore that country apart. He taught me to cherish justice but to maintain a safe distance from those who enforce it. Peace of mind is as noble as fear of the police is vile, he told me. My decision not to dope was always mine alone and was not something that was forced upon me. I think it is this claim that makes me stand out and that attracts annoyance at best and, at worst, the hostility of those who yielded only when threatened with police action.

I am grateful to the police for having proved and revealed to the wider world my integrity and, even though this may upset some, my singularity. The fact that I had earned my colours went down on record. Several of my team-mates, who were given the third degree, absolved me from any wrongdoing while at the same time admitting what they had been up to. 'Christophe Bassons wasn't doping. That can also be backed up by his results,' admitted Armin Meier. Willy Voet beatified me: 'Christophe Bassons? A saint!'

If it hadn't been for one or two mistakes on my part, I would have ended up with a halo. The judicial investigations progressed. The blacker the picture they painted, the whiter and more virginal I appeared! Inevitably, I finally ended up being noticed. Journalists were interested in me and sketched out an over-obliging portrait of this noble savage. They tracked me down to a hotel room in the Alps that had been transformed into an altitude simulation chamber. I was desperately trying to boost my blood values there without resorting to banned products. It seemed interesting to try, but slightly pointless at the same time. Those two weeks I spent inside a sealed room did more for my notoriety than all my years of medical abstinence.

Beyond that, however, what I had to say was of little interest, I'm afraid. It was a time of sordid revelations and staggering confessions. Talk of illicitly boosted haemoglobin flowed through newspaper columns. All I could offer was talk of my innocence and some mollifying, if confused thoughts. I did not have much to say except that I wasn't doping. My natural shyness restricted me to rather soppy comments. Brave boy that I was, when it came to everyone else, I didn't want to heap scorn on anyone.

My moral rectitude meant that I scarcely had anything interesting to offer that would titillate the general public. Consequently, microphones were pointed at more forthcoming parties. The period that followed the 1998 Tour was one of repentance. Penitents confessed their sins and revealed their acts of contrition. There was any number of confessions in the press. The more recalcitrant still managed to find ways to deny the obvious, but court hearings provided proof of institutionalised doping. The whole affair grew and grew, like ripples on the water after a pebble has been tossed into a lake. Gossip, the settling of scores and denunciations flourished. The great family of cycling was tearing itself apart in public. It was like one those books by Georges Simenon when the appearance of Inspector Maigret shatters the uncertain alliances that depend solely on what can't be said, on shameful secrets.

My place in this story was as the dumb bumpkin, the innocent up from the sticks who has seen everything but has understood nothing. I was different, as they say of those who are simple-minded. I had nothing to hide, and nothing to reveal either. But I have learned a lot. The detailed descriptions that others gave of certain practices have subsequently provided me with the missing clues to puzzles of years gone by. The forthright books written by the likes of Willy Voet, the soigneur at the heart of the Festina affair, and Erwann Menthéour, one of my colleagues in the peloton, weren't all that revelatory for me, but did serve as decoding devices that illuminated what was going on. Fifteen years later, the revelations and confessions about Lance Armstrong and his seven Tour de France victories are providing me with new details. I now use them as a means of establishing order in my mind, giving my memories a thread on which to hang. A scene that had initially been shot through a door that was only slightly ajar now appears full frame to me. I have the keys to decipher everything that was happening in the periphery of the shot.

The 1998 Tour provided me with a half-decent profile among the sport's fans. It also restored some of my worth among many within the cycling *milieu*. My career, which had seemed stillborn due to a lack of results, was suddenly revived. I was reallocated a role. I was the guarantor of the sport's future. I didn't mind that. I was convinced that cycling was on the road to a speedy recovery, and of the sincerity of its redemption.

I was stupid. It very quickly became apparent that the whole game was rigged. Cycling wasn't being reformed. It was simply adapting to new contingencies imposed from outside. I was nothing more than a figleaf, or even one of those masking agents liars use to conceal their fraud.

I didn't have to take a stand against this treachery. Others who were much better known did so instead. Jean-Cyril Robin sounded the alarm about *le cyclisme à deux vitesses* – cycling at two speeds. Cédric Vasseur also stood up with his diatribe against hypocrites. Several notable figures backed up their comments, starting with the president of the French Cycling Federation at the time, Daniel Baal. Over on the sidelines, I could only nod in agreement. They were much more impressive orators leading the cause. That suited me.

I could see boxes of drugs reappearing, but I didn't notice the silence returning quite as obviously. A shell slowly came down over the sport. As the races went by, criticism became less vehement and then died out, just like the embers in a fire.

The 1999 Tour arrived and was dubbed the Tour of Renewal. What had hitherto been implicit instructions became more formal: silence in the ranks! This was all part of rehabilitating cycling in the eyes of the masses, although it was perhaps as much about rehabilitating everyone's payslip. I understood the role that had been assigned to me. I had to bear witness to the good medical practices that had been put in place. My silence would be interpreted as a tacit agreement. Any praise that put my peers in the clear would have been very well received.

I had a lot to gain: I was owed a *bon de sortie*, as they say in the sport. This piece of cycling jargon is used to describe the right to roam that the peloton grants to a rider who wants to escape from the pack. Marc Madiot, my directeur sportif at La Française des Jeux, had suggested to me before the start of the race that I should spare myself as much as possible until we reached the section between the Alps and the Pyrenees. The profile of these so-called transition stages suited me, he said. A great connoisseur of the ways of the cycling world, he had no doubt concluded the rest of the pack would adopt a conciliatory attitude towards me. An exploit by Bassons, better known as 'Babasse' by his peers, would have been a good piece of propaganda during the Tour. If 'Mr Clean' managed to win, it would have been a sign that cycling had changed for the better …

Earlier in that year of 1999, I had a foretaste of this at another event, the Dauphiné Libéré, a stage race that serves as preparation for the Tour de France. I had claimed a stage victory thanks to a long breakaway, and it was hailed as a sign of cultural renovation occurring within cycling after the trauma of the Festina affair. I now know, thanks particularly to recent revelations made by Jonathan Vaughters, the overall winner and a team-mate of Lance Armstrong at that time, that while I was pedalling like a madman at the front of the race, a conclave was taking place within the peloton to decide whether or not it was a good thing for me to win this stage. These discussions had nothing to do with tactical considerations relating to my place in the overall standings. The focus was whether they should allow a rider who had refused to follow the peloton's rules to win the stage.

To stay in everyone's good books and ensure I got those precious *bons de sortie*, I had to say that everything was better in the bunch. I had to lie. I had to give my blessing to the farce in which I was a shameful performer. I actually had to disavow everything that I had been up to that point. There was a *quid pro quo*, based on me giving false testimony.

So I started to talk. Initially I professed just minor reservations. Then I became increasingly categorical. The dam broke. The words came in an unstoppable flow. Years of mute frustration caused me to boil over and swept away any reservations. I had kept my mouth shut for too long. Anger at the farce that got under way each morning and the fatigue that consumed me each evening steeled my resolve. The clear threats and the cold-shouldering I received, far from bringing me into line, fuelled my resentment. They transformed me into a desperado. Some of the lycra-clad hoodlums dubbed me 'Babasse the Balance', insinuating that I was sitting in judgement on the sport. I had nothing left to lose. Journalists kept coming to speak to me as my thirst to get everything off my chest remained unquenched. I'd been anointed as a just man during the 1998 Tour. In spite of myself, the 1999 Tour transformed me into a dispenser of justice. I had to proclaim the truth, whatever the cost. In the midst of this hostile environment, only the need to talk kept me in the saddle. As soon as they had managed to silence me, after 12 days of bravado, I fell from my perch.

I was surprised by the impact my statements had. Today I am re-reading what I said in newspaper clippings that are already yellowing with age. I would not change a single bit of it. However, I have the feeling that I wasn't saying anything that wasn't known already. I am surprised at the anger that my words caused, but this solitary little voice within the pack was only confirming the reality that nobody wanted to hear. I had infringed the golden rule that family disputes are always settled behind closed doors. I had laid everything bare to the outside world, which my peers regarded as the enemy.

Indeed, I think the scope of my remarks was also reinforced by the emptiness of those made by my peers: the vacuity of what they were saying was staggering. The crime I was guilty of wasn't giving vent to my frustrations, but doing so at an inopportune moment, when the idea had been to make everyone think that there was nothing more to say.

I was talking too much. The other riders criticised me constantly. But why did they remain silent, and why are they still silent? Doesn't the general public have the right to know what they talk about when they sit defeated around the dinner table each evening?

I didn't take part in the 2000 Tour de France. My new team, Jean Delatour, didn't figure on the list of those invited. We deserved to be there on the strength of our performances beforehand, but the director of the Tour de France, Jean-Marie Leblanc, didn't want us there. I think the fact that I was in the team had something to do with it. The team's management had stated its intention to include me in its line-up. This was an intolerable provocation. Since my escapades the previous year, I had become a figurehead when it came to the issue of doping. Consequently, I was not 'a welcome guest'. I use the term expressly, as it was the one employed by Monsieur Leblanc to justify the ejection of Richard Virenque in 1999. Despite this, Virenque was reinstated at the request of the international federation and, ultimately to the great relief of organisers, through some impressive legal wizardry. The Tour of Renewal kicked off with a neat sleight of hand.

In 2000, no miracle took place enabling me to take part in the race again. Bassons' ears didn't pop up out of a hat as if by magic. The wizards of cycling wanted to make me disappear completely in a puff of smoke.

So I remained on the sidelines. The Tour rolled on without me, carrying less of a burden than if I'd been there.

I hardly followed the progress of the race. I knew the plot in advance and the admiring notices it would receive. In fact, my team organised a training camp. We rode when the race was being broadcast on TV. This snub mitigated the frustration we felt.

It is not easy to escape the Tour. I heard the sighs of relief that the organisers and their cronies let out as the race's survivors paraded up and down the Champs-Elysées. Confidence has returned, the experts all chorused. It was the Tour of Renaissance, they affirmed, just as the 1999 race had been the Tour of Renewal. Their relief should have been pleasing to witness. However, nobody was there to contradict them. My absence certainly contributed to this newfound serenity. They did the right thing in not inviting me, because I would certainly have denounced the deception being enacted once again. How would I have been able to lie about it? I would have talked about it, written about it and shouted about it, even though plenty of people would not have wanted to believe me, preferring instead to be lulled into a false sense of security.

I am going to have to talk about this again, since nobody else has opted to do so. There may be a few people reading what I have to say who will understand me.

I only took part in one Tour, the 1999 edition. It wasn't a full Tour, though, more of a half-Tour in fact. Twelve days. I have two memories of it: the crowds on the first day and my loneliness on the last.

I am writing these lines for all those people who provide a guard of honour on the roads in July. I would like to make them understand that they are right to be there, that cycling is a wonderful sport, but that they are mistaken in some of what they think, and to enable them to see that the sport has misled them. The public has been hoodwinked about their idols. As they fall over each other in the rush for plastic trinkets that the advertising caravan sends flying their way, the fans have accepted riders who have been flung at them in a similar way but who are damaged goods. But how do you make them comprehend that what they are seeing is fake?

People congregate on the roads in July to celebrate the occasion. Opportunities like these are so rare. It is easy to understand why they rush out and watch the Tour as it shoots right past their door, why they jump with joy in expectation of its arrival. I once saw two quite elderly men fighting in a ditch over a plastic water bottle a rider had thrown away. In the end, one left with the bottle-top, the other with the bottle. Their behaviour was childish, but spectators do become children again when the Tour passes by.

But I sometimes wonder whether this naïvety doesn't encourage some people to take advantage. I would like to see the massed ranks stop bickering over shabby trinkets and start assessing their champions with an adult eye, and the fans using their good judgement to identify who is being honest with them and who is taking them for a ride.

Nowadays fame in cycling is worth its weight in gold. Some riders have understood this and cultivated the public's affections in order to ensure greater financial rewards from their sponsor. This situation obviously falsifies the relationship between spectators and the subject of their admiration, removing all sincerity from it. Popularity is becoming a self-supporting business, an enterprise in itself in fact.

I was cast out of the peloton in 2001. Maddened by that, I even sold my bike six months later. But now I'm back in the saddle once again, although purely for pleasure. My bike is not my livelihood, but it doesn't mean any less to me because of that. I will not dwell on the pleasure I feel when I'm spinning along on the road, intoxicated with the intensity of the effort I'm making, listening to my heart pounding. Millions of people experience this same intoxication. They understand exactly what

I am feeling. All I would add is that this rather rudimentary object, which can be difficult to handle, has survived into the era of the car. The bicycle is not just a means of getting around, it is a life-affirming activity that stimulates our bodies, enabling us to understand both our capacity as human beings and our limits.

Why is it that, at the age of almost 39, I still get such incredible enjoyment from riding a bike? When I was a professional rider, why did I persevere in that atmosphere of intense competition despite disapproving of it? Why did I get real pleasure from carving out a career path in the midst of that multi-coloured pack that antagonised me so much? I have long wondered about this paradox.

I found the answer by chance when reading the *Manuel de l'Educateur* (the sport instructor's manual). The chapter dealing with motivation really enlightened me. I am a hedonist when it comes to sport. The only reason I do it is for my own satisfaction. I put a lot into cycling because of the pleasure it brings me, because of experiences that make me feel so alive. The only reason I want to progress is for my own satisfaction. When competing I don't assess my performance by any measure other than the enjoyment I derive from it. Consequently, I would be happy to finish a place lower in the classification as long as I had beaten my personal best time.

Cycling also enables me to know myself better. I can explore the limits of my body and mind. This exercise in introspection is an end in itself for me, not a means for achieving success. I am constantly seeking to push my physiological and psychological parameters. Every step forwards is a victory – the only one that counts.

I think this is another reason for my aversion to doping, and probably the most important. Filling myself with drugs went against my approach. It would have cut all physical sensation from me, and consequently any pleasure. I didn't envy those robots packed with painkillers who climbed passes without feeling even the slightest itch. I didn't envy those pharmaceutically bloated machines that didn't know if it was really their own legs doing the pedalling or some alien who had slipped into their skin. I know that any outside assistance would provoke the same frustration within me as adding a motor to my bike. If mobylettes had been allowed on the Tour, I would still have stuck to my bicycle.

For me, opponents were and still are nothing more than a means to push my body to its very limits. I have a competitive spirit, but its purpose is much more about allowing me to improve rather than enabling me to win.

Fifteen years ago, my dream was to escape in the opening kilometres, to hold off the riders chasing behind me, drawing on every ounce of my reserves, and to collapse on the line without having either the strength or the desire to raise my arms. An easy success – one that had been bought, obtained via dubious associations, or by the use of some obscure pharmacy – was of no interest to me.

While victory was beautiful in my eyes, I loathed hearing people say, 'Only victory is beautiful.' On the other hand, the idea of being 'a good winner' is one that I revere.

Bearing this in mind, I think my pleasure was egocentric but not egotistical. If I was happy, then I could make spectators happy. They would surely get a lot more satisfaction from seeing athletes commit themselves fully rather than watching races where something is held back, or even faked. Isn't giving everything to the public the duty of the artist, and doesn't this apply even more in the case of sporting champions?

I don't completely agree with Baron Pierre de Coubertin, the father of the modern Olympics, whose creation has so betrayed him since his death. The most important thing is not taking part. It is to surpass yourself. That was why I enjoyed rubbing shoulders with the world's best. They provided me with a spur. But the only man I had to beat was myself. Competitive desire was inherent in me.

For many of the rest, the motivation was and still is extrinsic. Many of those I rode with and many of those I watch on television today view a rival as someone they must dominate. This stems from their experiences within the peloton. Victory is a way of establishing a comparative advantage, to boost a rider's superiority over the pack.

When a group flies by at 50 kilometres per hour, spectators only see a blaze of colours. They do not have time to pick out their favourites. Only success differentiates one rider from the rest. The commentator will say that the champion distinguished himself today: the meaning of that could not be clearer. Wins make it easier to divide the group, to have some riders stand out from the crowd. Beyond the race itself, wins also enable a rider to acquire a quite different social status. They offer fame, money, recognition. The indistinctness of the peloton effectively becomes a mirror of social mediocrity from which escape is essential at any cost. Doping is just another means to achieve it.

I was a bit of a one-off. I didn't claim to be either better or worse than the rest: I have just explained how this type of hierarchy made no difference to me. In his book, *Secret Défonce: Ma vérité sur le dopage*, Erwann Menthéour described me as 'extraterrestrial'. This was how the people in this two-wheeled world viewed me. But that perspective is skewed. If one person is riding normally and another is doping, which should we think of as the Martian?

If a polling agency were to conduct a survey among the population, 95 per cent of people would say that they would refuse to poison themselves in order to win. When I became part of the pro cycling scene, I would guess 95 per cent of professional riders were doping. (In the United States, a study conducted among top athletes showed that three out of four athletes said they would be happy to die before they were 40 if it meant getting an Olympic medal.) I find this disparity between popular opinion and the attitude of sporting champions appalling. I believe top-level sport has been usurped by people who are not necessarily the most talented or the strongest, but are simply the most determined or the most oblivious to danger. Sorcerers' apprentices who pretend to be doctors are then responsible for providing these kamikaze athletes with the physical means to achieve their goals. Although life expectancy is increasing within the general population, it is continuing to fall in cycling.

It is this situation, which is suicidal for the athletes involved and for my sport in the long term, which motivated me to write a book. In 2000, when I was 26, I wrote the first version of this memoir knowing I would be condemned by the peloton. My initial comments were also my testament as a professional, as by that point my situation seemed increasingly precarious, and was perhaps even untenable. I should probably have prefaced my remarks by declaring: 'I, Christophe Bassons, being of sound mind and judgement …'

Even though the deception carried out during the Armstrong years, when I was the pariah, has since been proven, I am returning at the age of almost 39 to this autobiography with the intention of providing a clinical examination of the cycling *milieu*.

I have chosen to use the word '*milieu*' because it seems most accurate to me in many of its senses. The peloton acts as a club, a framework for life, an ambience even. In many ways, it also seems to live up to the pejorative definition of the word: a group of individuals living on the margins of the law.

Cycling still offers lessons for life, drawn from city streets and the winding roads of the countryside. Unfortunately, this education is less poetic than it once seemed. Cycling hastened my move towards maturity. It enabled me to have a clear view of my life and what I wanted to do when I was in my twenties, at an age when other youngsters are floundering. But the few years of adversity I spent in the peloton taught me so much more! I saw so many things that I feel there is a lot I can usefully share.

My story can serve as an example. When I say that, please don't take it as boastfulness. I don't mean example in the sense of self-satisfaction in one's own achievements, but in the sense of serving as a lesson or warning. I do not think I should be viewed as a model to follow, a reference point, but simply as a good example. I need to explain what doping means for cycling, how it became not only a physical imperative but also a moral obligation. I have to explain the chain of events that led me to the point where my choice was to dope or to quit. I want to describe the degree of coercion that permeated the professional world, both to the youngsters who are coming into the sport with the duty to change old habits and to the old stagers who had the good fortune to live in healthier times. I want to relate how a tender boy blessed with some talent and a real passion for cycling, to the point where he wanted to make a career of it, found himself caught up in a mechanism shaped not by the toughness of the sport, but by the men within it. I particularly want to detail the steps on the pathway that leads someone to inject himself, not in order to win, but simply to exist within this family.

I want to shed a little more light on the hypocrisy that I have experienced. This is done so that, in future, a kid whose love for the bike leads him into the peloton doesn't end up experiencing the same disappointment I did.

It is for the sake of that boy or girl that I have to speak out.

Chapter 1

Love and *l'Eau Claire*

I became a professional rider on 1 January 1996. I was 21 years old. I was talented. I was ambitious. I was eager to be a success and convinced I would achieve this. I was one of those snotty-nosed kids who occasionally blossom and go on to become champions.

I had been courted by cycling's elite for the previous six months. In June 1995, while I was doing my military service with the Joinville battalion, the unit that has traditionally welcomed budding athletes (including footballers Michel Platini and Bixente Lizarazu, tennis star Henri Leconte, and cyclists Laurent Fignon and Richard Virenque), Yvon Madiot asked to meet me. He told me he had spotted me at the Circuit des Mines, where I had just won the opening stage. Generally, only the sport's cognoscenti are aware of this race, which takes place in France's eastern province of Lorraine and is considered a real test by directeurs sportifs because it allows talented young riders to cross swords with seasoned professionals. Yvon offered me the opportunity to sign a contract with the team he was putting together with his brother, Marc. The new outfit was set to be launched in 1996 and was sponsored by the La Française des Jeux lottery, a prosperous backer, who, it later became apparent, was a generous one too.

'You race like a rookie, but you interest me,' Yvon told me.

His offer caught me on the hop. Before meeting him, the idea of turning professional hadn't occurred to me. I had got my first racing licence in 1992 with the Union Vélocipédique de Mazamet, the club nearest to my home. I had joined them because the licence enabled you to get a reduction on the cost of entry to mountain bike events organised in the area. I was already showing I had impressive natural ability on the bike and was becoming more and more focused on the discipline. Some friends suggested that I give road racing a go. I took them up on that and began to stand out quite quickly. I won some races and earned myself a nickname – 'The Cannon'. I climbed up through the amateur ranks with ease, without stopping to wonder where this path was taking me. I continued with my university studies at the same time, with a view to finding myself a job. Consequently, I was surprised that someone was offering me the chance to make a living out of my hobby.

Over the following two months I got used to the idea. In fact, it wasn't long before I was viewing it with real enthusiasm. On 15 August, Yvon Madiot met up with me again during the French time trial championships at Les Herbiers in the Vendée. His project was taking shape; with a sizeable budget to play with, the team was destined to play a leading role. Madiot told me he had made contact with Bjarne Riis, the Danish rider who had just finished third in the Tour de France. He also mentioned that negotiations had been going on with the two Jalabert brothers, Laurent and Nicolas, who were not only from the same area as me, but had even emerged from my club. I also remembered the name of a German rider who was the same age as me. He was called Jan Ullrich. He had been the world amateur champion in 1993. He was a very promising boy. We both represented an investment in the future.

In order to convince me of the credibility of his project, Yvon Madiot also mentioned other riders, from both France and Italy, with a look of satisfaction on his face. I adopted what I hoped was a knowing expression as he recited a string of names as references. I didn't dare confess my ignorance of the sport for fear I might seem like a dimwit.

As much as cycling captivated me, watching a race on the television or perusing results in the paper bored me. My family simply weren't that interested in sport, and I rarely watched the Tour on television.

Sometimes I would cast a half-interested glance at a mountain stage or catch a glimpse of some coverage on the evening news, but on the small screen I was only able to pick out one rider from the labouring mass. That was Miguel Indurain, whose personality demanded my respect. He became my idol because of the aura he had, but I would have been totally incapable of reeling off his palmarès.

Everything that had gone before the Indurain era was unknown to me, shrouded in the mists of time, which cloaked for me the deeds of Fausto Coppi and Bernard Thévenet, Eddy Merckx and Laurent Fignon. Only Bernard Hinault stood out clearly from this muddled pantheon. Later on, I knocked Marc Madiot's self-esteem during the course of a meal when he was recounting a story about Paris–Roubaix.

'You won Paris–Roubaix?' I asked him.

'Are you taking the piss?'

'No, I'm not, honestly!'

'I won it twice, son!'

'My apologies, I didn't know.'

'Where have you been?' he asked, clearly upset that someone could be so naïve as to be unaware of the two biggest highlights of a career that he loved to talk about.

What I did retain, when reflecting on the long list of heavyweights mentioned by Yvon, was the simple fact that I had been chosen to be part of an esteemed assembly. I felt very proud of that. My self-esteem was also boosted by the terms of the contract. La Française des Jeux had offered me a two-year deal earning 25,000 francs gross per month. I made some enquiries after our first meeting and found out that the salary of a new pro was generally less than half this amount. Being offered such an attractive package meant much more than all the plaudits I had received. I ended up sharing unreservedly the fabulous opinion others had of me!

That same day I won the title and became the French amateur time trial champion. In this discipline, the rider's only rival is the clock, which means that it clearly establishes the intrinsic ability of each competitor. This success didn't help to get my feet back on the ground.

My new contract didn't go down well in one quarter. Michel Thèze, my coach at the Joinville battalion, was putting his own team together with a view to launching it the following season. He had been looking for backers for months.

At that time, French cycling was in a huge slump. Lots of teams were living on their wits, just scraping by, and they lived with the permanent fear that the sponsors they needed to enable them to keep going simply would not appear. As for the sponsors, they were cold-shouldering the sport despite the ongoing exploits of Laurent Jalabert, Luc Leblanc and Richard Virenque. Most of these riders had found sanctuary with foreign teams, based in Spain, Italy or Andorra, which had generous backers behind them.

Within this context of crisis, Michel Thèze had managed to get a number of investors in southern France to commit to establishing a team that would be called Force Sud. He was now trying to put together the roster for this team and was counting on me joining it.

When I told my coach I had already signed with a rival outfit, he went mad with rage, accusing me of deserting him. I was completely thrown by the virulence of his reaction and felt upset by it. The next day, after thinking it over, I reached a conclusion: the fact that my coach was so upset by my defection underlined my qualities even more. I was some kind of star who everyone wanted to get their hands on.

Two weeks later, I was hit by a bombshell. I received a call from an embarrassed Yvon Madiot. He told me his ship was not setting sail. Initially, I didn't understand.

'There won't be a team next season. The sponsor has withdrawn.'

My mind was swimming. I was reeling. I actually collapsed into a chair. I was so distracted I only half-listened to his explanations for the withdrawal. Yvon told me how Cyrille Guimard, who was also looking for financial backing for the following season, had hatched a plot designed to scupper the project. He told me about some ministers not agreeing with the deal, about scheming within the government.

The pursuit of sponsors was so fierce at that point that it wasn't simply a case of finding one of these rare birds. If you got your hands on one, you had to prevent it being pinched by a rival. The Madiot brothers and Guimard had hated each other for years. Yvon told me a few rather incoherent stories, characterised by rifts and low blows. I didn't understand anything about these long-standing feuds. I was aware of just one thing: our agreement was null and void. The young wolf was now without a contract.

I was completely distraught. It was the first setback I'd had since I'd thrown my leg over a bike. I railed against the betrayal. As an amateur, I simply rode the bike and I won. I was good, and without any other aspirations. But a dream opportunity had suddenly been laid before me, only to be killed off just as quickly. Three months earlier, I hadn't had the slightest idea of a professional career in cycling. Now it was my only aspiration. Was someone now going to prevent me from achieving my destiny?

Fortunately, Michel Thèze wasn't one to bear grudges. He offered me another chance to join him. I signed the contract immediately. The financial terms weren't as advantageous as those on the previous one. I was going to earn 15,000 francs gross per month, which was considerably less but still above average – not that I cared much about the money. The key thing was that I would finally be able to join the peloton, which had become my *raison d'être*, even before I'd had any experience of it.

Two days later, I received a call from Michel Gros, who introduced himself as the assistant directeur sportif at Festina. This team was based in Andorra and had been, and was still, home to some of the best French riders: Luc Leblanc, Jean-Cyril Robin, Richard Virenque, Pascal Lino. Details such as these might seem superfluous to many readers, but Michel still had to provide me with them. I can only repeat what I said before about my pathetic lack of knowledge. Gros had just found out that my agreement with La Française des Jeux had been rescinded. So he was offering me a two-year contract. His proposal was tempting, but I had just agreed another deal. Consequently, I had to turn him down. However, we agreed we would remain in touch.

In the space of three months, no fewer than three candidates had come forward with the aim of securing my services for their team. Being in such demand certainly inflated the ego of a country boy who had been sheltered from the temptations of the wider world up to that point. I soon forgot all about the false start with La Française des Jeux. However, it should have acted as a warning about the level of deceit within the sport and forced me to be more adult. But I was too full of myself to consider watching my step.

In September I won the world military time trial championship in Italy. The armies from some countries where conscription wasn't obligatory were quite open about bringing in talented riders for the events so that they could boost their prospects of success. I was shocked by such dubious practices. But they didn't prevent me from winning the title.

At that time, I viewed doping as nothing more than a minor irritation. I knew it went on in the amateur world, that it was a practice that some people fell back on. There were those who doped and there were those who didn't. But I hadn't thought about linking the practice with results, because I, Christophe Bassons, was winning without requiring even the slightest amount of illicit back-up.

I had seen the medical excesses that some of my companions at the Joinville battalion indulged in. They stuffed themselves with Guronsan, a stimulant, swallowing seven or eight tablets before a race. I'd also stumbled on some riders using early examples of the *flécheur*, a piston-like device fitted with a spring and slipped around a syringe. It could deliver subcutaneous injections as quickly as a wasp sting for those not keen on administering the needle themselves. This easy-to-use gadget enabled riders to look after themselves without requiring any assistance.

Novices would often faint when they first used them because of their heightened emotional state and the sudden nip of the needle. Then they would get used to it. I didn't really know what they were injecting themselves with: vitamin B12, iron, caffeine or something else. I heard a lot of talk about 'Keke', the nickname for Kenacort, which was a corticosteroid then in vogue.

I didn't ask for any explanations. Nobody offered me anything, and I wasn't bothered by what they had packed with their kit. I respected their right to make their own choices. I believed that feeling was mutual. I wasn't even that bothered about knowing that I had lost out to someone who was cheating. I was at the very same level as my rivals, I still relished taking them on and, when we weren't racing, still enjoyed fraternising with them.

As a world military champion, on my return to France I received a decoration from Charles Millon, the French defence minister, along with pole-vaulter Jean Galfione. The minister congratulated us for our successes in French national colours. My local MP presented me with another medal when I returned to the Tarn. I was fairly indifferent to being fêted like that. I gained pleasure from giving the best of myself and my victory had been a nice reward for the sacrifices I'd made. The baubles that were hung around my neck were only for the sake of etiquette. I imagine they must be lying around in a box somewhere now.

My only wish was to move quickly on, to enjoy my passion even more intensely. I couldn't wait to step up into the pro ranks, where I would be able to completely satisfy the simple need I had to give absolutely everything that I could. As well as experiencing a new environment, I was also going to discover myself. I prepared for the opportunity to explore the extent of my capacity as never before, to test myself in the ultimate competitive context, to advance my search to reach my absolute limit. I would have to bore down right into my body's core, dig out new reserves from my innermost depths, and unearth as yet unsuspected resources. I would go faster than I had ever gone before, so fast that no one would be able to follow me. I was pedalling on a cloud.

On 1 December 1995, I went to La Valentine, near Toulon, where Force Sud were having their first training camp. This first step filled me with excitement. I met my team-mates. There were a number of young guys and some older ones, such as Christophe Capelle, Thierry Bourguignon, Miguel Arroyo, Dominique Arnould and Pascal Lance. The self-assurance of these seasoned campaigners impressed me. They had the detached bearing of racers who had ridden the Tour de France and, therefore, knew the sport inside out. Just being with them gave me a taste of that elite I was on the verge of joining. Their faces showed signs of premature ageing, like anyone who has lived life more intensely than most mortals. Their skin was tanned by the elements that they encountered on the road, just like the old captains who sailed the seven seas. Their marble-white bodies were like a parchment on which I could pick out the scars left by the profession. I was ashamed of my baby-like skin, which betrayed my total lack of experience.

They only showed passing interest in the greenhorn who was gazing at them with such admiration. They were much more intent on assessing the potential of this new organisation. During the ups and downs of their careers they had experienced teams of every kind of level. They had known the opulence of outfits such as Castorama, from whom their directeur sportif, Cyrille Guimard, had squeezed absolutely every little resource, being the very capable businessman that he was. They had strayed into the impasse that beset Le Groupement, a team that emerged at the start of 1995 with world champion Luc Leblanc at its head: the façade came tumbling down six months later.

These old stagers immediately sensed Force Sud's lack of resources. They suspected that its finances were limited, which could mean difficulties at the end of each month and having to get by on credit. I noticed how they got gloomier the longer their analysis went on. They exchanged bitter remarks every time they noticed something that didn't add up. It was obvious to them that there was no chance of a smooth road ahead on a team with so many inherent failings. Their experience enabled them to pick all this up, whereas I could see only abundance.

I was bowled over by the kit that was handed to us when we arrived. In my club at Mazamet, I only had one jersey to last a whole year. Now I was collapsing under the weight of tracksuits, cycling shorts, gloves and socks. In my room, I went through all of the gear I had again and again, running my hands through it as if I'd just uncovered buried treasure. This impressive bundle of kit suggested to me that we were in for a long-running adventure. I didn't understand my team-mates' warnings. I understood them even less when I saw the equipment we'd be using. Brand new frames and an infinitive range of wheels, rings and sprockets left my jaw hanging. I couldn't wait to try these precious machines.

Before that, Michel Thèze summoned us to a welcome meeting. He made a few introductory remarks, then got down to the nitty gritty:

'I want to be absolutely clear – the use of EPO is totally forbidden here.'

Erythropoietin, or EPO. Nowadays, this molecule is so well known by the general public that it has become synonymous with doping, although wrongly I would say. Its efficiency had already been well established: the product increases the number of red blood cells that carry oxygen to the muscles, effectively topping up the body's fuel reserves. Thanks to this extra boost, the legs gain greater endurance and work more efficiently. Its secondary effects are less well known. By modifying the composition of blood plasma, this additive can lead to thrombosis and embolisms. By mathematical effect, it also diminishes the level of white blood cells, weakening the body's defence mechanisms and thus increasing the threat of illness. Since its use became embedded within sport at the end of the 1980s, this medicine designed for use on patients who have just undergone surgery has caused numerous deaths among athletes.

At the end of 1995, I wouldn't have been able to deliver such a biology lesson, although even now it's incomplete as the long-term effects of overdosage with EPO are still unknown. EPO didn't then have the notoriety that it does today, in the wake of numerous doping affairs that have raised universal awareness of it. These initials were being mentioned within the amateur ranks, but this panacea was still hidden behind a fog of lies that I wasn't intending to penetrate. Soon, however, I was going to be able to judge its effect, having seen actual evidence.

One of Force Sud's backers was a laboratory that was promoting homeopathic products. As a result, the riders were all taken to see a doctor nearby and he drew some blood from each of us. At the end of the training camp, we went back to his consulting room. The doctor had drawn up a balance sheet for each of us and handed it to us with a prescription for homeopathic medicines based on individual requirements.

Sitting in the waiting-room, I watched my team-mates return one by one with a plastic bag filled with medicines. I noticed an ironic grin on some faces as they examined the contents of their little bags. The jokes came thick and fast in between mocking laughter.

'This is the magic potion, guys.'

'These pills come from Lourdes.'

'With this, you will be able to beat the hour record.'

Then my turn came. After I had been told the results of the analysis, I was handed five or six boxes together with instructions on how to use the products.

'I don't agree with this,' I told the doctor.

'But it's as efficient as EPO!' he responded, mistaking the reason for my refusal.

'No, what I mean to say is that I refuse to dope myself.'

'But this isn't doping, it's homeopathy. And don't forget about your sponsor. At least take the boxes with you and decide what you want to do with them.'

I didn't want to show any lack of solidarity so I left with my packages. I went back to my parents' house in Labastide-Rouairoux, where I was still living. I put the whole lot in my wardrobe without opening them. Unless someone has tidied them away, they must still be there now.

I didn't need any artificial assistance. The training camp bolstered my self-confidence. When we went out on group rides, I came back feeling that I was at the required level. The old guys seemed to accept me as one of their peers. I really enjoyed their joviality. Thierry Bourguignon's gift of the gab and his talent for repartee impressed the timid boy who could scarcely string two phrases together without blushing. I gradually overcame my natural taciturnity in order to join in with the general bonhomie. I found being part of the group really appealing. When I returned home I was already desperate to see my new comrades again at the first race.

Michel Thèze had put together a winter training programme for me, and I stuck to it with relish. I lined up for my first race in early February 1996. The Etoile de Bessèges was a five-day race in the Gard region of Languedoc-Roussillon. I hardly slept the night before it started. My heart was pounding when I arrived at the start. As I took in the hustle and bustle of the pre-stage events, excitement began to build inside me. Then the peloton was off. Wrapped up within the cocoon I was now a part of, I savoured every metre raced, with every sense on alert. I noticed a rider who stood out because of his elegance on the bike. He was turning the pedals with disconcerting ease, as if the laws of gravity, equilibrium and wind resistance didn't affect him. I noticed his name on his race number. Fabio Baldato was a renowned Italian sprinter. Surreptitiously, I stuck to his wheel so I could admire the fluidity of his pedalling. Like a performing monkey, I tried to imitate his cadence.

I carried on with this mimicry throughout the first stage. I had an instructive day. The ease with which I followed the peloton's rhythm encouraged me to be more daring the next day. I positioned myself up towards the front, where adventure loomed. In the first few kilometres, a man attacked. When he did, I jumped on the pedals and went off in pursuit. Some other riders followed and soon there were five of us clear. I looked back and could see our advantage was building.

I was thrilled by my daring and focused on committing fully each time I went to the front of the line. I span my legs to the point where I was losing my balance. In our small group was Jean-Claude Colotti, a veteran coming to the end of his career. This member of the old brigade got irritated at seeing me pedalling flat out in too small a gear. 'Bloody hell, stop spinning it like that! You're going to suffocate,' he growled.

Our escapade was cut short before the finish. The massed ranks descended on our little quintet. As it did, I realised the extent of the peloton's power compared to that of individual riders. When the sprinters' team-mates organised a pursuit behind a breakaway group, it was as if a huge and irresistible steam-roller had been set in motion. It was a well-established fact in cycling that the bunch would always overpower an individual. A breakaway rider gets much more tired than a rider sheltered in the midst of the pack. Not only does a breakaway rider act as a hare for the hounds chasing in the pack behind, but he is penalised by the constant battle with wind resistance. There is also another explanation for this happening, as I learned later. Medical preparation homogenised the ability of riders, effectively locking down races. It blurred the idea of a rider's form ebbing and flowing. There were fewer abandons from races, as well as far fewer breakaway victories.

I wasn't aware of these notions at that point. I was intoxicated by my first foray, which had resulted in me climbing onto the podium for the first time to receive the jersey of best climber. On the final day, my parents came to watch me. Their presence and obvious pride in their little boy thrilled and motivated me. Once again I chose to be adventurous in the opening kilometres. There were two of us to start with, but I found myself all on my own after my companion punctured when we'd been away for 37 kilometres. I rode for another 100 kilometres on my own, before being reeled back in, inevitably, three kilometres from the finish. But what did that setback matter? I had passed my entrance exam and had proved my worth right away. The next day I could expect glowing citations in the press.

Raymond Poulidor – whose name I did actually know! – praised 'the arrival of a new talent', calling me 'a future champion' who had 'endurance and courage'. In its review of the new pros at the start of the season, *L'Equipe* said that I was 'undoubtedly one of the riders with the greatest potential among the new wave' and even 'an all-round talent'. As I remember, I allowed myself to enjoy this glorification of my ability. After the 1999 Tour, I would effectively end up being regarded as 'a little rider' by the cycling fraternity. How quickly opinions change.

The Etoile de Bessèges ended gloriously. On the final morning, Festina's Michel Gros took advantage of the chaos at the start to slide up to me while my team managers were distracted elsewhere.

'We made you an offer. Just to let you know that it still stands.'

He started to walk off, smiling rather enigmatically, and saying over his shoulder, 'We should stay in touch. Your team won't be around for long.'

I took this remark seriously. We hadn't received our salaries for January. Force Sud's management had claimed there had been a delay in getting the team's accounts set up. This blunder was soon sorted out. But February and then a good part of March passed without us receiving a centime. The guys started to moan. Thierry Bourguignon led the revolt. There were an increasing number of union meetings. Michel Thèze went looking for news from the backers and returned with promises and a vague schedule of payments. The more experienced riders believed they knew what this combination meant. They thought the sponsors were going to try to drag things out as far as the Tour de France. If we were selected for that race, our backers would pay the money outstanding. If not, they would drop us. The financial guarantee that they had lodged with the French Cycling Federation when the team had been registered would act as our redundancy.

The thinking behind these calculations should have been instructive. However, as I still lived with my parents, I was indifferent to these financial problems and this lesson in cynicism. All I was concerned with was racing. I had no worries about my future.

I was very tempted by the noises Festina were making. Competition had knocked the rough edges off me. However, I started to take much more notice of the hierarchy among the teams, shown by the resources each of them had available at stage starts and finishes. When we parked our very basic vehicles alongside the specially modified buses that belonged to the big teams, the gloom that descended upon us was striking.

At the end of March, Force Sud lined up in the Critérium International, a two-day race of three stages that was organised by the Société du Tour de France. This was the moment for us to show ourselves if we hoped to feature in the summer's great event. I was extremely motivated. The race was taking place in the Tarn around my home town of Mazamet.

On the start line I found myself among a number of big guns: Bjarne Riis, Richard Virenque, Luc Leblanc. The only one missing was my idol, Miguel Indurain. I felt I was mixing with cycling's high society. The speed at which the race was run heightened that impression even more. The opening stage was flat. It concluded with a sprint at the end of an interminable finishing straight. Our little band got into battle formation with the aim of leading out our favourite, Christophe Capelle. It was the first time I had been involved in this breathtaking exercise. The peloton packed tighter and tighter together. I hung on near the front, waiting for my turn to set the pace at almost 60 kilometres per hour. I was intoxicated by the speed. The plane trees alongside the road flew through the periphery of my vision at an incredible rate. I had never gone as quickly on a bike. I finally pulled aside, my part of the work completed. I couldn't see the battle between the sprinters. Crossing the line, I heard that Capelle had won. We all gathered together in the closed-off area beyond the finish to congratulate each other. That evening we were all in a party mood. As I lay down in bed that night, I thought to myself: this sport will bring me nothing but satisfaction.

The next morning, before the start of the first part of the split stage, a white-haired man with a cordial air approached me. Pierre Chany was one of the most renowned of cycling journalists. He had been knocking out stories for *L'Equipe* for years. He had followed every edition of the Tour since the Second World War. He had rubbed shoulders with all the great names, and his friendship with Jacques Anquetil was well known. Yet the close relations he had with many major figures didn't prevent him from maintaining a critical perspective on the sport. Even before drug controls were introduced at the end of the 1960s, he had been scathing in his criticism of the damaging effects resulting from the use of amphetamines and other stimulants. He had been the mouthpiece for Anquetil when the great champion confessed that he used stimulants, in an era when others denied the facts in a simpering fashion. His professional integrity had always enabled him to avoid producing the kind of lies that certain low-rent members of the press corps deal in today. Having long since passed retirement age, Chany was still writing the odd piece in *Le Dauphiné Libéré*. By doing so, he satisfied his passion for cycling and made clear his admiration for the riders to the wider public. He would never have dressed them up as fairground freaks, unlike some star-makers and star-breakers who came along later. Smooth talkers with the smile of a preying mantis, these journalists would swear to you that they loved the riders. They would produce magnificent eulogies for placement on the tombs of their heroes, who had been taken away too soon.

Pierre Chany approached while I was getting myself ready to race at the back of a car.

'Christophe, I am proud to meet you.'

I was slightly embarrassed on hearing this. I didn't know about this gentleman's prestige and only learned about his many achievements later on. It was simply his age and dignity that made an impression on me.

'You've got the class of cycling's old school,' he added. 'Watching the way that you race I can see something from another age.'

He told me how much he had enjoyed my escapes during the Etoile de Bessèges. He had been completely enchanted by my effrontery, he said, and since then he had followed my progress with interest.

'Continue like that,' he concluded. 'Try to remain distinctive.'

With that he moved on. He died a few months later on the eve of what would have been his 50th Tour de France. I feel a certain egotistical regret at his passing. I would like to know whether he would still have appreciated my originality today. How would he have judged the battle I took on? Would he still have backed my cause during the 1999 Tour, or would he have denounced my escapades?

After Chany had left, Michel Gros came up, accompanied by another man. He introduced himself as Bruno Roussel as he shook my hand. Festina's directeur sportif then said something which gave me another lift.

'What you are doing is really impressive. We're interested in you. There's a contract waiting for you when you've made up your mind.'

Bucked up by that, I went off on my bike. The compliments kept coming. I was snowed under by praise and that gave me even more ideas. But my body was about to bring me back down to earth. As soon as I took my first pedal stroke, I felt a sharp pain in my knee. I was paying for the excesses of the day before. Rather than easing off, the pain got worse as the kilometres passed. Incapable of pushing on the pedals, I quickly found myself back among the team cars following the peloton. I was experiencing the infamy of being spat out of the back of the bunch for the first time. I felt humiliated. I found myself alone, wandering through the countryside, frantic with pain. I swayed from one side of the road to the other. A driver who had been held up slowed to ask if I wanted any help. I refused. I soldiered on to the feeding station, where I was forced to abandon. I was fuming because I wouldn't be able to take part in the final time trial that afternoon. I had been expecting to get a fuller idea of my worth in that test. I felt humiliated by the debacle and was furious at my sudden impotence.

I returned home in a dark mood. I had to take good care of my knee. I knew from a past experience that still played on my mind that I couldn't deal with it any old how.

Back in 1993 I had been affected by an allergy and went to see a doctor of some repute. That professional prescribed an intramuscular injection of Kenacort, a corticosteroid-based product.

'But that's not allowed. I will have to stop racing,' I told him.

'No, there's no problem. *Ça passe.*'

That same phrase, '*ça passe*', was used within the peloton. It indicated that, although the product featured on the list of banned substances, it would not be picked up in dope controls. Therefore, there was no need to worry about any sanction. The good doctor was implicitly repeating a well-known cycling maxim which went '*pas pris, pas dopé*' – if you're not caught, you're not doped. I don't know if this doctor still shares this philosophy: he is now one of the team responsible for urine tests at the Tour de France.

At the time, I had agreed to have the injection. I needed to be pepped up. Out of curiosity I went out on my bike and noticed the exhilarating effects that this corticosteroid produced. Training rides were absolutely blissful. During my sorties, I had picked out certain sections that were like testing areas – a steep hill here, a long flat section there, a particular series of bends. I regularly tested my form and took note of how I was feeling at these points. I also worked out a time trial course where I could assess myself. On each occasion, the Kenacort-fuelled performances were convincing. The medicine improved my performance and reduced my fatigue. I returned home on the verge of succumbing to a terrible temptation. In the end, I decided to stop racing for two weeks, at which point the effects of the product began to diminish.

Like many athletes who make acute demands of their respiratory system, I was sensitive to allergies. I had asthma as a child, but later became desensitised to it. But it remained a weakness. Since that episode, I had managed to deal with it without using Kenacort.

In 1994, I went back to see the same man. A lack of iron had been detected in my body. I needed to get my level back up again. The doctor prescribed some injections of Fer Lucien. This medication was also misused and also featured among the panoply of well-established doping products. This time I refused the injections. The doctor was annoyed by what he saw as my senseless concerns.

'If you refuse to have the injections, you will just have to take the capsules.'

That's what I did. I don't recommend the experience. The liquid left an abominable taste of rust on my tongue. I retched when I was swallowing it. However, I preferred this torture to an inoffensive prick. It was only designed to improve my health, but I knew it would mean crossing a line. Kenacort, Fer Lucien, and then what?

In 1993, corticosteroids had instantly seen off the pain that was affecting me and had improved my performance. Three years later, I refused to go back down that path. I would undoubtedly have finished the Critérium International using that medication. I would have taken part in the time trial. I would even have finished well up, as you didn't need to take much for it to have an effect! I would have been the revelation of the race. The papers would have suggested my name was one to follow. The elasticity of my conscience would have resulted in me convincing myself that this wasn't cheating. A doctor's note would have provided the ideal balm for my scruples and my fear of the dope control. I had a problem. I needed to take care of it. What could be more normal than that?

But then, how would I be able to hold back? Wouldn't I end up using it when I had even the slightest twinge? I knew all about the beneficial effects of corticosteroids. I would soon learn how their abuse led to dependence on them. Lots of users were hooked on them. Use of the product caused the body, or more precisely the suprarenal glands, to stop producing cortisol, a natural hormone vital to the body's equilibrium. Once the body could no longer produce this hormone, synthetic substances had to be used to top up the required levels. The gland broke down, sometimes beyond repair. Consequently, those affected had to replenish their body with this precious element on a permanent basis, otherwise they would end up with a deficiency. Among other effects, a shortage plunged them into a deep depression. Later on, I would witness scenes of despondency and anger that had a purely chemical origin.

Yet I still had to find a remedy. I knew that the doctor was going to prescribe something that I didn't want to take. My reservations caused me to go instead to Toulouse, where I had a meeting with Marc Bichon, a doctor in the rugby world. That sport, I believed, had been spared the ravages of doping. Dr Bichon didn't recommend any kind of illicit remedy. He diagnosed an offset patella. He assured me that the problem wasn't all that serious. I could continue to train as long as I didn't put too much strain on the fragile joint. He advised me to stop racing for two weeks. He also suggested that I adjust my shoe plates in order to modify my position on the bike and relieve the strain on that delicate area.

Just as he had predicted, the shooting pain disappeared after a fortnight. It has returned every year since then. The preventive measures that I've taken have gradually made it less acute. But the affliction is still chronic and comes back every spring, like the swallows. Again like them, the pain doesn't arrive on any fixed date. I've just had to get used to this imponderable. When it returns I pull out of any races, no matter what their importance, until the inconvenience passes. I've had to pull out of some of the big Classics because of it. This rather fundamentalist approach surprises some. But the beneficial effect it has reassures me that it is the only way to avoid getting onto a slippery slope. I've seen too many unsuspecting athletes finally agree to have a first innocuous injection, which is justified as therapy, and then they are never able to do without the syringe.

I took advantage of the rest that my knee demanded by sorting out my immediate future. What was effectively my voluntary work for Force Sud was beginning to weigh down on me, especially as I had a mouthwatering offer from Festina … I had some legal arguments ready to justify the switch, principally the fact that my agreement with Force Sud had been broken as a result of their non-payment of my salary. As it was, I had no problem getting the National Union of Professional Cyclists (UNCP) to terminate my contract.

I quickly got in contact with Bruno Roussel. The terms that he offered me turned out to be less attractive than those he had previously dangled in front of me. My salary would be about 12,000 francs a month – but it was better than riding gratis, as I had been doing up to that point! Roussel was well aware that market forces weren't working in my favour.

I wasn't going to take offence at this hardnosed approach. After all, I wasn't beyond reproach myself. By negotiating this new deal, I had broken a pact drawn up with the other riders on the Force Sud roster. We had promised each other that we would show solidarity in adversity. And here I was, leaving them in the lurch at the first opportunity. Because I didn't want to see my dream career disappear once again, I was acting like some awful egotistical brat. However, I didn't feel guilty for long. Other riders, I noticed, were also negotiating their own future. The mutual agreement we'd had was nothing more than a smokescreen. It was every man for himself.

All team spirit had evaporated. The team wasn't going to survive for much longer. In the end, it folded before the summer, and several unfortunate riders ended up jobless. As for me, I continued on my glorious path.

At the end of April, I signed a contract tying me to Festina until 31 December 1998. I had a meeting with Bruno Roussel and Michel Gros at Meyzieux, on the outskirts of Lyon. That was the location of Prosport's technical HQ, Prosport being the Andorran company that oversaw the watch-making company's cycling activities.

The two men took me around the HQ. I was impressed by the set-up and by their attention to detail. I could soon understand the reason for the disdainful looks of my new team-mates when confronted with Force Sud's odds and ends. There were good teams and less good teams. With Festina, I was about to experience the absolute best.

My guides also told me about the different personnel and their respective roles. We had two doctors whose job was to keep an eye on our wellbeing: one Spanish, Fernando Jiménez, and the other Belgian, Eric Ryckaert.

Before signing my contract, I made it a point of honour to clarify my position.

'I know that there is doping within cycling. But there is no question of me resorting to it.'

'Don't worry, we've got a rule that we don't suggest young pros go down this route for the first two years,' Bruno told me. 'But I want you to understand that it is possible. If you do change your mind one day, bear in mind these two doctors. We don't want guys doing their own thing in a corner somewhere.'

'Possible or not, I'm refusing,' I restated rather grumpily as I signed the contract.

Bruno Roussel looked at me intently. There was a trace of a smile on his face.

'I'm happy to hear you say that. It reassures me.'

His response wasn't tinged with cynicism. I was going to find out just how complex a personality Bruno was. A free spirit, he was tarnished by an environment in which directeurs sportifs are often former pros who have long since become accustomed to the reality of the *milieu* and are too familiar with the way it works to be able to consider doing things differently. He was a Breton, the son of Ange Roussel, a cycling coach renowned for his rectitude. He had long argued against unsavoury practices at his former RMO team, and had initially maintained his stance at Festina. He finally gave in to ambition, to fatalism and, particularly, to the will of the riders.

Bruno Roussel was viewed with condescension among his peers. But in a lot of respects, I found him to be far more capable than those whose experience of life barely extended beyond the sport. The experiences he had had before coming into cycling had added a great deal of depth to his personality. It was possible to have a conversation with him about things beside cycling, cars, women and money. I believe he always admired my tenacity. He also understood my arguments, because he used to have the same views himself. I remain convinced that his lack of conviction about doping led to his downfall. He scarcely offered any resistance to the police, unlike other directeurs sportifs, whose duplicity was far more deeply ingrained.

'I can win without taking anything,' I insisted irritably.

'Yes, definitely,' said my new boss.

I could win without doping. I was convinced of it. One man would support me in this opinion: Antoine Vayer, the team coach. I had met him at the Critérium International. He had accompanied Bruno Roussel when he had followed up his initial interest in me. I had scarcely paid any attention to the guy, who weighed me up like some kind of small-time hustler. I had no idea that he would soon become my only ally.

Once the contractual formalities had been completed, Vayer brought me to his base in Laval. He took me into a centre for sports medicine, where I went through an impressive battery of tests, clinics and questions.

My physiological capacity was weighed, measured, extrapolated and calculated. Festina's other riders had also gone through this dissection of their athletic abilities. Printers spat out an infinite number of mysterious curves and fantastic tables, plus reams of abstract figures. At first glance, I had the definite feeling of being treated like a guinea pig. Then my interest was piqued by this methodical inspection. I could see that this was nothing less than the scientific application of the introspective and empiric approach I adopted on my training rides.

On the third day, in my presence, Antoine Vayer picked up the phone and called Bruno Roussel. He had reached a verdict.

'He's got a big engine, you're right. He has got the same physical capacity as Bernard Hinault.'

The coach then went through a few pieces of data, which I gathered confirmed his assessment. I revelled in the comparison with Hinault. The figures were saying that I had enormous potential. I knew that, both by instinct and by having seen my rivals pedalling with their tongues hanging out behind me. He only needed to ask me!

This examination had another aspect to it besides establishing my worth and quantifying the extent of my talent. It also enabled him to get right down to the nitty gritty. Antoine Vayer could use this knowledge to draw up a training programme adapted to a specific athlete and to their individual objectives on the calendar.

A good amateur rider in the early 1980s, Vayer was a bike fan who had studied physical and sporting education at the same time. He had opened a training centre in western Normandy that was the equivalent of the football academies that turned out star players. A number of decent riders emerged from the set-up. He then became the personal trainer to several professionals. Among them was Pascal Hervé, who benefited from Vayer's work and warmly recommended the guy to his boss, Bruno Roussel.

I've already explained how our directeur sportif had a more open mind then the majority of his colleagues. Tackling things in a new way intrigued him, and he had already tried a number of different approaches. His curiosity had encouraged him to investigate osteopathy. Festina had also employed a nutritionist, Denis Riché, who was an uncompromising censor of our daily menus. The team had also taken on an ergonomist, Armel André, who worked on positioning on the bike in the wind tunnel with a view to reducing wind resistance as much as possible. Bruno Roussel was looking at every angle. I think he wanted to dilute the impact of the only science then in use within the peloton: the science of medicine. He was desperately searching for a remedy to the pharmaceutical dependence of his protégés, or, at the very least, ways of enabling them to reduce their dosage.

Most of my colleagues viewed the benefits of these interlinked disciplines as an addition to pharmaceutical assistance rather than as a replacement for it. They devoted plenty of time to them, but regarded them as a passing fancy. Soon advances in medical research and the advent of more potent performance-enhancing products rendered all other avenues of exploration redundant.

The constraints imposed by the nutritionist or the coach were regarded as worthless distractions. They were rejected one by one. The riders started to regard the presence of these men, who knew so much but weren't compromised, as a nuisance: their virginity made them dangerous. Denis Riché slipped away in 1997. Antoine Vayer was confined to working with those riders who wanted his help. Bruno Roussel reluctantly took note of these rejections, aware that their move to the sidelines sounded the death knell for a new form of cycling.

One anecdote encapsulates this ambiguity very neatly. At the end of 1997, Antoine had tried to point up the importance of his results to Bruno after one of the riders he coached, Laurent Brochard, had won the world road race championship. Roussel regarded the coach in silence for a moment and then said to him:

'You know, Antoine, which is the most important: a good coach or a good doctor?'

The response was obvious and didn't please either of the two friends having the discussion. In the chaos of the time, the doctor won the scientific duel, his art triumphing completely over that of the coach. It was going to become extremely difficult to stand up to this dictatorship.

Chapter 2

Cycling is a Breeze

I first wore my new jersey on Sunday, 11 May 1996 in Paris–Mantes, a race open to both professional and amateur riders. There were just two of us representing Festina. I was accompanied by Bruno Boscardin, a Swiss sprinter who was apparently the quickest in the field. Our tactic was simple. I controlled the race as it unfolded, setting the rhythm and neutralising any breakaways. My team-mate's finishing speed provided the finishing touch to all this work. First race, first victory, first prize: 10,000 francs. The 'big engine' was ticking over very nicely.

Bruno Roussel appreciated it. He asked me to head to the Alps the next day. A training camp had been organised there with the aim of doing some reconnaissance of the Tour de France stages. My team director intended to acquaint me with his best guys, whose sole focus was July's big race. As I responded to his summons, I realised that he was already offering me a minor role in this group.

On the evening of 12 May, I arrived in the car park of a luxurious hotel in Val-d'Isère. There were gleaming German cars all around. 'Well, son, you're in the big league now,' I said to myself as I surveyed them. Somewhat intimidated, I carried my things up to my room. There I met Patrice Halgand, another young buck whose value was being assessed by Bruno Roussel. I had known him at the Joinville battalion and his familiar presence reassured me.

I went down to the dining-room feeling as anxious as a country squire about to make his entry into the court at Versailles. The others had already sat down for dinner. I noticed Richard Virenque, Laurent Brochard, Christophe Moreau, Laurent Dufaux, Emmanuel Magnien, and many other faces I'd studied in the team's publicity photo on the journey down. My arrival scarcely provoked any interest. All I got were dismissive glances before they went back to their conversations. I went around the table, shaking my team-mates' hands. Then I greeted the backroom staff, who traditionally sat apart. Many of those present were accompanied by their wives or girlfriends, which was very unusual to see in a world where misogyny ruled.

I sat down at an empty place and was soon forgotten. My neighbours joked among themselves as if I didn't exist. While I waited for our meal to arrive, I started gobbling the bread, to calm my nerves as much as to ease my hunger. I took one piece after another from the basket and chewed them greedily.

Antoine Vayer could see what I was up to and cut in: 'Have you finished making a pig of yourself?'

'But it's really good, this bread.'

With my distinctive south-western accent, the word '*pain*' came out as 'païngue'. My distortion of the word and infantile response provoked general hilarity. The others started to make fun of me. Adopting stupid voices, they imitated my pronunciation. I was ashamed and at the same time happy that I finally existed in their eyes. The incident had sealed my entry into the group. The jokes finally dried up and the conversation returned to habitual subjects: cycling, cars and cash. Usually, another topic would produce all kinds of bragging: girls. But the presence of women at the dinner table made this a difficult subject.

The next day we tested out the Tour's time trial course. Then we set out towards the Italian ski station of Sestrières, following the route of what was likely to be a decisive stage of the race. The reconnaissance began at an easy pace. It soon took on a playful aspect. We all acted as if we were rivals, inventing intermediate sprints, imagining acclaim from watching crowds. The speed picked up with each dummy attack.

Joyful shouts gave way to diligent silence. The group really believed it was in a race.

I became intoxicated by this competitive atmosphere. On the final climb up to Sestrières, I went to the front of the group. I acted as the model team-mate setting the pace for his leader. I really ended up believing that was what I was doing, pressing on the pedals like a hard-working domestique. To my great surprise, my progressive acceleration provoked no response. Logically, the others should have attacked. So I turned around and saw my team-mates strung out down the hill behind me. I was filled with pride and a rush of energy by the chaos I'd caused.

Only Richard Virenque was still on my wheel. On the final ramps, he attacked and opened out a 100-metre gap. The team leader was eager to assert his authority by being the first to arrive at the hotel. But that evening I was reassessed.

'He's not too bad, this kid. I think he can help me out. Can you try to put him in some races with me?' Virenque told Bruno Roussel, who was eager to pass on the news of my promotion to the new rank of lieutenant.

To show his respect for me, the champion invited me to a cyclosportive event, the Virenque du Verdon, which was organised by his fan club. Fifteen hundred people rode it, all of them delighted to be rubbing shoulders with their idol. In the midst of this collective hysteria, I could really assess the extent of his popularity.

When we were on the start line, Richard said that he wanted his brother, Lionel, to win the event. A few of those in the know pointed out the preferred candidate's lack of physical condition. Virenque cut in. 'That's why we will have to help him,' the event's figurehead said. Along with Laurent Brochard, I was assigned the role of escort to the designated victor. Our main task was to push him up the hills, where none of his rivals dared raise a voice of complaint against this evident cheating. Our efforts came to nothing, which was just as well from a moral point of view. But my uncomplaining commitment helped to further boost my value in my new boss's eyes.

After this brief interlude, my apprenticeship restarted. I lined up at the Midi Libre and then at the Dauphiné Libéré, two stage races that serve as preparatory events for the Tour de France. This mini-programme was due to be completed at the Classique des Alpes, a race that suited climbers. Virenque's desire to have me riding at his side had been granted, although partly because Bruno Roussel also wanted to assess my endurance in longer races. He couldn't wait to find out whether they would suit me.

But there was an unpleasant surprise in store for me. The rhythm of the whole peloton had picked up substantially in my absence. As the days went by, I struggled to stay with the pace being hammered out. At the same time, my team-mates strolled through each day without suffering the least amount of fatigue.

Some warped reasoning helped me to reassure myself. I still managed to stay with the peloton, even though was I always well to the back of it. On the opening day of the Dauphiné Libéré, I just missed out on getting into the break of the day. In the prologue the day before, I had recorded a better time than all the riders who did make it into the escape. That evening I worked out that if I had managed to get into that group, which had stayed clear, I would have been the race leader of the road. If …

The Dauphiné's Alpine stages completely disillusioned me. I was limited to very much a background role in the mountains. The braggart who had been in evidence at Sestrières disappeared without trace. I told myself that I had allowed my thinking to run out of control during the training camp in the Alps. The others had held back while I had given the very best of myself. I had been hoist with my own petard. My team-mates' quality had risen, while I started to doubt my own ability.

During this long and hard battle, I had at least gained one memory to savour, as I had crossed paths with Miguel Indurain for the first time. On the start line one morning, I discreetly sidled up to him, sliding my bike in alongside his in as nonchalant a manner as possible. I could speak a bit of Spanish and had already worked out a few words that I could casually say to him. Now that I was confronted by him, however, I didn't dare speak. I contented myself with contemplating his regal demeanour. He seemed even bigger than I had imagined. I felt intimidated by his height, impassive regard and imposing features. I felt tiny beside this giant figure who could have been cut from marble. He gave off a sense of almost child-like mildness that, rather than providing reassurance, seemed to make him even more distant from me. A barely perceptible half-smile played permanently on his lips. His gentle gaze passed over everyone's heads and seemed to be lost on some summit to which only he had access. How could I have dared to disturb him on his Olympus?

We had just one thing in common: just like him, I went to bed at 9.30 in the evening on race days.

I emerged from this long examination in a state of physical exhaustion and low morale. However, Bruno Roussel came to congratulate me on the final evening.

'You've done really well to finish these two races. I am happy with you.'

He reminded me that I was only just 22. My margin for improvement was huge. As a racer, I was still in gestation. He pointed out that my Spanish idol had taken considerable time to fashion his now indestructible physique. I had to persevere. He told me to watch the Tour de France closely that summer and learn what I could from it.

'It could be instructive,' he told me.

I was encouraged by his compliments and this promise of what might be. As he left my room, he made this final comment: 'You never know, it might turn out to be true. In the end, you will be able to compete without taking anything.'

It had been a month in which I had not only been knocked into shape from a sporting perspective, I had also gone through a cultural initiation. After the stage each evening, I had noticed an odd smell as I approached my soigneur's room. Initially, shyness held me back from asking what it was. I was afraid of making a fool of myself, but I was being prudent as well. I was entering a world that I knew was filled with all kinds of unmentionable practices. Within the cycling *milieu*, the function of the masseur is often confused with that of the soigneur, a vague role for which no formal qualification was required. I knew that this generic expression was a cover for all kinds of hypocrisy. Some soigneurs were dopers, others were simply masseurs. I still didn't know who was who in this game where so many roles were not what they seemed. I didn't want to commit a *faux pas* that might get me into hot water.

The question continued to eat away at me, hanging in the air as stubbornly as that strong scent. One evening, as I lay on the massage table, I found I couldn't hold back any longer. I adopted a light-hearted tone.

'There's a really peculiar smell in here. Where's it coming from?'

The guy responded without the slightest hesitation, telling me that it was Becozyme I could smell. He told me that this vitamin, which is injected intravenously, had an immediate restorative effect. He also told me about intravenous therapy, in which bags of substances were transfused into the arms of riders after periods of intense effort. He also mentioned other pick-me-ups that aided recovery. As he kneaded my muscles, the soigneur gave me a lesson in aspects of the sport that were unknown to me.

'Do you want to try Becozyme?'

The question surprised me.

'I'll have to think about it,' I replied. 'I'll see.'

I mulled his offer over for the rest of the evening. There was no rule against having such injections. I was worn down by fatigue after a hard day in the mountains, during which I'd ruminated over my lack of power in the *gruppetto*. This Italian word is used to describe the riders who get dropped on the climbs and come together in small groups with the aim of uniting their efforts and finishing within the designated time limit.

The following day, I found myself rowing hard again in what is the cycling equivalent of a lifeboat, out of my head with fatigue and a long way from my dreams. I finished exhausted and demoralised. The soigneur didn't repeat his offer. Modesty prevented me from bringing it up again formally. Should I have done so?

Wiser as a result of the explanation the soigneur had given me, I surveyed the comings and goings in the corridors with a more knowing eye. At that time, nobody paid any attention to me. I was transparent and inoffensive.

I would bump into soigneurs who had rolled thick napkins around their wrists and hands and were going from one room to another. I could see that some funny business was going on despite this modest attempt to conceal it. Impunity was leading to carelessness.

Mystery surrounded the contents of these makeshift muffs. I would only find out the details about them later on when I read Willy Voet's autobiography, *Breaking the Chain*, which was published in 1999. In that book he reproduced two extracts from his diary that corresponded precisely with the Midi Libre and Dauphiné Libéré in 1996. Day after day, as those distinctive fragrances hung in the air, the devoted team servant noted down in minute detail the products used and doses given, and who received them. His notes showed that EPO was flowing freely – 2,000 units to this person, 4,000 to that – and that growth hormone was as well. Looking back at this methodically compiled almanac, I'm staggered by the quantities listed, bearing in mind that these would be nothing compared to doses administered during the Tour de France, which followed soon after.

All of a sudden, I could understand why there was such a difference in the levels of the men I had left for dead at Sestrières and who, just a week later, were strolling past me in a race.

I also realised that I had only seen a tiny amount of the seedy activities that were going on at that time. I was a home body, and usually I stuck very much to my hotel room in order to recuperate. I spent most of my evenings flat out on my bed, my mind empty and my body limp. Incapable of concentrating, I watched the most stupid programmes on the TV, constantly zapping from one channel to the next, waiting until it was time for dinner or to go to sleep.

In the adjoining rooms, some of my neighbours got their strength back with an instant pre-dinner hit that came thanks to a needle in the arm. They would have another injection before they went off to sleep, and yet another when they got up the next morning, before a final small one in the bus just before the start. That meant they began the day fresh and full of energy, while I would start each day a little more run down and guaranteed to finish the stage senseless with fatigue.

Did my knowledge only extend as far as intravenous drips, Becozyme and recuperative products at that time? My regular soigneur at Festina was Laurent Gros, Michel's son, and he was totally unaware of the dodgy activities that were taking place, which was why he looked after the new pros. I wasn't likely to learn much about the hidden practices going on by spending time with him. However, I started to get to grips with a new vocabulary thanks to information gleaned on races where other members of staff looked after me. Acquitted with this lexicon, I was able to decode certain conversations a little better.

My understanding increased still further during my time behind the scenes at the French time trial championship, which took place at Malbuisson at the end of August. I had been entered in the event along with Laurent Brochard and Christophe Moreau. The evening before, we did a reconnaissance of the course. Willy Voet was with us. It was the first time he had acted as my soigneur. He worked almost entirely with Richard Virenque, to whom he was completely devoted, as well as with the other Tour de France regulars, who were nicknamed 'the barons'. The Belgian soigneur, with his little round glasses and shiny, bald head, had a real gift of the gab, which I liked. We hit it off with each other that evening, thanks in part to the intimateness of the gathering. At the end of my massage that evening, he said to me:

'Do you need anything for tomorrow, kid?'

'No, nothing, thanks.'

'OK, that's good.'

The next day, one of the rooms we'd been staying in had been reserved so that we could use it as a changing room during the event. As I was among the early starters, I went to warm up before my team-mates. I then returned to the room to pick up a dry jersey. It was empty as the other two riders had gone to warm up by that point. A full syringe was lying on the bedside table. I never found out if it had been left out for me as a discreet gift from Willy, or if it was intended for somebody else. I went off to the start. When I returned to the room for a shower, the syringe had gone.

I found out later what the potion was that Willy used to mix up. Before time trials, riders would inject a mixture of caffeine, which is a stimulant, and Solucamphre, a bronchial dilator. This was the magic formula that Dr Ryckaert advised me to use in 1997, promising me it was harmless.

I didn't acquire any kind of ghoulish fascination as a result of these discoveries. I was like a 19th-century ethnologist clinically deciphering the peculiar habits of tribesmen in Papua New Guinea. I didn't have the slightest intention of putting a needle into my arm. My surest motive for restraint was pride: I was convinced I could succeed without resorting to doping, the weapon of the weak.

To me, my team seemed like a monolithic structure that would serve as my stepping-stone towards success. I couldn't find the slightest fault in the organisation, nor the smallest weakness in its collective focus. The set-up was built around one man: Richard Virenque, who I was completely dazzled by. He was like a benevolent despot, and the rest of us were vassals within his kingdom. We were happy to campaign alongside the rider whose exploits in the Tour de France's polka-dot jersey had everyone in raptures. We lined up proudly beneath his red and white standard. Our master would say: 'I have to be well placed at this point,' and we did everything we could to make sure he was. When he said 'Ride', we would ride. When he said 'Attack!', we would attack. We only had one response: to do as he said, even if the strategy seemed flawed. Pascal Hervé was the captain who spurred us on with yells of encouragement. He and Richard almost always shared the same room. As they lay on the two beds, they cooked up the race tactics that Bruno Roussel could do no more than rubberstamp.

I witnessed a further example of this feudalism during the French championships, which took place in Castres at the end of June. It is the tradition in French cycling that when a rider becomes the national champion, he hands over his victory purse to his team-mates and even tops it up with another 100,000 francs from his own pocket. The blue, white and red champion's jersey not only provides the champion with huge pleasure for a season, but also quite substantial financial rewards.

The evening before the race, Richard gathered us all together.

'I will put 500,000 francs on the table if I become the French champion.'

That might seem an enormous commitment, but it really wasn't. The contracts in force at Festina laid down that salaries would be reviewed every season to take victories into account. The subsequent indexation of salaries was established by a precise formula. Victory in a minor race resulted in a monthly boost of 1,500 francs. Victory in a Tour de France stage or success in the French championship would lead to a monthly bonus of several tens of thousands of francs. Add in the marketing value of Virenque being in the national jersey, and the bonus is incalculable.

After dangling the carrot, Richard waved his stick.

'Bear in mind, though, that I will select those riders who deserve to share the sum I'm putting on the table.'

The warning was directed at those who might have had even the vaguest intention of providing any support to Jean-Cyril Robin, who was the French idol's only notable rival. Robin had been signed in 1995 to fill the gap left by Luc Leblanc. Robin and Virenque were united only by their mutual dislike. Worn down by Virenque's imperious attitude and Roussel's weakness when it came to his leader's diktats, Robin left Festina the following year, just as Leblanc had done at the end of 1994. The rule of King Richard was absolute.

As it was, our ruler didn't get the chance to decide which of his faithful subjects deserved to split his bounty that year. Despite starting as favourites, our army was defeated by its own arrogance. A guy from GAN, Stéphane Heulot, took the title.

Then came the Tour de France, the pinnacle of the season and the keystone of the sport. In line with my mentor's request, I followed it closely as it unfolded. The good student was soon showing the commitment of an eager fan. Watching on television, I got fully behind our brave warriors. I admired the pugnacity of Richard Virenque and Laurent Dufaux, who finished third and fourth respectively in that race. My partisan feelings were, however, tempered by the regret I felt at seeing Miguel Indurain struggling. The myth of his godlike invulnerability crumbled and I watched the great champion toil on the climbs like a mere mortal.

I interrupted my viewing to meet up with Antoine Vayer in Bordeaux. I had to do some tests at the velodrome there. Bruno Roussel had conceived the idea that I would try to break the French hour record. So the coach provided me with an aerodynamic bike and got me riding around the track while he looked on with his stopwatch, making me stop and then start again like a show-pony performing in a circus. He came to the conclusion that I could not only break the record but could even go beyond 50 kilometres in the hour. That afternoon, we paused to watch the Tour stage into Pamplona, Miguel Indurain's home town. Laurent Dufaux won it and we jumped into each other's arms, shouting with joy.

Bjarne Riis's overall victory on the Champs-Elysées reminded me of the aborted launch of La Française des Jeux. Jan Ullrich's second place provided me with even more reason for reflection. At the same age as me, the German was already flourishing in the heat of July. I couldn't wait to join him on the sun-baked roads. I felt that Bruno Roussel had that destiny in mind for me.

Bruno looked after me like a protective godfather. My first professional victory owed much to one of his acts of paternalism. I was taking part in the Mi-août Bretonne, a series of eight races organised around Lorient. It was one of those local races that endeavour to keep the passion for cycling engendered by the Tour going strong right through to the end of the summer. During a stage on Saturday, 10 August that was due to finish at Trégunc, I was in a break with another prospective talent, Dominique Rault. We had quickly managed to build a solid lead on the peloton. At one point, as he was going past me to take up the pace-making, Rault asked: 'Well, what are we going to do now?'

The meaning of the question was clear. I knew all about these confabs where a price was put on victory. The weaker rider often tried to come to an arrangement. It was then a matter of providing him with an incentive to keep collaborating. If not, the other rider would stubbornly sit on your wheel and leave you with a dilemma: should you continue to do all of the work yourself and run the risk of your reluctant companion preserving his resources for the sprint, or should you follow your companion's example and refuse to contribute to the break, effectively condemning it to failure? There was one way to avoid this no-win situation: pay up.

I should have said to him, 'We're not going to give you anything,' and simply waited to see how it played out at the finish. But I said, 'You'd better speak to Roussel' – just as a kid would say, 'You'd better speak to my dad.'

Dominique Rault eased up alongside my team car. Then he came back to towards me, his face a picture of innocence, and went back to setting the pace. Six hundred metres from the line, I attacked. My breakaway companion didn't react, although I can't say if that was because he couldn't or because he didn't want to. I don't know what had been hatched between Rault and Roussel. I have never tried to find out. I had claimed my first professional success and didn't want to consider the possibility that it might have been tarnished.

I could sense that Bruno had big goals in mind for me. Like a wily farmer, he was patiently nurturing my ability, not wanting to spoil a fruit packed with promise by acting too soon. His plan to bring my talent to maturity then took me to the Tour de l'Avenir, a race that lasted about ten days and was effectively a nursery for under-23 riders with the Tour de France in their sights. I made an honourable start but then made a premature exit. I abandoned on the fourth day due to exhaustion. Moreau, Halgand and the rest of the band surrendered at more or less the same time. Our mutual lack of form was put down to overtraining during a camp before the race. At least that is what our leaders claimed. They would never have questioned the value of a medical product even if taking too much of it had resulted in them being 'blocked' when on their machines. Their claims about overtraining marked the start of a whispering campaign against Antoine Vayer, whose methods and privileged relationship with Roussel came into question. This crank was starting to take himself too seriously with his talk of fractional rhythms, cardiac braking and muscular regeneration!

One advantage of living a cyclist's life is that the sheer pace of it prevents any deep thinking. The disappointment of the Tour de l'Avenir was soon forgotten. A few days went by and I was already looking ahead to a new challenge, the Grand Prix des Nations, an event for time trial specialists. I finished it in seventh place, up with the best, and felt reassured once again.

This good performance, added to the fourth place I'd taken in the French championships at Malbuisson that I mentioned a little earlier, resulted in an unexpected extension to my season. I was selected for the French team for the world championships, which were set to take place in Lugano in early October. I was given a starting slot in the time trial event and named as a reserve for the road race. My first professional season was ending with a grand finale.

Time trials had an effect that few of the general public were aware of. They sent the demand for real estate soaring. Competitors battled each other to hire garages that were close to the start line, in order to avoid the makeshift facilities thrown up by race organisers, which were open to the elements and the gaze of passers-by. In the years before the use of buses made frantic perusal of classified ads irrelevant, these little havens enabled riders to prepare themselves away from public view. Like the other teams, the French had rented a pied-à-terre in Switzerland.

I finished 17th in the event, 4'23" down on the winner, Alex Zülle, and 31 seconds behind my team-mate Christophe Moreau. There wasn't much chance of me getting a start in the road race, which meant I didn't really bother with training. I took advantage of this little holiday to treat myself to an indulgence I had to keep a tight rein on throughout the year. I was a regular visitor to the town's chocolate museum. I went there three times, I think, coming away each time with a little something to give to my team-mates. I was buying their friendship to an extent, like a little boy who wants to get on with the bigger kids.

The championships ended with victory for Belgium's Johan Museeuw – I don't think my delicious bars of chocolate played any part in the French team's defeat. But this sporting setback didn't stop us partying. We ended up having a wild night out in Lugano, but I had to abandon our tour of its nightspots prematurely. I wasn't used to drinking lots of alcohol, and the effect of that combined with the amount of chocolate I'd eaten sent my stomach spinning, which brought an abrupt halt to my evening. I was the butt of everyone's jokes as I headed off to the hotel.

But what did it matter? I really felt I was part of the family now. I had the same relish for my career that I had for my squares of chocolate.

The riders lived in their own world, one in which there was far more money than outsiders could imagine. I was fascinated by the flamboyance of my peers, by their complete scorn for conventions. At that time, I was fully aware that our net salaries at Festina were almost the same as our gross earnings. We had no social security cover, which meant there was nothing to protect our health or our pensions. I was enthralled by the way riders lived day to day. To me their happy-go-lucky attitude made them seem like artists. I only realised later that I had misread them and that they were egotistical millionaires who had signed up for private insurance on the quiet.

I also didn't know that Andorra's social security department had just struck the team off for excessive use of medical products ...

I was mistaken about all kinds of things from start to finish. One evening during a winter training camp at Gréoux-les-Bains, Pascal Hervé was refused entry to a nightclub because he was wearing a tracksuit. So he stopped a guy who was walking past and swapped his Festina watch, which was worth several thousand francs, for this gent's jeans. He got undressed in the street, pulled on the jeans and made a triumphal entry into the nightclub as if it were a badge of honour. I was shocked. It went against my belief in the value of money, which stemmed from being brought up among people of modest means. It was only later that I realised just how much contempt this bit of bartering showed for human dignity. It was the way everyone made fun of a guy who clearly didn't have much money and couldn't refuse such a tempting offer. There was no generosity of spirit or goodwill towards him, just condescension.

Like the others, Pascal Hervé earned tens of thousands of francs per month. He had so many tracksuits he didn't know what to do with them. As for the watch, he asked the sponsor for another the next day and they provided it at half price. The following year, the watchmaker circulated a threatening letter. It stated that watches would now be distributed using a system of quotas. It appeared that two guys had ordered 50 charm bracelets and had passed them on to a reseller. These big shots weren't lacking in commercial acumen.

Soon after that, Richard Virenque invited us to his wedding, which was to take place at the start of the following year. I saw his gesture as reflecting his nobility as team leader. I found out later that the groom had negotiated an exclusive photo deal with the magazine *Paris-Match* in return for a considerable fee that guaranteed them our presence. In 1998, he would crow about negotiating another scoop with the same magazine. On that occasion it was pictures of the outlaw packing his bags after his eviction from the Tour de France. Only by then had I come to understand the decadence of this cycling aristocracy. Once knocked off their perches, they were quite happy to sell off their honour for a few notes. Cyclists didn't have any particular set of rules that kept them in line, as I naïvely believed. In fact, they didn't have any at all.

At the end of 1996, I had not yet had my eyes opened to all this by adversity. I hadn't received the slaps in the face that would eventually make me see reason. I still couldn't see how such behaviour simply indicated the total dissoluteness of the personalities involved. Their over-the-top, fuck-you attitude and the hint of debauchery fascinated me, a 22-year-old guy who had been brought up in quite a puritanical way and had been encouraged to respect social norms. I was ready to ditch my antiquated principles to become part of this madness and mayhem. I was happily marching into this rotten world.

Only my refusal to dope still set me apart. But for how long? My conviction that I could win clean was wavering, even though I didn't fully realise it. I hitched my wagon to the sport at the end of the EPO boom, when use of this product was at its height. Some crazed fools were registering an haematocrit (red blood cell count) of 58 per cent at specific points in the season, which was close to 20 points above the level for a normal person. Bjarne Riis had just earned a nickname after his victory in the Tour de France. It was circulating on that very evening, amidst much disgust and envy: 'Mr 60 per cent'. It's difficult to hang on to a train being driven by engines like that.

The stakes were enormously high, but the rewards even higher: money, glory, the Tour … In addition, impunity was practically assured, which only pushed temptation even higher. EPO, corticosteroids and a large part of the rest of the cycling pharmacopeia were not detectable at the end of 1996. This brings us to Francesco Conconi, the pioneer of Italian sports medicine, the man behind the exploits of Francesco Moser, who pulverised the world hour record in the 1980s and in doing so dragged cycling into the vanguard of medical science. The spiritual father of Michele Ferrari and the rest of the Italian doctors who dominated the peloton in the 1990s before the judicial authorities took an interest in them, the courageous 'Professor' Conconi actually spent his spare moments assisting the International Cycling Union (UCI) in its battle against doping. Thanks to substantial research, the Italian scientist worked out a method to detect EPO in anti-doping controls. The problem was that ten litres of urine were required for an accurate reading … The level of hypocrisy was ridiculous. The credo within the cycling fraternity was simple: a cyclist is doped when he is declared to have tested positive at a control. This effectively meant that cyclists were never doped. The UCI, the supposed regulatory authority, was nothing less than a blind shepherd that allowed the peloton to run wild.

Was I on the verge of succumbing to temptation? Could I have ended up 'charging' myself, just as other prudish souls had done before me? I will never know. Instead, a woman entered the picture. She took my hand and led me to where I truly wanted to go.

On 13 December 1996, I met Pascale Cabezuelo at Pont-de-l'Arn. We were both at a party that had been organised for local athletes. We ended up on the same table, and not completely by accident. We had known each other at high school, after which our paths had diverged. It was clearly apparent that the break hadn't been total as we instinctively sat next to each other.

Pascale was involved in artistic roller skating, which she simply described as 'roller skating' to give it a bit of gravitas and wipe the sarcastic look from my face. She had competed at the highest level of this sport before moving into coaching. I won't hide how small my regard was for this discipline, which seemed to consist of doing graceful pirouettes in leg-irons.

Pascale felt the same disdain towards cycling. To her it was an absurd pastime that consisted of following white lines in the road and repeating the same mechanical movements ad infinitum. She detested the sport, and did so even more once she became better acquainted with the cycling *milieu*. She rarely came to see me when I was racing. She showed little interest in how I'd got on when I returned home from racing or when I called her in the evenings from hotels, which used to annoy me on those occasions when I was lucky enough to be in contention. She just politely asked for my news, like a worker's wife asking her husband how his day in the factory had gone.

Her total indifference undoubtedly immunised me against all temptation. Pascale was involved in a sport that had little financial support, and therefore plenty of principle. No one would swap a luxury watch for a pair of jeans in roller skating. My girlfriend was quick to point up the vacuity of a world that I thought was marvellous.

Riders' wives often shared the dreams of their other half. They became part of the *milieu*, either by affinity or as a result of becoming trapped by the easy financial pickings. Being with a champion provided them with glory by proxy. Social status came as one of their wedding presents. It was easy to be seduced by this. Naturally, wives worried about the medical excesses they either witnessed or suspected. But, at the same time, danger was ever-present in any case. It was there when their husband performed a daredevil descent of a mountain pass at full speed and went within a hair's breadth of flying off the edge and into the void below. Doping was another risk that came with the job. They worried about these perils but didn't have any intention of denying their husbands their passion. Their silence can be regarded as an expression of love.

Parents react in the same manner. Mine always supported my stand against doping. They reaffirmed their support for me at my worst moments, drawing great personal pride from this. It was as a result of this that my mother saw my normally level-headed father get angrier than he had ever been before. Cyrille Guimard had just come out with some unpleasant insinuations about me during the 1999 Tour. Hearing his words on the radio, my father was furious. He wanted to write an inflammatory letter to Guimard for what he regarded as slanderous comments, deliver it to him himself and then tear it up in front of him. My mother had a real job calming him down.

But I don't think I would offend them by saying that my parents would have closed their eyes if I had decided to dope. Just as they understood and supported my stance against doping, they would probably have accepted the opposite scenario. If they had stumbled in while I was injecting myself, I would have said exactly what other riders did: 'Pah, it's only water and a few vitamins. There's no danger.' Whether convinced or not, they would have averted their eyes. I could have repeated the words of Michele Ferrari when he was asked about EPO: 'It's no more dangerous than ten litres of orange juice.' They would have taken my word for it. Nowadays, do people not say that taking a few grams of creatine is akin to eating several kilos of red meat without the comparison shocking anyone?

During the 1996 season, my parents completely shared the dreams I had for my career. They were proud of their little boy, who was a celebrity in the Tarn and would soon be known much more widely. But would they have been able to stand in the way of my plans? I'd had all of my inoculations and was an adult. What would one jab more or less matter? They would have been worried about their beloved son when they got to hear the rumours of the suicidal habits within the peloton that were doing the rounds; they would have been all the more anxious at seeing me celebrating on a podium. Lots of other parents reacted in exactly this way.

I'm sketching out a portrait of honest people who have simply been overtaken by events. I am not talking about the criminals who prepared the syringes for the children of these honest folk. These poisoners, who were very much part of the cycling scene, were like children who have been abused and end up inflicting the worst cruelties on their own offspring. Child-killers are well aware of the evil they are carrying out but consider it the natural state of things. Unfortunately, I know all too many of these depraved people, who are ready to say: 'You will take dope, my boy!'

That Friday, 13 December, I found my balance in life. Pascale is a strong character, someone who is not driven by the desire for money and honours. It was Christophe Bassons she loved, not a promising cyclist with a rosy future. She has supported me in the best of times and in the worst. She picked up half of the burden I was carrying even before a priest asked us to make our marriage vows. She shared my darkest moments. More than anything, she made me keep believing in my principles when I was ready to toss them out of the window.

Along with Antoine Vayer, my parents and a few others, Pascale provided unwavering reassurance, which kept me on the straight and narrow in my quest to compete without doping. The backing of all these people enabled me to stave off temptation. However, at the end of 1996, I was still so desperate to be accepted within the cycling *milieu* that I would never have dared to denounce it.

In early December, the team gathered for a training camp at Gréoux-les-Bains in the Verdon. To describe these gatherings as a training camp is rather misleading. Rather than physical exertion, they were intended more as a period of relaxation at the end of a hard season. The schedule essentially consisted of sorting out administrative issues such as licences, preparing the publicity campaign for the following season, testing out the latest equipment innovations and meeting new riders. Another key focus was the settling of accounts and distribution of prize money.

The prizes earned throughout the year were put into a single pot. Each rider's share was then decided by the number of racing days they had completed during the season, no matter what the level of the races and the results they had obtained. As a matter of fairness, a percentage of the winnings was also handed over to the backroom staff. This was about 15 per cent of the total. The system was time-proven and simple. Yet, it still threw up a few complications that needed to be discussed. Sometimes the meetings went on for days as a result of the quibbling involved. It was rare for much generosity of spirit to be shown. However, Pascal Hervé did surprise everyone one day with his magnanimity.

'I think we should give the staff 20 per cent,' he suggested.

Richard Virenque quickly supported this motion, which the two men had no doubt cooked up between them. Voices were raised against this show of generosity. It was argued that on other teams the usual ratio was between 10 and 12 per cent. In the end, the share handed to the staff was 18 per cent.

I now have some doubts about the philanthropy of those who instigated this reform. Willy Voet's autobiography later shed some light on this. Reading that, I learned about the risks that some of the staff were running in tracking down products and transporting them across borders. Clearly it was felt that these efforts should be rewarded.

I also made another discovery during these financial discussions. The sum that we were sharing out didn't correspond to the total amount of prize money won throughout the year – far from it. Almost 600,000 francs was missing. The money spent on buying medical products had been deducted from the pot. In other words, the money spent on doping was openly accounted for. Expenditure for the Tour accounted for a quarter of this amount.

What do you think I said about this – me, the 'Mr Clean' of cycling, the destroyer of doping? Nothing at all. I kept quiet and pocketed the 45,000 francs that were handed to me, which was quite a sum for a new pro. It was the price of silence as much as a reward for my exploits.

I was still one of cycling's well-behaved kids at that point. Much later, I looked back at what I said to a reporter from *Tarn-Info*, a local paper, in November 1996. The journalist had asked me about two riders who had tested positive for nandrolone. 'I would prefer not to express any opinion on their suspensions,' I had replied. 'I don't want to talk about it. Sometimes journalists make mistakes because they have a tendency to want to put together an article that says something about themselves. Personally, I think EPO will soon be banned, and if the French Cycling Federation starts analysing blood, then this will advance things in this area.' My comments were perfectly in tune with most people's thinking within the cycling *milieu*. It was nothing more than perfectly delivered waffle. No one could have said it any better! Thanks for making that point, Christophe Bassons!

Chapter 3

The Illusionists

My 1997 season began with a great trip. In mid-January I flew across the Atlantic to take part in the Tour of Mexico. Our sponsor was trying to break into a new market, so the watch-making company asked us to take part in the event as part of its promotional drive. I had never been outside Europe before. Now Festina were taking me to the New World. From my perspective, cycling was in a good place.

We landed four days before the start of the race, but I never made it that far. During a training ride, the pain in my knee came back. As a result, I had to cut short my trip without seeing much of Mexico at all. For me, the country retained the postcard image of beaches with fine sand, sombreros and spicy sauces. I didn't know that for some travellers the country provided other less well-known benefits. The pharmacies in Tijuana and other towns close to the border with the United States were effectively doping supermarkets where riders could stock up during the winter and get their cure 'on the road'.

My programme for the season wasn't overly disrupted by this setback. Bruno Roussel slotted me into the group of riders who were preparing for the Tour of Italy, where Pascal Hervé was set to be the leader. I think that was another important step in my introduction to the sport, the Giro being the second biggest event of the year after the Tour de France.

Our preparation for the Giro picked up pace at Tirreno–Adriatico. I could see from the very first day why it was regarded as the fastest race in the world. The peloton rode in a frenzied way from the very start to the very end of the stages, stretching out into a long, ribbon-like line in which it was almost impossible to get to the front. Being distanced by only a few metres almost automatically condemned a rider's hopes for the day. I clung on in order to avoid this dishonour. I particularly remember a 30-kilometre section alongside a lake on one of the stages. The riders were in Indian file, almost in one long line. I was riding *à bloc* (full gas) and was very close to exhaustion. I kept telling myself that this nightmare was soon going to end, but the torture persisted. I think I cried that day. As I got onto the massage table, the soigneur realised the state I was in and offered me some means of recuperation. I flat out refused.

'You're pale, Babasse,' one of my team-mates declared.

'You're right, he's whiter than white!' another chipped in. 'Our Babasse looks really done in.'

The teasing continued all through dinner. I don't know if it was a coincidence, but that night I was sharing a room with Pascal Hervé for the first time since I had joined Festina. I was knackered. I only wanted one thing and that was to lie down and sleep. Pascal was sitting opposite me.

'I've heard that you don't want to be injected with the recuperatives. You're in one of the most difficult races in the world here. You will find it hard to finish if you don't look after yourself like you ought to. Like everyone else.'

His tone was friendly. Then he became much more blunt: 'You are in a team. We do what we do in order to win money. It would be good if you could also bring some in for the rest of us.'

I was right at my physical limit, incapable of arguing. 'I'll see' was all I could say in response. I was racked by uncertainty. Did I have the right to follow my own path? Moreover, did I want to suffer like this for nothing?

The race picked up again at the same rhythm. I was pedalling in a fog that was becoming thicker and thicker. My reactions were getting blunted. On the seventh day, the last of the race, I had a mental blank on a bend. I fell and crashed into a metal dustbin. It could have been a lot more serious.

When I returned to France I felt as shaken by Pascal Hervé's friendly admonishment as I had been by my crash. For the first time, one of my colleagues was making me face up to my responsibilities.

Distraught, I spoke about it with my parents and Pascale. They told me: 'Get some more advice.' It was the wisest thing they could have said to a young guy on the edge of exhaustion. Any talk of moral responsibility would have had the opposite effect to the one desired. Antoine also came to my rescue. 'I can tell you that you will get there without it,' he assured me.

I think my poor performance at Tirreno–Adriatico denied me a starting slot in the Giro, where Pascal Hervé went on to distinguish himself by wearing the leader's pink jersey for several days. 'I'll see' was all I had mumbled. It wasn't a good enough response.

At Tirreno–Adriatico, my cultural journey through a shadowy world had continued. I came across my first centrifuge. The machine, which was quite big, had been put in the bus. A blood sample would be placed inside it. The machine would begin to spin, separating the plasma from the red blood cells. The haematocrit (the level of red blood cells) could then be established using a grading system. During the Italian race, Dr Ryckaert carried out this test on all of us twice. He was getting used to using it.

That season was set to bring about an innovation. The widespread use of EPO had led to riders trying to outdo each other in their dosage. Red blood cell counts were getting too high. Those willing to take the craziest risks were imposing their law and were pushing the peloton towards collective suicide.

Team doctors were wondering what to do, not because they had finally reacquainted themselves with the text of the Hippocratic oath, but more through fear of a fatal accident ruining their careers as dopers. Plenty of the riders were concerned too, as they were being forced to up their dosage to remain competitive. Finding itself unable to rein the maniacs in, the International Association of Professional Cyclists (AICP) agreed to allow what was effectively the imposition of a speed limit.

There had been growing support for fixing an upper limit for red blood cell counts. Now the bar was fixed at 50 per cent, which was still ten points above the usual norm. In the end, a margin of tolerance resulted in 51 per cent being set as the actual level. The craftiest riders worked out how to be just below the limit, as an incorrect calculation could push them over it. It would have been annoying to end up getting sanctioned for being a few imprudent tenths of a per cent above it: after all, the sport's police were as liable to error as anyone else.

The UCI was, like a mother, full of indulgence and compassion for its wayward children. This attempt at coercion was not intended to suppress the practice of doping, but just to make it more civilised. Readings above the upper limit didn't result in any disciplinary action being taken, as was the case if a urine control produced a positive test. Instead it resulted in the rider having to stop work for two weeks. The miscreant wasn't regarded as a cheat, but as someone who was ill and needed to be looked after …

However, precautions still needed to be taken. The controls were carried out at dawn. The results were available almost immediately and the enforced absence from work meant that riders couldn't take part in any races. Positive dope tests had the undeniable advantage of launching a drawn-out procedure during which riders could continue to compete. Suspensions, if there were any, would occur at the end of the season. They were served out discreetly in the midst of the winter break.

There was also another good reason for being prudent. The public and the press, who were no longer as easy to fool, had made the connection between riders being prevented from competing and their being up to no good. That's simply how people were thinking.

The first blood control, carried out by the UCI's doctors, took place on the opening day of Paris–Nice. Bruno Roussel was woken up at six o'clock and was asked to present four random riders from his eight-man team. This early-morning call didn't surprise him: the UCI's representatives who had been staying in the same hotel overnight had warned him about this eventuality the previous evening. As a result, a wave of panic had swept through the hotel's corridors. Those flapping were like bungee jumpers, whose adrenalin shoots up even though they are not running any risk of hitting the ground.

Naturally, I was hauled out of bed first and led the way for the rest. I had suddenly assumed some importance within the group. I was Mr Loyal, who had to ensure that the others gained some time, enough at least for the artists to prepare for their appearance on the scene. I went down with the express mission of keeping the gentlemen carrying out the blood tests busy for a while. While I was doing this, the others were making a detour into the doctor's room to undergo a private test that would establish their level.

One careless rider delivered a reading above 50. While the others continued with the delaying tactics that I'd started, the doctor fixed him up with a glucose drip. This diluted the blood and, as a result, reduced the red blood cell level. All of the controls undertaken on Festina riders were negative.

There's another detail I should mention: when I went down to the ground floor and into the room where the tests were carried out, there were some TV cameramen already waiting there for me. Everyone had got wind of this supposedly random control. Although it was little more than a masquerade, three of those picked out for testing from other teams did deliver results over the limit, including Frenchman Erwann Menthéour. We had avoided the trap with disconcerting ease. I couldn't understand how others had ended up being caught.

The tragicomedy that played out that morning gave me a huge amount of satisfaction. For five minutes, the hotel corridors were transformed into a street theatre, with all manner of feverish activity, doors banging and loud swearing. I was the only one who remained calm while my team-mates were running around like headless chickens, their eyes still full of sleep. You could have been forgiven for thinking we were on the *Titanic*, with passengers dashing about between cabins.

It wasn't long before the team issued everyone with lifejackets. I remember quite soon after this incident going into our rooms and finding coat-hangers dangling from the handles on the window. They had been bent and twisted into a hook shape so that they could be used for a very different purpose to hanging up clothes. If there happened to be a surprise dope control, they could be used to hang up the bags of glucose solution that were always stored under the beds. The methods used to prevent detection kept being improved, and blood controls became a routine issue that everyone had to deal with. Riders as well as teams began to have their own centrifuges. About the size of your hand, they quickly became an essential part of a cyclist's kit. They didn't even bother to hide them. One day, I noticed one lying on the window ledge in a hotel room.

I admired the ability of my peers to be able to sleep despite the very real possibility of a dope control taking place. Centrifuges and drips effectively became their teddy bears, providing reassurance when they were in bed. But what kind of sleep could these strange kids really get? I don't think they enjoyed the sleep of the righteous.

In spite of the simple precautions taken in the face of these inspections, sporadic exclusions from racing still took place. Festina never worried about such an eventuality and I think other teams were as clued up as ours about the ruses that enabled them to stay a step ahead of the sport's policemen. So on what criteria were the sacrificial victims chosen, bearing in mind that most were usually nothing more than also-rans?

Later on I learned that some of the more habitual dopers couldn't get their red blood cell levels down after a while. Pumped up with EPO, their blood became resistant to treatment. They couldn't dilute it even with litres of glucose water. As a result, their red blood cell count became incriminating. Some experts believe it was this scenario that led to the exclusion of Marco Pantani from the final days of the 1999 Giro d'Italia, when he was wearing the pink jersey of race leader.

Before too long, a new way to cheat the tests emerged: doctors provided medical certificates attesting that the poor wretches who had been caught out had been wrongly incriminated. Their haematocrit had risen naturally, either because they had spent too long living at altitude or because of a congenital defect. In just a few months, some members of the peloton had reached a physiological specificity that Himalayan sherpas had taken centuries to achieve.

I came from the plains in the Tarn region. My natural haematocrit was always somewhere around 40. I never had a dose of EPO that might have suddenly transformed me into a potential conqueror of Everest. I had nothing to fear, nor anything to reproach myself for. However, I wasn't happy with the blood tests nor with the more standard urine tests. I found it humiliating to have to undergo this assessment. But my conscience ensured a personal mandate to comply that was just as strong as the procedural pseudo-injunctions.

As time went on, I viewed the stress that some of my peers were under with a somewhat less than fraternal sense of jubilation. I'll admit this even began to have a rather unsavoury edge to it. When the press presented me as a paragon of virtue and put me on a pedestal, a sense of doubt gnawed away at me. What if someone tried to entrap me?

I read about Dieter Baumann, a German athlete who had been depicted as a model of integrity. He loudly condemned the damaging effect of doping within his discipline. He ended up testing positive for nandrolone. Ever since, he had claimed that an injustice had taken place, but his protestations sounded just the same as those made by everyone else who had been caught out. Baumann insisted the product had been put into his toothpaste without his knowledge. He railed about a plot, just as all of the others do. In the end, his federation acquitted him, giving him the benefit of the doubt or because there had been a procedural error, I don't know which – so many well-known cheats have been spared punishment by a similar show of leniency. Baumann was allowed to keep on competing, but his stance had been tarnished. The rebel had been brought to heel and the man had probably been broken.

I confess that from that time on I was paranoid every time I underwent a control. I don't feel any more serene today. I am always worried that my name will be drawn out for a random test at races. Even having a clear conscience doesn't provide me with any sense of security!

The team had beefed up its roster at the start of the season. Up to that point, it had only been concerned with the intense delights of the Tour de France and the mutual love-in between Richard Virenque and the race's fans. But now Bruno Roussel was nurturing some new dreams. He wanted his team to be in the action right through the year. This new ambition had resulted in him getting a boost in his budget from the team sponsor. That was the theory at least, but was it more a case of him building up grandiose plans in order to cover the constant need for money that stemmed from the greed of his troops? Whatever the case, the directeur sportif was now in a vicious circle that was hastening his eventual fall from grace.

The idea of preparing a crack force for the Giro emerged from this nascent megalomania. I have already explained how I was sidelined from this objective, having had a sense of foreboding about the plan. I had been switched into the group earmarked for the spring Classics. This was another testing ground for Festina, another way of bolstering the team's rather meagre palmarès.

Bruno Roussel had attracted Gianluca Bortolami to the team with this goal in mind. He was an Italian *rouleur* and one-day specialist who knew what it took to tame the Paris–Roubaix cobbles and resist the devilish winds of the Belgian flatlands. He had been tempted away from Mapei, at that time the biggest team around. No doubt our directeur sportif was hoping that Emmanuel Magnien, Bruno Boscardin, Laurent Brochard and this prestigious recruit were going to form an expensive but successful quartet, and perhaps even challenge Virenque's omnipotence, about which Roussel had a bad feeling.

I had expressed my interest in the Classics to Bruno Roussel, who, obliging as ever, had accepted this whim of mine. As I saw it, these one-day races offered a significant advantage: they didn't depend on the need for recuperation. The downtime between each race would, I thought, enable me to regain my full physical capacity without recourse to artificial means. Brimming with hope, I headed for a hotel in Neuville-en-Ferrain, where our campaign headquarters was due to be located for a month. Situated on the Belgian border, our base was just a kilometre away from the place where Willy Voet would be collared by the customs authorities prior to the 1998 Tour de France.

Upbeat to start with, the atmosphere quickly turned sour. The campaign was characterised by defeat. As our losses stacked up, Bruno Roussel became irritable. He criticised us for our lack of results in a tone I'd never heard from him before. The pressure he loaded on our shoulders was hard to bear.

The defeated men attempted to justify each new setback. There were signs of revolt among the ranks. Dr Ryckaert had limited the use of EPO because of the threat of blood tests. Rumours were going around about a new product, PFC, perfluorocarbon, which had been tested on American soldiers during the Gulf War. It had the same properties as EPO but didn't raise haematocrit. It made it a doddle to get through blood controls. But our doctor had banned its use, believing the secondary effects of its usage were dangerous – rightly, as it turned out: one rider almost died because of a dodgy batch. The peloton also buzzed with the news that some synthetic haemoglobins produced clear physical benefits and remained undetectable.

Throughout the 1990s, our Belgian doctor had built up his reputation through his knowledge of EPO. His star was fading thanks to the arrival of a new range of pharmaceuticals that he viewed with scepticism. I think it was around this time that he acquired a new nickname that both stuck to him and discredited him: Dr Punto. This new tag made reference to one of Fiat's smaller models and was a derogatory comparison with Dr Ferrari, who had the ability to turbo-charge a rider's capacity.

Gnawing jealousy used to explode to the surface at mealtimes. Some of our group had found out that the squadron preparing for the Tour had access to a new product that was impressively effective. They complained about not having access to it and raged indignantly. Why them and not us?

Once again I must point out that it was Willy Voet who shed light on this for me in his autobiography. There I learned that the product, dubbed 'P' at Festina, was Clenbuterol, an anabolic apparently imported from Portugal. 'Banned from sale in France, Clenbuterol is one of the most effective hormones when it comes to producing muscular mass,' explained my expert guide to doping. I prefer to transcribe his words in this instance. I've got no expertise in the matter and wouldn't like to commit any kind of blunder in terms of nomenclature. But there was no doubt this product was effective, to judge from the size of Djamolidine Abdoujaparov's thighs. He tested positive for the product during the 1997 Tour de France. I was astounded by the physique of this colossus every time I got close to him. To me, his craggy face, the muscular bulk bulging through his jersey, and his expressionless, almost brutish features were an exact embodiment of strength. He had the indestructible appearance of those neo-realist representations of Communist heroes that were in vogue in the Soviet Union, from which he had emerged.

The Soviet sprinter, who took Uzbek nationality following the collapse of the USSR, had won a medium mountain stage during the previous year's Tour de France. That had provoked surprise among the race's commentators, but no more than that. However, I believe that result was one of the most remarkable consequences of doping and the most convincing when it comes to countering those people who still dare to talk about the placebo effect. Medical preparation enables climbers to win time trials, *rouleurs* to be victorious on mountain passes and sprinters to win the toughest Classics. It does away with specificity, while at the same time levelling out ability. Previously, only a rider blessed with exceptional class could aspire to be a complete athlete. Today, an ordinary rider can become an all-rounder with a little bit of chemical remodelling. A little bit of a boost here with EPO, a bit of strength added there with growth hormone, and a tad more endurance thanks to corticosteroids, and off you go, young man.

One final thing should be added before I continue with my account: Djamolidine Abdoujaparov tested positive seven times that same year before finally being sanctioned.

Put on an unwanted diet, my team-mates shouted conspiracy. The soigneurs did what they could to put an end to their griping. The day before the Tour of Flanders I went down to join the other riders for breakfast. I could hear laughter resounding around the dining room, and when I walked in I was stunned by what I saw. The guys' faces were deformed by horrendous puffiness. A bad batch of corticosteroids had resulted in water retention. They looked like characters from a second-rate horror film. The monsters were laughing about their deformities.

I was alarmed by their lack of concern. I was going to be alarmed for other reasons the next day when I lined up in the great Flemish Classic. The pack set a hellish pace on Belgium's back roads. Everyone fought for position, elbows flying everywhere. I had to bump up against my neighbours in order to ensure that I stayed in the saddle. I fought tooth and nail to ensure that no one slipped onto the wheel of the rider in front who was providing me with shelter. I had to use my elbows constantly in order to avoid being sent into the roadside ditch.

A crosswind produced a horrific lottery in the form of echelons. In order to get some shelter from the gusts coming across the road, each rider took up a position at an angle to the wheel of the man in front.

Little by little, the peloton fanned out across the road. The moment would arrive when the whole width of the road was filled. The next rider couldn't insert himself into the line without riding onto the pavement or into the spectators at the roadside. Finding himself without any shelter, he would quickly lose a few metres. A split would open that soon became almost impossible to close up. When an echelon formed, there was an all-out fight to avoid losing out and ending up with your nose right into the wind. Riders would have to sprint again and again to get up to the front of the group in order to avoid the consequences of a split. As the speed inexorably rose because of these accelerations, the riders squabbled with each other. It was a bit like a chariot race, where absolutely anything was permitted. I really enjoyed this almost circus-style racing. However, I soon realised that without medical help I was not playing the Ben Hur role, but that of one of the Christians who've been thrown to the lions. It was too fast for me. I abandoned at the feeding station.

Paris–Roubaix was finally approaching, and I was quivering with anticipation. This race fascinated me more than any other. It was always said of 'The Queen of the Classics' that 'you either love it or you hate it'. I instinctively knew I was going to love it. Training rides on the course only helped to convince me of that. I felt at ease on the cobbles. My experience of mountain biking had prepared me very well for such treacherous terrain and made me well aware of the very particular laws of equilibrium related to cycling.

The morning of the start arrived at last. It was chilly, one of those pale days on the cusp of winter and spring. The soigneurs were loading all the kit into the team cars before heading to Compiègne, where the start was set to take place on the broad avenue outside the château. Dressed only in T-shirts, some of them were dripping with sweat as they worked. They snorted like angry bulls as they bustled back and forth. I looked on, wrapped up in several layers of warm clothing. I was astonished by their resistance to the cold and mentioned this to a team-mate, who laughed and told me: 'They've charged up.'

The prospect of a big race provoked this kind of collective frisson. It affected the backroom staff in the same way as the riders. They doped themselves in proportion to the level of the race.

The race began. I felt at ease on the first sections of cobbles. After three sections I even ended up at the front with about 50 other riders. My job was to help Emmanuel Magnien and Gianluca Bortolami, and I stayed close to them without any difficulty whatsoever. After the frenzy of the Tour of Flanders, I was pleased to be feeling so comfortable. This really was a race that suited me.

Then Emmanuel punctured. Like a loyal soldier, I gave him my wheel. I had to wait a long time to get some help for myself in the chaos. I fumed as I stood holding my useless machine. Eventually a neutral support vehicle arrived. I was eight minutes down when I finally got back under way. There was no chance of me getting back up to my team leaders. I wasn't any good to anyone. My race was over. I abandoned at the next feeding station.

However, I was satisfied with my Roubaix debut. I felt proud of myself that evening. The race was undoubtedly made for me. I couldn't wait for the next edition to roll round. But a team-mate tempered my optimism. He explained how the race only really started at the fearsome cobbled section of the Arenberg Trench, which was just after the place where I had packed in for the day …

My first experience of the Classics left me with mixed feelings. My performances hadn't been stellar, but they hadn't been awful either. Just before the spring campaign, I had cracked the head of my fibula after slipping over on some ice. I needed some time to recover from this and I probably wasn't at my top level. That was why I was having problems staying with the pace. My enthusiasm remained intact. I could still find plenty of reasons to remain optimistic.

Spheres are the predominant geometrical shape in cycling. They are everywhere. Even the calendar is like a never-ending and almost unchanging loop, within which there are other spinning spheres that are just as intangible. At the very centre of everything is the Tour de France, known by the French as *La Grande Boucle*, meaning big buckle or loop. Everything else revolves around this hub, the various cogs interlocking and creating forward momentum. Consequently, the mechanisms that drive the calendar resemble a bike.

Complementing this idea of geometrical perfection, the Four Days of Dunkirk closed the Classics cycle that had begun a month earlier with the Three Days of De Panne. After this race, the preparatory cycle for the Tour de France would start.

At Dunkirk, I found more reason to be optimistic. I finished fifth in the time trial, 21 seconds down on Frank Vandenbroucke, who had been anointed successor to Eddy Merckx by the Belgians, and 37 seconds down on the day's winner, Johan Museeuw.

That evening, Eric Ryckaert asked to talk to me as I was coming out of the shower.

'You finished fifth today,' he said to me. 'You rode a great time trial. You're really blessed with some potential.'

He paused. I liked Dr Ryckaert. I found he had a human touch and was sincere, unlike his colleague Fernando Jiménez, who was as slippery as an eel. I sat down on the bed to hear what he had to say. It was an important moment. I could already sense where this conversation was heading.

'You've got potential,' he repeated, 'but you will never make the best of it if you refuse our help. You would undoubtedly have done better today if you had agreed to have an injection before the start.'

The doctor revealed the results of the blood tests that had been carried out on me during Tirreno–Adriatico. I hadn't even thought to ask about them since they'd been done. My haematocrit had gone down to 37.5 per cent. He told me that I had finished the race on the verge of anaemia. I immediately understood why I had been in such a bad state at the end of that race, almost on the point of passing out. The doctor continued.

'It is more dangerous to ride with a haematocrit of 36 than it is with one of 50. You can't expect anything if you don't agree to push your level back up.'

He then told me something that Gianluca Bortolami had confessed to him. 'If Bassons was at 50 instead of 40, he could win Paris–Roubaix.'

'Just consider that if you agree to take EPO, Christophe, you would earn ten times more money.'

At that time I was earning 13,500 francs a month. Other riders had salaries well above 100,000 a month, not to mention the 500,000 that Richard Virenque was already receiving.

'You could earn a lot of money, Christophe,' the doctor affirmed.

Our conversation lasted for half an hour.

In the face of his flattering and persuasive comments, I could only come up with some fairly vapid objections, such as 'I don't agree.' I felt I had been cornered, which was hardly helped by what was becoming my standard reply: 'OK, I'll think about it.'

Bruno Roussel was told about the meeting and my obstinacy. Pressure was also being applied in a different way. I had effectively missed my last chance of making the team for the Giro, which was starting a fortnight later. Having grown tired of waiting, Bruno Roussel had drawn up a new programme for me. Instead of riding the Tour of Italy, I was relegated to the Tour of Luxembourg and events in the Coupe de France series. I was also passed over for selection for the Midi Libre and Dauphiné Libéré. I was being punished.

Was there any chance of being a success without resorting to doping? The ruthlessly revealing results provided by the doctor's centrifuge kept bringing this question back to me. A few weeks later, during a race of ten days, my haematocrit dropped from 41.5 per cent at the start to 36 per cent on the final day. I was the only one of the team to experience this inevitable drop in my level. The levels of the others remained between 47 and 48. Thanks to the knowledge I'd gained, I now knew the reason for this consistency. I was well aware of the merry dance done with coolboxes each evening in the hotel. I finally knew how it all worked!

My team-mates now joked about me more than ever:

'You look pale, Babasse.'

'You seem tired, old man!'

'Take some vitamins – that will sort you out!'

My conviction that I could succeed was being worn down. The drawn-out agony I went through at this race convinced me that I needed to draw a line under the longer stage races; that I had to yield, given the rules of the game. On the other hand, I still firmly believed that I could have some success in one-day races. I was only ready to abandon half of my dream. Hope is the last thing to die, as a Russian saying goes.

While we were racing in the Alps I spent a lot of time talking with Philippe Gaumont. The guy had a reputation for being a bit of a yob, but he always seemed like an honourable man to me. He didn't skirt around the issue when the topic of doping came up. He flaunted his positive tests like tattoos. He took responsibility for his actions and their consequences without whining, equivocation or denunciations.

My performances had, it seemed, attracted the attention of his employer, Cofidis. He had been asked to express the esteem they had for me.

'If you want to join our team you can,' he said to me one day. 'But you must know that members of our team *fait le métier.*'

That was how I found out that my position had become known outside my own team. I had never said anything openly about it myself, but clearly my stance was already well known within the pro peloton, which left me to think that it was quite unusual.

By this time I'd fully grasped how ingrained pharmaceutical excess was in the professional cycling community. Its members weren't doping just to win, but to exist. Philippe Gaumont told me about competitions that took place within his team. Those involved would take Stilnox tablets, which are very potent sleeping pills, together with very strong coffee. Initially, the effects of these two things counteracted each other, but in the end they combined. The user would then reach a higher state. 'After you've taken 12 tablets, you're completely floating,' Gaumont told me.

Around that time, I raced in three criteriums where there was absolutely nothing at stake, in Calais, Amiens and Aubervilliers. I noticed that some of my fellow racers seemed to be more exuberant than usual, to the point where they looked like they were going to crash on every corner. I put this wild behaviour down to these illicit games that they revelled in when they mixed up unlikely combinations of substances. In principle, events like these did not have a doping control. However, the organiser of the event in Calais had got wind of a medical inspection. He dashed around letting all the racers know the news so that they would rein in their intake of drugs.

The wheel of time was still turning and it brought us back around to the French championships, which took place in Montlhéry. At dinner the night before the race, our group was split between two tables, one for those taking part in the Tour and one for the rest of us. It was an indication of the split that had occurred.

Richard Virenque wasn't expecting much from a course that was perfectly designed for *rouleurs*. It suited Emmanuel Magnien much better. Virenque only arrived on the morning of the race, his skin yellow and his features bloated. He found he was unable to stay with the pace right from the very opening kilometres. Suddenly, he started to vomit.

I was not going much better than him. On what was a flat circuit, I could barely stay with the pack. I was getting worse rather than improving. I had the feeling that my body wasn't up to the job. I had lost every little shred of morale.

The Tour de France got under way soon afterwards, but this time Bruno Roussel didn't ask me to follow it closely. There wasn't even the slightest chance that I would be part of this festival of excess in the near future. I went on holiday to Spain with Pascale, my sister Valérie and her boyfriend, Denis. We stayed in the outskirts of Barcelona.

I followed the Tour with detachment for two reasons. I felt distant from it, almost like a stranger, despite my team's success. Festina excelled in every one of the mountain stages. The team took several victories and Richard ended up on the second step of the podium. The French public was in a trance-like state. Virenquemania was at its height. The team's collective performance didn't surprise me. I had noticed that the guys were in particularly good shape and brimming with confidence when I had encountered them at Montlhéry. But I didn't draw an ounce of personal pride from their performances. On the contrary, I felt that a great divide was opening up between this elite and me. I couldn't even put it down to my age: Jan Ullrich had just won the Tour de France.

All the same, training was making me a better rider. Antoine Vayer was tracking my progress on his computers and regularly showed me the upward curves that indicated my performance was improving. But the exploits of the likes of Laurent Brochard, Didier Rous and Neil Stephens on the Tour demonstrated the exponential improvement brought about by their medical preparation. I ended up regarding these team-mates as strangers I simply didn't know. In my heart of hearts, I delighted in the fact that their heroic deeds were boosting the team's prize kitty. It amused me to think that I was earning money while I was kicking back and resting.

I returned from Spain … a little less white than I'd been when I'd gone. Also my haematocrit had gone back up, and my morale had risen too. The conversations I had had with Pascale had reinforced my convictions. I had told her about the possibility of succumbing to temptation.

'I don't think you should,' she kept telling me. 'What I want more than anything is for you to keep me informed as to what's going on.'

In August, I raced in the Tour du Limousin, which was won by Laurent Brochard. While I was working for him, I realised that the impression I had got from watching the Tour de France on television was spot on. Laurent had never been as strong. Six weeks later, he was crowned world champion in San Sebastián.

Bruno Roussel and Michel Gros were still intoxicated by the dizzying successes they had enjoyed during July. One evening at dinner, they kept telling us that we were the best. We were unbeatable, they said. If it hadn't been for the fact that our rivals got so afraid of us that they ganged up against us, Richard could perhaps even have taken the yellow jersey. That eventuality will come in time, etc, etc.

'He has neither lord nor master,' Bruno affirmed.

With regard to my own position, I didn't exactly feel like I was on top of the world … 'Some stride along the crest of the road, but I'm down in the very bottom of the ditch,' French comedian Fernand Reynaud once said in a sketch about a roadworker. That was me, one of the very smallest fish in the peloton. I was the lackey without any real future. I did my share of the work for Laurent throughout the race, sweeping the road clear before his wheels. But, when we got to the stage finales, I put away my dustpan and brush and disappeared into obscurity among the also-rans of the classification.

One evening, Michel Gros came into my room. It had been a baking hot day. Everyone had been knocking fluids back like there was no tomorrow. Each of us had dropped back in turn to the team car and returned to the bunch laden with bottles, which we handed out. *Chasser la canette* is the traditional term for this, harking back to the days when riders would rush into bars and grab any can of drink to hand for their leaders. At the finish, I drank litre upon litre without managing to quench my thirst. I was so parched I felt I could have drunk every drop on the planet.

'You should try a recovery injection,' Michel said to me. 'It would stop you getting dehydrated.'

'I'd prefer not to.'

'But it's only a recuperative, for heaven's sake. Take it and you will remain competitive!'

Michel has always been someone you could have confidence in. Although doping was generalised at Festina, as Bruno Roussel would later confess to a judge, it wasn't all-pervading. Some guys tried to avoid getting pulled into dodgy practices, or at least as much they could. Michel was one of them, as was his son, Laurent, and another masseur, Rik Keyaerts. As team insiders, they knew exactly what was going on. There was no way they could have been unaware of it. But their convictions, together with a dose of good sense perhaps, plus a feeling that this kind of effrontery couldn't go on for ever, meant they kept themselves at arm's length. Like me, they would eventually have the last laugh. In the meantime, they were relegated to support roles. They endured the condescension of those who had been artificially transformed into little emperors by cheating. The haughty contempt we, the pariahs of the syringe, had to put up with brought us closer together. Laurent and Rik became my confidants on those evenings when their massage failed to ease my dejection.

Michel certainly wasn't a doper. So hearing him sounding off like that when faced with my pigheadedness got me thinking. He was right: a recuperative was nothing at all. Why was I sticking to my guns so categorically? Didn't I have the right to give it a go? Would testing this out just once mean that I had succumbed, that I was hooked and would end up a junkie? Give it a go, you idiot, and then make up your mind!

This time I was sinking. I only had a single lifeline to hang on to.

'OK,' I told Michel. 'But first I have to talk to my girlfriend.'

I called her as soon as Michel left my room.

'Are you really sure you want to do it?' was all Pascale asked me.

It was a good question, the only valid one in fact, and one that I was no longer asking myself as my own will seemed to be lacking in the face of their authority. But I certainly wasn't sure I wanted to yield. I was allowing the suggestions of others to undermine my own convictions. Their attempts to persuade me were eroding my stance. The deftly offered and apparently fraternal suggestions, along with the criticisms made by the management, were like an acid eating away at my foundations. On the other side was sweet Pascale, indispensable Pascale! She had put forward one simple question in the face of their claims. This insidious little dance was nothing more than a cover for their high-handed attitude. Once again, Pascale had prevailed. I wouldn't take a recuperative, and I would tell them that if I had to.

But I didn't need to. Michel didn't bring the issue up with me again. He had offered his point of view – or perhaps acted on orders. He respected my decision.

But what exactly was my decision? 'Are you really sure you want to do it?' In truth, I wasn't sure of anything, my darling, my beloved Pascale. I was in the throes of a complete intellectual breakdown. Accumulated fatigue and contradictory claims had loosened my grip on my free will. I was drifting back and forth in a current made up of other people's opinions, incapable of resisting or opposing any kind of argument. I was no longer capable of thinking for myself. Contradictory pieces of advice were rattling around in my head. My fiancée was dead right. But the smooth-talking Ryckaert's words were still resounding in my mind. 'If you had agreed to have an injection before the start, you would have done better,' he had told me. Even Antoine didn't know what to think any longer. Forgive me, Pascale! I have to give it a go.

The cycling calendar turns like a never-ending thread on a screw. After a few spins of the wheel and pedal strokes you're heading on towards the next race. At least that's what it seems like when you find yourself back in the same place you were in a year before. You spend all day riding like a condemned man, only to find yourself back at another start line the next day, your computer set once again to zero. The races, the towns and the hotels keep coming back, and eventually they become so intermingled that it's hard to differentiate them. Ultimately, the rider starts to feel like a traveller who stays in the same place. Only the memories and successes collected along the way remind him that he's moving forwards. But I was only accumulating memories.

At the end of August, I found myself back in Malbuisson for the French time trial championships. I was even staying in the same gîte as the year before, back in the same room where we had previously got ourselves ready. The bedside table on which I had noticed the syringe was still there. A year earlier, I hadn't considered touching it. On this occasion, I went to see one of the backroom staff before the start.

'I really want to try an injection,' I told him.

The guy looked at me. 'Are you sure?'

'Yes, but I don't want Solucamphre, just caffeine.'

'OK, if that's what you want.'

The guy didn't question my rather intriguing request. He took an ampoule out of his medical kit. He asked me to sit on the bed and hold out my arm. He put a pillow on my knees and put my elbow into it. He tightened an elastic tourniquet around my forearm in order to make my veins stand out. When he could see that they were sufficiently prominent, he swabbed me with cotton wool that had been dipped in alcohol and inserted the needle. The whole operation took only a few seconds. I just stared at my clenched fist. I didn't dare glance up and catch the eye of the guy doing all this, because I was afraid he would be able to read the defeat in my face.

I had lost. The *milieu* had won. I felt humiliated. I had failed to stick to my commitment never to have an injection unless I was ill. I had taken the first and undoubtedly the hardest step, one which it was generally impossible to turn back from. I knew that Christophe Moreau had also refused that first prick of the needle for a long time. He had only agreed to have an injection in 1995. Then, he had changed dramatically. I was taking the same path. How long before I would resort to drips and intramuscular injections, packed with all kinds of medical products, both banned and otherwise? Small doses of caffeine were permitted by the rules. I hadn't infringed them – which was fine! But I couldn't delude myself. I was a potential doper, just like the rest. I looked at the arm that would soon belong more to the doctor than to me. The swollen artery would now become the passageway to all kinds of experiments.

Then I cried out with terror. An enormous blister had formed. The guy had missed the artery and liquid had gathered under my skin. My nerves had undoubtedly been responsible for this misjudgement. I watched horrified as the inflammation kept getting bigger, and implored him to do something.

'There's nothing that can be done. You just have to wait for it to go,' he told me. 'I missed the vein. Do you want me to try again?'

'No, no, no!' I yelled as I dashed out.

I had to get to the start. I felt that everyone would notice the bump. With my mind still spinning, I pulled on some armwarmers, which were bound to attract attention in the middle of August … I was ashamed and panicked. I finished up in seventh place, having recorded a terrible time.

The feeling of shock did at least bring back my mental autonomy. I swore to myself I would never go down that path again.

In September I once again lined up in the Tour de l'Avenir, the stage race reserved for so-called *espoirs* – young talents. Was I still one of them? At 23, wasn't I now in the category of riders classed as irretrievable disappointments? The only race Babasse was leading was into the middle of nowhere. Your applause please for our impressive champion, the pick of the losers! He deserves it. He knew exactly how to fool those around him. He had made them believe in him, only to come unstuck when even very little was expected of him. What a magnificent failure! He had chickened out, betrayed the confidence that had been placed in him. His place as leader of the losers was well deserved. Bassons was their king, he was cycling's biggest reject. Bassons the anarchist who didn't want to do what everyone did, the punk who didn't want to use the needle. No future!

Cycling can serve up some astonishing twists. Fourth place in the prologue behind David Millar looked as if it was going to relaunch me. Was I really as mediocre as I thought? Did I have a future and a right to be there? I felt like my old self again. That set me on the road to an impressive performance that concluded with another fourth place on the final day. The most astonishing thing was that I had finished in satisfyingly good form. After ten days of racing, my legs still felt good, I was still turning the pedals with great *souplesse*, and I wasn't dead with fatigue. I was on the way back.

Just as I had experienced a change in fortune, so did the Breton rider Erwann Menthéour, although in his case for the worse. He crashed two days from the end and waved goodbye to a race he had dominated. His career practically ended there. He fell into an awful state of depression, which was more the consequence of medical excesses than sporting disappointment. Menthéour found some relief in writing, and in 1999 he published *Secret Défonce*, a warts-and-all account of his career. In it he confessed to absolutely everything he had done and revealed how doping had improved his performance but destroyed his psyche. He had started down that path by taking a simple recuperative.

My season was coming to a close. I had done 28,000 kilometres on the bike, and I hadn't progressed a jot. I even felt that I was going backwards. This wasn't some kind of optical illusion: the other riders were flying past me. I had finished the Grand Prix des Nations time trial in more or less the same time but in a much lower place than the year before. I had finished behind Richard Virenque who, since the Tour de France, had produced some excellent performances in a discipline that he had hated not long before. Having failed to blow the whistle, I had not been selected for the world championships.

I had taken one victory in 1996. But I didn't have even a single line to add to my CV for 1997. The page remained quite blank, almost virginal. It seemed that I had picked out a page for my palmarès that was simply far too big.

I still had the ability to lie to myself. I dug up good reasons for below-par performances. It is almost a given that a professional's second year is not as good as his first. However, the third season is often one of confirmation. Richard Virenque no longer counted on me for support. In fact, he barely spoke to me. I had disappointed him just as I had undoubtedly disappointed Bruno. But finishing the Tour de l'Avenir without being almost totally wiped out provided a tiny bit of hope that I might be able to complete a big stage race and perhaps even complete *La Grande Boucle* itself.

I had another reason for sticking with my life in the saddle. I was still tolerated within the pro scene. My stance was no doubt well known, but I was the only one harmed by it. My dream-like, almost poetic fantasies attracted nothing more than amusement. For my part, I was proud of why I stood out but didn't want to become isolated. I still felt part of the family. That October in San Sebastián, Laurent Jalabert won the world time trial championship and Laurent Brochard became the world road champion. A neighbour and a team-mate had distinguished themselves and I was happy for them.

The winter break bolstered my pipe dreams. Autumn is a holiday period for cyclists. The supporters' clubs take advantage of the downtime to organise rides in tribute to their champions. Pros who live close by come along to the festivities, which conclude with a dinner that goes on well into the night. Every year I used to go along to two celebrations organised by Laurent Jalabert's fans – honour to whom honour is due.

Before one of these sorties, we were all in the same room together getting changed. The atmosphere was relaxed, the conversation full of bawdy jokes. Then one person was asked: 'Have you got the gear?'

'I sure have,' he said.

The guy took a flask out of his bag and it went around the room, everyone pouring themselves some before they passed it on. Among the people in the room was an ex-rider. He had been left partly disabled by an accident. The others refused to let him have the flask, insisting it wouldn't be good for him. The guy was whining on about getting a dose. Seeing him pleading for it made me realise just how hooked it was possible to become.

Then it came around to me.

'Are you going to try it?' the guy next to me asked.

'This is Babasse's christening!' someone else shouted.

I have never dared ask what the flask contained.

Ever since the previous season, I had been lucky enough to have my own fan club and a similar end-of-season tribute. The first time my fans turned out to support me was at the French championships in 1996. They put up banners and painted my name on the road. Having your name daubed on the tarmac like this is a rite of passage for any pro.

My ardent fans didn't hold my lack of results against me and organised the second Fête des Ténors on 8 November. Most of the professionals in my region accepted the invitation to come. Laurent Jalabert was going to be there, as were his brother Nicolas, Christophe Rinero, Didier Rous, etc. I was proud to see them all come together for me. The frustration I had felt at the end of the season dissipated with this show of camaraderie.

Tradition provides the framework underlying the whole sport, and it demands that riders spend Christmas with family and close friends, and the New Year with each other. As a result, end-of-year festivities are split between two families.

Consequently, I took Pascale, Valérie and Denis to a New Year's Eve party at my team-mate Didier Rous's house in Montauban. Most of the gang I've just mentioned were also there with their partners and friends.

The dinner was a blast, but past experience of what went on at these end-of-season shindigs kept me on my guard. At the end of the meal, some of the guests slipped into the kitchen. I discreetly followed to see what they were up to. Someone had pulled out the now familiar flask. Some of its contents were tipped into a cafetière.

I quickly headed back to the table and managed to whisper to Pascale and Valérie that they should avoid having any coffee. I also declined when it was offered to me. But we didn't manage to warn Denis. He drank a cup. A rather shy man by nature, he soon began to talk very loudly. The evening took on a new tenor as a wave of excitement swept through the room. People were yelling, laughing, singing. Denis was very much part of this frenzy. At seven the next morning he was still dancing, even though the music had long since finished.

As I watched all this unfold I noticed that I was very much part of it. I normally went to bed early, but it was seven in the morning and I still didn't feel the need to sleep. I was laughing my head off at the most ridiculous stories. I was slapping everyone around me on the back. I had drunk more alcohol than usual, but that couldn't explain my new-found stamina. Usually, drinking too much sent me to sleep. I realised that I had been tricked.

I don't know if I had *pot belge* that evening, the devilish cocktail concocted with amphetamine, caffeine, cocaine and heroin. It could have been some other equally explosive mixture designed to spice up exactly this kind of gathering. I simply didn't know. I didn't ride the next day and none of the others did either.

Ultimately, I was satisfied that I had been initiated. I was like the others. I was their friend. I even felt that I was now more than ever a part of that brotherhood known as the peloton. But I still didn't want to see the rottenness eating away at this family.

However, the cycling fraternity was already being shaken up without anyone fully realising. A new minister of youth and sport, Marie-George Buffet, had been appointed in June 1997 and she had made the fight against doping a priority. As a sign of allegiance, the Tour had already offered her the head of Djamolidine Abdoujaparov. A Cossack who was over the hill had been tossed to a Communist minister. The guy had been sacked by his Belgian Lotto team together with the guilty soigneur. That would keep the lady happy, they assumed.

During the winter of 1997/98, the police carried out a search during the Grenoble Six-Day track event. They seized products that had been hidden under a mattress. A judicial inquiry was quickly opened. A soigneur of Belgian origin was already concerned that it was all going to come out. Cycling was dancing on the edge.

Chapter 4

Blood and Tears

I began 1998, which was set to be the year of revelation, dealing with the effects of *pot belge* and my fascination for the cycling scene. The sensations caused by this double hit soon dissipated, though. I gradually regained my lucidity. It wouldn't be too long either before the general public was brought out of its collective hypnosis.

The atmosphere at Festina worsened day by day. The team had never been as strong in terms of ability, but also never as unstable. It had been strengthened by the recruitment of Alex Zülle, a Swiss who had been headhunted from the Spanish ONCE team. Winner of the Tour of Spain, he was a serious threat to Virenque's hold over the group.

The substantial fee expended on Zülle signalled a new spending spree. Money was flowing into the team, but only certain parts of it. The stars were becoming increasingly demanding. Salaries were rocketing. For these divas, the hotels were never luxurious enough, there were never too many support staff and the equipment was never stunning enough. This luxurious lifestyle put a strain on the sponsor's not insubstantial budget. Using some sporting jiggery-pokery, Roussel was selling victories at races later on in the season in order to sate the constant demand for extra cash.

Now our backer's patience ran out. Zülle's arrival resulted in an ultimatum from Festina's financiers. The sponsor was insisting that the huge sums that had been swallowed up had to produce a victory in a major race, or else the directeur sportif's days were numbered.

Richard had the hump with Bruno for having imposed Zülle, a star blessed with just as much class as he had, on him. He felt betrayed, even though Bruno had done nothing more than respond to our backer's bidding. The relationship between the two men, which not long before had been extremely close, had cooled and become testy.

An incident that had occurred during a training camp in Hyères at the end of the previous year had demonstrated the bitterness that characterised the deterioration in their relationship. We had to start using a helmet that our standard-bearer wasn't happy with at all. He was already reticent about wearing any kind of head protection and thought this new headgear was too bulky.

Laurent Dufaux was the first to try on the new piece of kit. Seeing him in it provoked general hilarity, which only made Richard, who was very concerned about his image, even more determined not to wear it. Remember that the fans' brown-haired favourite would soon dye his hair grey so that his groupies could pick him out more easily. He also had white socks made to measure for him.

'I will never wear that bowl,' he insisted. 'I don't want to look ridiculous.'

'You can talk, with your effeminate shoes,' Bruno joked.

Richard was extremely offended. He instantly raised his voice – well beyond the point you'd expect over such a minor issue. This angry outburst illustrated the animosity that had built up between two colleagues who had previously been all but tied at the hip. Their antagonism would become as strong as their friendship had once been.

During this same get-together, the discussion about how to split our prize money had inflamed the bad feeling within the group. The meeting was always likely to be stormy. Whereas the Tour de France riders had been good during 1997, the Classics group had been mediocre. In the eyes of the former, the system that we had in place guaranteeing equal shares was effectively an act of charity.

Pascal Hervé spoke. He explained that July's heroes had shone precisely because they had agreed to the sacrifices that others had not consented to. Consequently, there was no question of sharing the pot.

He proposed a new method of splitting the money. There would be two envelopes: one would contain the prize money from the Tour, the other the prizes accumulated during the rest of the season. A share for the backroom staff would be taken from each one, as well as the money to cover medical costs. What was left in the first envelope would be distributed only between those riders who been on the Tour team, while the contents of the second envelope would be split pro rata in the usual way. Incidentally, he also revealed that July's kitty had already been paid into the accounts of the nine riders concerned.

This proposal, and more especially the fact that the rest of us had been presented with a *fait accompli*, produced an outcry. The discussion turned venomous. Infuriated, I cut in to give my opinion.

'Fine,' I said, 'I agree with the way that Hervé wants to split things. However, I would ask for each individual to pay for his medical products. I don't see why I should pay for stuff that I have no recourse to.'

An icy chill fell on the room. Everyone looked at me. In an instant, thanks to my proposal, guys who had been tearing strips off each other moments earlier were united in absolute horror.

'That's too difficult to work out,' Roussel finally said in order to break the weighty silence.

The dispute resumed. The negotiations lasted more than a month before Bruno brought the matter to a close. The established method of distribution would be applied one last time. The Hervé-Virenque method would come into force the following year. With this judgement of Solomon, our directeur sportif was trying to reconcile the two parties. But the divide that opened up in 1997 had become unbridgeable.

As for me, I had turned everyone against me. For the first time, I had openly come out against the system. I had done so in the heat of anger and because of the sordid squabbling over money. I had shown my colours behind closed doors. Despite this, I was on my own and had suddenly become a figure of suspicion.

Like drugs eating away at the body, doping was slowly destroying the team. Festina became bedlam and, more worryingly, a laboratory of hellish practices.

Alex Zülle arrived with his own soigneur, Marcello Torrontegui. The Spaniard, Dr Michele Ferrari's test-tube baby, had looked after Tony Rominger when the Swiss rider was pulverising the hour record for fun. Compared with this expert, Willy Voet's star suddenly faded. A kind of contest began between the different soigneurs, as they tried to gain the esteem of their favourites.

This arms race was exacerbated by the eviction of Eric Ryckaert. Since the winter, he had been doing battle in the Belgian courts. The police had searched his office, near Ghent. They were interested in the doctor's ancillary work, with no link at all to Festina. However, Bruno had ordered his staff to destroy everything in the archives that contained a reference to his name. The outlaw had been removed from the team's technical staff. He had disappeared from the new edition of the team presentation brochure. Overtaken in terms of science, he had become dangerous from a legal standpoint. The management were looking for a replacement, and other, more efficient and discreet dopers, had been approached. While that search continued, Fernando Jiménez became the team's only registered doctor. But he couldn't watch everything that was going on. It was every man for himself, and an 'anything goes' attitude took hold. The resulting mayhem led to numerous blunders that resulted in unwanted publicity.

I worked hard through the winter months. The experience of the previous two seasons had taught me that I could only hope for victories at the start of the season. Medical programming provided me with a brief opportunity in February and March, when my opponents were still in preparation mode. By early April, it was already too late.

Antoine's computers confirmed my visual impression. The team's coach had developed what he called the lactic profile test (DLT). Its particular virtue was that it enabled a comparison to be made between athletes via a series of exercises undertaken in the lab or on the road. Those subjected to it had to endure a number of torturous exercises with the aim of making their body cough up its absolute parameters. A ranking could then be established.

In early December 1997, just as the holiday period was ending and just before medical protocols got under way, I was in second place. After another test in late January, I was only seventh in the ranking. By April, I was way behind the rest.

The injustice taking place could be quantified by means of other parameters, including VO2 max at threshold, another piece of scientific barbarity, which requires further explanation.

Perched on a home-trainer, we were required to make progressively more strenuous efforts while wearing a mask that extended out like a trunk. The pipe running from the mask was connected to a computer. A gradual increase in pedalling resistance would inevitably result in you struggling to get your breath. The lungs, heart and blood were no longer able to supply the muscles with the oxygen they were demanding. Due to this lack of oxygen, or anaerobic effect, your legs would begin to secrete lactic acid. This resulted in pain and, before too long, cramping. This torture meant you could measure the maximum (max) volume (V) of oxygen (O2) that the individual could absorb at the moment when they reached an anaerobic state (the threshold). Consequently, the consumption of the human engine could be calibrated. It was possible to deduce from this the capacity of the 'engine' and, therefore, of the athlete.

To refine the assessment, the figures were then divided by the weight of the athlete in order to obtain a value per kilo. Drawing again on the car analogy, it was therefore possible to establish differences in power output required to move the vehicle forwards.

Another test that we regularly had to submit to enabled an assessment to be made of our power. Still on the home-trainer, you had to produce a violent effort that left you totally breathless. The amount of energy you had produced at this anaerobic point could then be estimated in watts.

At their best in 1998, my VO2 max at threshold reached 85.1 millilitres of oxygen per kilogram, while my power at threshold was 400 watts. An accumulation of training and competition enabled me to improve these figures by about 10 millilitres and about 15 watts between the end of the holidays and the point where we were racing and training full-time.

Yet, between December and May, one of my team-mates managed to raise his VO2 max at threshold from 65 to 91. His power output at threshold increased from 325 to 430 watts. He had consequently increased his potential by a third in just four months ... Treatment with EPO, growth hormone and anabolic steroids had significantly boosted his endurance and strength, while other drugs had seen the weight drop off him, leaving his body fat level at no more than 5 per cent.

Antoine might just as well have burned his physiology manuals dating from the late 1980s, where it was stated that a VO2 max of 80 and a power output of 350 watts signified an exceptional individual.

I'll just point out again that I produced readings more or less equivalent to those of Bernard Hinault, who won the last of his five Tours de France in 1986. In a little more than ten years, the characteristics of an extraordinary champion had become very common values. Following this same logic, it might even be fair to say that Michel Platini would have been playing in the second division at that time rather than being the world's best footballer, as he had been in 1986!

At the height of his career, Lance Armstrong said he could put out 500 watts at threshold. That exceeds by nearly 50 watts the output achieved in 1995 by Miguel Indurain, who was, it should be noted, six kilos heavier. Some of those who have succeeded Armstrong can sometimes register power outputs that are even higher. The gap between generations is widening ever more quickly. It is becoming a chasm that divides athletes from the rest of humanity, amongst whom any increase is more sluggish over a much longer period. Standing above *homo sapiens* we now have *homo 'sportivus'*, who has a much higher physical capacity but is reckoned to have a shorter life expectancy. Rather than being a reason for antagonism, this gulf has instead resulted in the deification of athletes.

Language – and medicine! – are evolving just as quickly as my sport. Because of his aggressiveness Hinault was nicknamed 'The Badger'. Since then, the meaning of the word has changed and in slang it now means 'nerdy'. I, Christophe Bassons, am the new 'badger' of cycling …

Bruno Roussel knew all of these figures. My stubbornness in refusing to 'boost' my performance seemed like a real waste. This anomaly also made me unclassifiable. I was a modest rider with huge potential. In other words, I was a failure, only good for being tossed overboard. But if I deigned to finally play the game, there was a bright future for me. No wonder he despaired of me!

While he waited for me to make my mind up, my boss drew up a race programme in second-level events, which reflected his disenchantment. The GP Marseillaise in the south of France, the Majorca Trophy in Spain, the Laigueglia Trophy in Italy, the Tour du Haut-Var and Classic Haribo in the south of France once again, Het Volk and Kuurne–Brussels–Kuurne in Belgium, and then Cholet–Pays de Loire in western France … I was sent to every point of the compass, bounced around like a pinball. I acted as the stopgap, the rider who filled out the roster at races. To round this off, Bruno was sending me to the Tour of Chile, at the very end of the world. From this it would be fair to assume that he was telling me to go to hell …

In Majorca, I hit it off with Alex Zülle. During this race, the Swiss raised eyebrows with an unprecedented gesture. Despite being our leader, he dropped back to the cars to go and get water-bottles to hand out to his team-mates. This act of humility earned him the friendship of some of the group. Virenque would never have reduced himself to this role of water-carrier. On the contrary, he wanted those who hoped to gain his favour and a place in the Tour de France to be sycophantic and servile.

Alex was devoid of arrogance. He had a gentle and quiet nature. He spoke German, but the language barrier wasn't the main thing that made him quite reserved. His myopia and, particularly, his naïvety kept him apart from the real world. He never seemed to know where he was going, or where he was being taken, and his blindness caused him to have a lot of crashes. He quickly went down the medical slippery slope. He proved too weak to dare to resist the system.

Even today, I regard Alex as a man of real heart and an exemplary champion apart from the stain that was left by the 1998 Tour. I was really sorry to see him involved in the affair. He confirmed that he didn't know how to lie. He was also one of the first to admit he had had recourse to doping at Festina, and that this had also been the case with his former employer, ONCE.

I got a further insight into the gulf that separated Zülle from Virenque during the Flemish Classic, Het Volk. I had escaped in a small group, which was a joyful experience that I was becoming unfamiliar with. To my great dismay, Richard Virenque then led the pursuit, flouting the rules of racing that have it that you sit tight when one of your colleagues is up front. When he joined the breakaway, he ordered me to set the pace and then attacked on the Muur de Grammont, the main difficulty on the course. This hill is one of cycling's mythical places, a ramp that the cycling Sisyphuses battle their way up every year with the same difficulty. He led the race over this test then abandoned on the descent. That evening, he boasted to the press about having shown himself in the toughest part of the race.

As for me, despite the futile work I'd done for him, I managed to finish in a respectable position. Shortly after, I had another decent finish at Kuurne–Brussels–Kuurne. I did not delude myself with reckless ideas.

We were just getting into March. I now had just a month in which to distinguish myself. After that, I would be eclipsed. However, the hard winter training programme that Antoine had laid out for me had at least brought about this upturn.

This good run of results had an unexpected consequence. Once again, it seemed, Bruno Roussel was ready to show a bit of faith in me. He pulled me out of the Tour of Chile and put me into the group preparing for Paris–Nice and the Critérium International.

I still wonder today about this return to grace. Did my directeur sportif want to give me one final chance to prove that it was possible for me to win by sticking to my own methods? Or, on the other hand, was he thinking that my good performances could be put down to a better attitude that was finally going to push me to *faire le métier* – do the job the right way?

Nevertheless I was furious that soon I would have to step back into the shade, after having felt the first warming rays of spring. I wanted to seize the opportunity I was being offered and have my moment in the sun. My good resolutions withered. I was reeling again. I could at least try a recuperative! Weren't they nothing more than sugar and water? I was lying to myself, of course: there was much more than just a watery syrup at stake.

I called my parents to describe my torment to them. They told me that one single flirtation didn't seem that dramatic. I just had to try it and then form an opinion, they said. Thankfully, my parents presented exactly the reasoning I wanted to hear. I also presented my plan to Pascale.

'It's up to you,' she said. 'The important thing is that you feel happy about what you're doing.'

Frankly, I didn't feel happy at all. Those close to me had not exercised their right of veto, but my conscience was still nagging away at me as Paris–Nice got under way. I waited another two days.

Finally, I went see one of the medical staff in their room. 'I want to try a recuperative.'

'What product do you want?'

'Water and glucose only.'

He then cracked open two vials and drew their contents into a syringe. I sat down, took the pillow and stretched out my arm on it. This time the needle went right into the artery.

I went back to see the same man again before the end of the race.

Bruno would probably have got to know about my new frame of mind. He was all sweetness and light to me now. He once mentioned the Tour de France to me. He was, I think, looking for allies for Alex Zülle. The Swiss had no hope of getting any support within Virenque's clan, who had real contempt for the man they had dubbed 'The German'. I was getting on better with Alex all the time, but the better my relations were with him, the more atrocious they became with Richard and his vassals.

It wasn't long before I had to endure the consequences of this open hostility. During the Critérium International, Pascal Hervé and Christophe Moreau attacked me at the end of a stage. The two of them accused me of not having done my fair share of the work for Christophe, who was the designated leader for this race.

'Never, at any point during the race, did I see you at an important moment,' Pascal Hervé raged.

'If it had been Virenque in my position, he would have put you into the ditch for acting like that,' yelled Moreau.

I was devastated, less by my team-mates' criticisms than by their sudden change of mood since the start of the season. Hervé had been extremely helpful during the Tour of Majorca: he gave me the benefit of his experience, telling me how he saw the race going the following day, his intuition proving correct on each occasion. Richard, on the other hand, was frosty at the Tour du Haut-Var. I could have sworn I was happily accepted by the band around me during Paris–Nice. Two weeks later, at the Critérium International, the same guys were making me a scapegoat.

In my opinion, this kind of mad behaviour had two explanations. I think the unbridled use of chemicals over the previous few months had had psychological consequences. The euphoria that was created, either directly by the drugs or indirectly by the success they resulted in, helped to inflate egos, as well as bulking up muscles. The indiscriminate use of chemicals transformed personalities, enclosing minds within some artificial paradise. Those who used them started to behave like addicts. Their mood was unstable, shifting from excitement to depression without any clear reason.

Virenquemania was also dizzying minds. Thanks to the adulation of the crowds the French champion and his cronies had eventually lost all grip on common sense. They were no longer able to build up normal human relationships because of the cultish reverence with which they were regarded. All they felt was contempt for the rank and file who circulated beneath their pedestal.

The following afternoon I had confirmation that I wasn't the only one subject to their emotional instability. The Critérium International ended with a time trial on the Sunday afternoon. Before the start, I was warming up on one of two home-trainers at our disposal.

Virenque came out of the bus, immediately drawing a crowd and raising cheers from the fans. Dozens of people were clustered along the barriers that surrounded the area where we were getting ready.

Richard came up to me and asked me to get off my bike, insisting it was reserved for him. I refused, explaining that I had started my warm-up routine. Annoyed, he then turned to the mechanic, Jacky Bordener, and began insulting him. He accused him of letting me do what I wanted, and called him 'an absolute nobody' and 'a bloody idiot'. The guy tried to explain himself, stammering an apology. Looking on as if it was some kind of fairground performance, the crowd watched the poor wretch, whose head went down in the face of the invective directed at him. I was sickened to see this 50-year-old man being humiliated. I got off the home-trainer and got on the other.

'Take it if you insist,' I told him.

Richard immediately became aware of the childishness of his attitude. He wasn't quite so keen to take it from me now. He gave me a black look as he got on to his toy. The new standing that I built up in the minutes that followed changed nothing. My excommunication from the Tour had been decided.

What importance could this have? April was already upon us. Like sap rising in the trees, the haematocrit was ascending in riders' blood vessels. I didn't expect anything from the Classics, which were characterised by a meteoric rise in the average speed. Fatalistic, I expected the peloton to leave me languishing. I wasn't disappointed. Tour of Flanders: abandon. Gent–Wevelgem: 65th. Amstel Gold Race: abandon. Trophée des Grimpeurs: abandon. Even Paris–Roubaix provided me with no respite during this funereal passage: my bike broke down 50 kilometres from the finish and I couldn't find anyone to fix it. Abandon.

I was humiliated, crushed, especially as I felt my Pygmalion was on the verge of disowning me. Once again, Bruno was irritable towards me. He made me race more than was right, as if he wanted to push me over the edge. I clocked up 35 days of racing in three months.

One evening, acting like some evil stepfather, he created a scene during dinner because I had my elbows on the table. It wasn't like him to act like some starch-collared old biddy. I suppose he was just using it as an outlet for his anger. As well as being a perverted talent, I was a personal failure for him. He couldn't blame me for not doping: his personal conviction prevented him from doing so. Consequently, he picked me up on trivialities.

I realised that the water and glucose recuperatives I was taking were nothing more than snake oil. I was still as 'white' as ever. My comrades reminded me of that ad nauseam. I knew I would have to put something else in my syringe if I wanted to be able to continue.

The Four Days of Dunkirk completed this calamitous series. Once again I had to peel off my race number, this time on the second day. The pain in my knee had returned. The problem with my joint was partly psychosomatic on this occasion. I was simply cracking up.

I returned home for a fortnight's convalescence. I rushed over to Pascale's. As I came through the door, I collapsed into her arms.

'I can't go on like this,' I said. 'I'm going to stop completely. I'm going to call them and tell them that I'm ending my career.'

My fiancée persuaded me to hold off. 'You've got two weeks off to rest. Just wait a bit before making your decision.'

Cuddling and scolding me in turn, Pascale devoted those two weeks to motivating me. The long walks we both loved to take became an opportunity for her to express her concern and annoyance. She told me about the efforts she had made to persevere with her studies and top-level sport at the same time. She had slaved away in order to appear in five world championships, without any hope of making a penny from it, just for the sake of her passion. As a spoiled child of the professional world, I had the chance to turn my favourite sport into an attractive profession.

'I know what it's like to have to fight,' she declared, hoping to provoke my male pride. 'Think of your father, too.'

I had thought about him. For 12 years, Ariel had got up at four every morning. Between 5 and 8 a.m., he clocked in at a wool factory. From 8.30 to 12, he was a mason and worked on building sites, even when it was cold enough to split stone. He had lunch, then picked up his trowel again between 1.30 and 5 p.m. Then he returned to the factory at 5.30 and stayed there until nine in the evening. So what right did I have to complain?

More than anything, Pascale reminded me of the pleasure I got from the bike. I had ended up forgetting that. I was simply lamenting my fate and obsessing about the injustices that had befallen me.

After a week had passed, I reacquainted myself with this mode of transport again. The pleasure that comes from pedalling returned immediately. I went back to criss-crossing the roads of the Tarn. I knew its landscapes by heart. I had a soothing memory associated with each of them.

* * *

I was born on 10 June 1974 in Mazamet. We lived in another town nearby, Labastide-Rouairoux, on a small council estate in the Planotte neighbourhood. When I was 15, my mother, Françoise, who didn't want to see me driving a car or motorbike, gave me a mountain bike to replace my old bike.

I used to play tennis then. I had tried basketball first of all, but I was a pretty poor player. I was more gifted with a racket. I got a licence and achieved a decent ranking. I used my bike to go to school and to my training sessions. My friends were on mobylettes, and I really had to pump my legs to keep up with them.

A French teacher at my school, Gérard Bastide, advocated modern teaching methods. A post-1968er and disciple of the French Renaissance philosopher Michel de Montaigne, he preferred minds to be stimulated rather than just filled. In his eyes, the bike had huge educational value. He organised rides to explore the gorges of the Tarn, the Caroux and the Sidobre, and the outcrops all around them. Up there, he elaborated on his literature lessons for us, believing no doubt that the authors' words would have more impact when delivered to us sitting with the heavens above us and the earth below. Our teacher made us look at life from a different perspective and encouraged us to enjoy it. We used to pedal with even more gusto on our way home.

In 1991, my father's friend Alain Bertrand, who worked in the same factory as him, took me out riding. He was considered one of the best cyclotourists in the area. He had just bought a mountain bike and took me with him to test it out. When we got home, he told me that I had a good deal of ability.

'I would like to see how you fare on the road,' he said to me.

The following weekend, he worked out a route for us. I borrowed my father's classic bike, an old model with toe-clips. I put on my shorts – I didn't have any cycling shorts – and off we went.

'Stick right on my back wheel,' he advised me.

After ten kilometres, I went to the front. Our jaunt lasted 70 kilometres. Others followed. Patrick Zalovo, a friend who was five years older than me, started to come along with us. As we rode, we improvised finish lines and pretended we were racing.

At the end of that year, Patrick and I went to take part in the Roc d'Azur. This mountain bike race included champions and unknowns as it was both the final of the European Championship and a mass rally at the same time. I finished third in the junior category.

Friends then advised me to take out a licence, which I did in 1992 with the Union Vélocipédique de Mazamet, my local club. As I have already said, I had just one reason for doing so: if you had a licence, entry to mountain bike events was cheaper. However, the club president, Robert Vidal, asked me to do some road races. The first took place in Bizanet, in the Aude, where I finished fourth and best junior. The following week, the president signed me up for the Challenge Midi-Pyrénées for juniors. With hairy legs I lined up on my bike with the toe-clips. Six of us ended up at the front. I felt strong, but I punctured and lost a minute. The others sped on. Using all my energy, I managed to get back up to my companions in the break.

'Thanks for waiting for me, guys,' I yelled at them.

Already a vindictive young man …

I had expended too much of my strength in the pursuit. I finished second in the sprint. The region's technical adviser, Jean-Claude Decoopman, had been watching the race. He asked me to take part in the national junior challenge in Brittany the following week.

I shaved my legs, I put clipless pedals on my machine and headed west. I finished seventh in the time trial.

Shortly after that, I participated in a race at Bretenoux in the Dordogne. I saw four guys escape. I countered, quickly caught three of the escapees and immediately went past them. However, I never managed to get on terms with the fourth guy who had stolen away. I crossed the line feeling disappointed about this setback. But once over the line I discovered that only three riders had actually escaped in the first place. I had taken my first victory without even raising my arms.

I was then asked to take part in two training camps organised by the national junior coach, Bernard Bourreau, with a view to going on to the world championships. At the end of the camp, he told me that I had been selected for the competition, which was taking place in Greece. I was handed a French national tracksuit and team bag.

I returned proudly home. I announced the good news to my parents, but they seemed embarrassed. A little annoyed, I asked them the reason for this lack of enthusiasm. My father told me that Bourreau had called while I was in transit to say that in the end I had not been picked after all. The coach felt that I lacked experience for competition of that kind. It was an immense disappointment, but obtaining my baccalaureate soon wiped that out.

I enrolled at the University of Toulouse to do a diploma in civil engineering, with an option in public works. My getting on this course made my parents so proud; they saw it as a successful end to my schooling. I was also thinking about how things were mapping out for me. My studies were time-consuming, so I was only training once a week. My results on the bike reflected this, but I didn't care. I still got so much pleasure from riding. I spent the holidays pedalling. This enabled me to get a few results in September. I ended up coming fourth in the French Espoirs Road Championships, which took place in Marmande.

I then went back to swotting for my exams.

Winning or losing didn't matter to me. I enjoyed it all so much, and I loved the atmosphere at the races. We were an inseparable band of mates. At the weekends we sometimes did an eight-hour drive, six of us crammed into a car, to get to some distant event. We had so many hours of fun just getting there.

Then attention switched to the races. I got real pleasure from attacking on my own soon after the start and trying to defy the peloton chasing behind me. More often than not, they did catch me, but sometimes I stayed away to the end. If I had raced with greater economy, I would certainly have enriched my palmarès. But all that mattered to me was the thrill of riding without restraint.

This indiscipline enraged my coach, Claude Puech. When I squandered my chances of victory like that, he would get extremely angry. He'd be grumbling as he hoisted my bike onto the roof. Then he would get behind the wheel and wouldn't say a word to me during the return trip. It made me sad to see him in this state. I felt bad for him. I used to promise that I would be more tactically astute the following week. I rarely kept my word. My passion encouraged me to attack as soon as I got in the saddle. Babasse 'The Cannon' didn't know how to play it smart.

Claude and his wife, Marie, were among those lovers of cycling who spend every weekend on the road to satisfy their passion. He kept telling me that I had the same qualities as Laurent Jalabert, whom he had already trained. He even claimed that I was better than him as a time triallist. My coach could see a future in sport for me when I was still only thinking about having fun. He tried to sharpen my competitive appetite and curb my mad dog instincts. But he never encouraged me to dope, as some pseudo-educators do.

The amateur world was obviously not immune to such practices. Claude sometimes gestured with his chin towards some rider with a certain reputation.

'Look, see that guy, he's not winning under just his own steam.'

My trainer showed blatant contempt for the '*chaudières*', or 'boilers', as these locomotives who stuffed themselves with drugs to go faster were known.

More than anything, I hated the mafias that I soon found myself up against. These were organised gangs of often experienced riders who used to rig races. One of them would escape while his accomplices would control the opposition, using more or less legitimate means. More than one recalcitrant rival found himself lying bloodied in a ditch, his hide ripped by the road, for having tried to stand up to them.

They were modern-day highwaymen who plundered criteriums because they had the biggest prizes. By doing so, they earned themselves tidy little sums that sometimes reached as much as several tens of thousands of francs a month.

Thanks to my mania for jumping away as soon as we took the first pedal strokes, I had had these triads on my back. I didn't care in the slightest about their tactics, but this hostility cost me more than one victory. I lined up one day in a criterium in Rodez that had been fixed by one of the cliques. When I went to the front of the race, one of these gangsters in cycling shorts tried to push me onto the pavement. I managed to stay upright, and in response I jammed the bully-boy against the kerb. The guy began to sound off and threaten me. A nice slanging match ensued in the middle of the countryside.

'We will not let you get clear, asshole,' he promised me. 'You will not win.'

'You won't either,' I replied.

I then dropped back into the heart of the peloton. Once there, I found myself alongside a young rider I got on well with, a lad called Martin, who had a fearsome reputation as a sprinter. I went back to the front and hammered out a fierce pace. The speed I was riding at prevented anyone from escaping. In the final kilometres, I still had enough strength to lead out my ace, who won. The winner came up to me afterwards to thank me.

A few weeks later, during another criterium taking place in Graulhet, I was caught in an ambush. There was a dark, narrow street on the course where there was no room for the fans. Whenever we went into this dangerous back alley, several of these bandits would try to knock me over with a shoulder shove or by swerving. I held for a while, but I soon had to abandon with my nerves shredded.

I knew the mafias were not content with just fleecing the fans. They also ran the trade in doping substances among the young riders. Some of these cutthroats were former professionals who had maintained their links with the trafficking network. Just once, one of the dealers tried to lure me in. I refused. The open war I waged with these con artists subsequently saved me from further temptations.

Despite my deplorable lack of cycling intuition and the hostility of the gangs, I produced some good performances. As a result, the national technical director, Patrick Cluzaud, suggested that I did my military service with the Joinville battalion. I had successfully obtained my university degree, and the idea of spending a sabbatical year pedalling during my military service really tempted me. In the Parisian suburb, I met lots of young guys whose only thought was to turn their sport into their career. I, however, was one of the rare birds there who felt they were indulging their passion and fulfilling a civic duty that also soothed the soul. While I was there I befriended Eric Salvetat, who was a year older than me. He never turned professional. I don't think that was ever his goal. We shared the same convictions about doping, and I think he immediately saw the incompatibility of our beliefs with what was required in that career, while I simply refused to see how difficult it would be to adhere to this line. He became a sports teacher in the Landes region. We now work on many projects together. During my long years of isolation, I missed his presence.

I was still an amateur when I met – and upset – Richard Virenque for the first time. The race took place in Quillan in 1994. On about 15 August, a local committee had organised a post-Tour criterium in which a few of the stars from the Tour de France were making an appearance. Some amateurs were also invited to fill out the line-up. I had had to cough up 600 francs to make up the numbers.

According to the rules of these events I should have been no more than an irrelevant bit-part player. However, youthful enthusiasm impelled me to refuse a mundane role as a spear-carrier and move stage front. I managed to contest some intermediate *primes* with Djamolidine Abdoujaparov. Later, I got into a five-man breakaway that included the Italian Claudio Chiappucci and Richard Virenque. The scenario had been set up beforehand – but there was an intruder in the group! I realised too late that I was annoying everyone. Several professionals told me off after the finish. These reprimands upset me: I thought I'd done well.

The following year, I was again asked to play the role of one of the stooges. On the start line, I once again found myself alongside celebrities who had made names for themselves on the TV over the previous month. I felt like a big kid rubbing shoulders with such esteemed company.

One of the older riders then came up to me: 'Look here, son, I'm warning you. Don't you dare try anything like you did last year, or it will turn out badly for you. You stay at the back. Understood?'

This warning intimidated me. From the beginning, following a plan that had been previously agreed, Virenque and Dufaux made an attack. The idea was to get the crowd going, but also excite the small businessmen watching so that they would put up prizes on every lap. But in the adrenalin rush, I forgot the instructions I'd been given. I made an attack of my own and went off the front all alone. The rest of the cast weren't that bothered, seeing it as a show of caprice by a greenhorn who didn't get much publicity. These professionals had no desire to tire themselves out in one of those criteriums where the only objective was to earn a bit of money. Consequently, I managed to open up quite a gap.

When they didn't see me dropping back, the pack started to chase me down. The announcer had also realised that things were going pear-shaped. I was torpedoing the main event. Each time I went through the finish, I was pocketing *primes* that had been put up for the stars to win. The master of ceremonies then announced that the prizes would also be awarded to the second rider through on every lap. A second race was effectively organised behind me. But I didn't care about these bonuses.

I was in heaven, riding flat out at the front, with everyone else chasing my tail. On what was a short circuit, so that the public could get frequent sightings of the champions, I soon ended up almost three-quarters of a lap ahead.

Nobody was really interested in me when, on a descent with 15 kilometres of racing remaining, I crashed. The main body of the pack were soon bearing down on me. As soon as I had been caught, Richard Virenque gave me a dressing down. Then Laurent Dufaux took me to task when I went to collect the money I had won.

'Don't you understand that it is us that everyone has come to see, not you? It was up to us to make the race.'

'I don't see why the public should be deceived,' I replied.

My grandfather, Joaquim Bassons, once told me: 'One day, you will be champion of France, but I will not be there to see it.'

I did indeed become French time trial champion in 1995. I placed the winner's bouquet on his grave. He had died of cancer the year before, aged 89.

My grandfather was born in Spain. His family was fervently Catholic and rather conservative. Joaquim was an altar boy on Sundays. When the civil war broke out in his country, however, he joined the Republicans, who were opposed to the coup d'état carried out by Franco. He was taken prisoner and spent some time in Franco's concentration camps. He escaped, got into France and ended up in so-called detention camps, where the French government coralled immigrants who had lost everything and whom it viewed with suspicion.

Joaquim became a glassblower in a factory at Saint-Pons-de-Thomières. He pieced his life back together on this side of the Pyrenees. He later recorded his memories in Spanish in large books, of which he published a few copies. As well as writing about his life and the war, he also visited schools and spoke to children who were studying the period about the atrocities that had taken place during the conflict.

He was a proud man, and even more proud of his grandchildren. I think I was his favourite. He wrote poems for me that I've never shown to anyone except Pascale.

The day before his death, I went to the hospital. We chatted for one last time. I cried when I left. This is still the most painful memory of my life. The way I see it, the difficulties that the cycling world put me through will never be anything like as significant as that tragic time.

After his death, some friends gave me an enlarged photo that showed me in my cycling kit with him. I hugged the frame and cried when I saw it. Joaquim was my first fan. He sent articles to the local papers when I had any kind of success. He believed in me.

He was known for his strength of character. I inherited it, without realising it at first. My parents have always protected me. For a long time they made every decision for me. I was shy, almost invisible when I was nothing more than a kid from the country whose life ran easily like a smooth-flowing river. But once I got embroiled in the cycling *milieu*, my capacity for holding my ground, my stubbornness, came naturally. These qualities were there without me realising, lurking inside me, ready to spring up when life demanded it.

In moments of difficulty, I always recall my grandfather's rectitude. I ask myself what he would have done in my place. I thought of him during those two weeks of depression in 1998. He would not have appreciated my state of mind. He would have encouraged me to rebel. I had no right to betray the confidence he had placed in me. For his sake too I had to press on.

Chapter 5
End of the Cycle

I left home with just one idea in mind: to try to do all I could to be happy in my racing. 'If all is good in your head …' Pascale kept telling me when we talked about recuperatives. I had my answer ready: my head would never be right if I had a syringe in my arm. They could keep everything they had – their injections, their IV drips, their centrifuges and all their paraphernalia of woe. I was going to let them have all of that, as well as the victories that it seemed went hand in hand with them. There was no question of me puncturing my skin to please them.

My return reminded me that my decision to keep racing wasn't mine alone. It also depended on my employers. They were ones paying for my services.

Nevertheless, I decided to adhere to my new resolution from the very first race. The Pru Tour lent itself well to my philosophy. This race meandered through the picturesque British countryside for ten days. Being dispatched to Britain by Bruno was like being sent into exile. But I was actually in heaven. The organisers had worked hard at getting things right and had booked us into luxury hotels. The island had another advantage in as much as hardly anyone spoke French. I couldn't bear the cloying hypocrisy of the peloton, and the language barrier protected me from it. I could ride in silence, without having to make small talk with people in whom I'd become less and less interested. To add to my good fortune, Antoine Vayer was parachuted in as directeur sportif. That meant I was protected from any questionable practices. However, the insanity of doping didn't take long to cross the Channel.

Roussel called Vayer out of the blue. He told him that Christophe Moreau had tested positive at the Critérium International. The product involved was Mesterolone, an anabolic steroid that was easily detectable. The culprit had accused Festina soigneur Jean Dalibot of providing him with this product. Dalibot was with us on the Pru Tour. Roussel was worried because Laurent Lefèvre was in very good form at the British race – he was afraid that Dalibot had given the young athlete the same product. Bruno asked Antoine to search the soigneur's belongings to find out what he had with him. Another positive test would have been catastrophic for our reputation. No search took place.

In line with one of the noble customs of the *milieu*, the soigneur denied he had been at fault. The soigneur's role is fundamental in cycling. He is the father, the nanny, the devoted friend, and even the silent recipient of anger if required. It's difficult to understand the central role of this caste within doping if you don't take into account the intensity of the relationship that gets established between them and the riders during the half-hour they spend on the massage table each day.

Yet I have always been amazed by the contempt in which some riders held the backroom staff, not only at Festina but also in other teams where I worked. Masseurs and mechanics were regarded as minions. They had to carry suitcases up to the rooms at night and bring them down again in the morning, and sometimes even pack them up when a thoughtless rider hadn't bothered to sort out his mess. In the evening they waited on tables at dinner, fetching bread and water when their overlords demanded them. These little emperors felt they had a right to this kind of mollycoddling, and even the right to demean the staff, who had to yield to their every whim. It would never have occurred to them to say thanks or show any kind of politeness.

'Willy, go and get us some bread!'

'Jean, get your arse in gear!'

'Shit, Laurent, when's the waiter planning on bringing us the next course? Go and tell him to get a move on!'

I have always refused to get involved in this kind of degrading behaviour. I carry my own suitcase and go and get what I need if something is missing.

Their lack of qualifications, the precariousness of their employment status and their veneration of the cycling world encouraged soigneurs to accept servitude in exchange for salaries that were far from extravagant. The last to bed, the first to get up, these jacks-of-all-trades bent over backwards for their protégés, with whom they had a complex relationship that included affection, admiration and submission. They accepted as inherent in their role the need to compromise themselves for their champion and carry the can for him. I never understood how they could accept playing the role of scapegoat. In addition to servitude, they had to put up with ingratitude and opprobrium at the first hint of trouble.

Christophe Moreau was allowed to line up in the Tour de France. As for Jean Dalibot, he was punished by being laid off. The sacrificial victim sank into a deep depression. Then he was discreetly brought back into the set-up. However, he kept complaining to his boss about the lack of support he'd received against his accuser.

The Moreau affair sat alongside the dossier on Brochard: the world champion had tested positive for lidocaine, but a medical certificate turned up opportunely that justified the use of this medical product for therapeutic reasons. Left to their own devices, these ingénues took reckless risks. The increasing number of those involved in the whole doping process also led to overdoses or to links with characters of a dubious nature, which resulted in riders getting worse rather than improving. This was why Bruno Roussel put in an emergency call to Eric Ryckaert, who had to control this dangerous and appalling mess in the big races. Paradoxically, this reorganisation and the centralisation of products in the hands of specific people would eventually result in the downfall of those behind this system.

As for me, I continued on my merry way. I was sent to the Tour of Switzerland in June. I had once again retreated into my shell and had adopted a degree of indifference. I took the chance to take in the Swiss countryside as I sat in the *gruppetto*, even if it meant finishing last.

Was it still really necessary to follow this band of fanatics who didn't share my zen-like state at all? How can you get any pleasure out of riding when others are smothering the life out of you with their excessive pace? For these very unusual kind of Buddhists, the only thing in a permanent levitative state within their ethereal sphere was their haematocrit. I continued to be held back by the harsh laws of gravity and physiology. Once again I finished the Tour of Switzerland anaemic.

I kept coming up against this issue of a blood deficiency. If my rivals had ridden just two or three kilometres an hour slower, I would have had no trouble staying with them and maintaining my form. If their haematocrit had fallen naturally due to the effort they were making, I would have had no need to constantly draw on my reserves. Their cheating didn't only prevent me from winning. It endangered my health. I could do nothing in the face of this shitty behaviour. The disgraceful actions of others were causing me to suffer like a dog, and I was brimming with impotent rage at the injustice of it.

I could not continue. I had to find an answer or a way out. But how could I boost my blood significantly without resorting to EPO? I found myself at an impasse.

The question was all the more relevant as I had a meeting with Bruno Roussel to renegotiate my future. My contract was due to expire at the end of the year.

Once he had felt curiosity about what was behind my ill-tempered opposition to any cheating, but that and his amused indulgence had now passed, and he was basically just annoyed. It was clear that the rest of my career simply depended on the limits of his patience and also on the fact that my monthly salary of 13,500 francs was hardly a burden on the finances of one of the world's richest teams. In more ways than one, I didn't count for much.

I met Bruno the day before the French championships, which were taking place at Charade, in the Auvergne. Antoine attended the meeting. Bruno didn't beat around the bush.

'I need to know what you intend to do in the coming months regarding EPO. This is a handicap for you ... and for the renewal of your contract. I need to know your intentions.'

So I played my last card.

'Together with Antoine, I've decided to test out a hypoxic chamber. It should boost my haematocrit by five per cent.'

The coach then took the floor and launched into an impassioned plea for this technique. He explained how it involved sleeping in a depressurised chamber where air is in short supply in order simulate being at altitude. Blood naturally begins to produce red blood cells to compensate for the lack of oxygen. For decades, athletes had known the virtues of altitude training camps to boost the efficiency of their breathing. This was a scientific application of the principle, which enabled the simulation of very high altitude, above 3,000 metres. Hypoxia had famously been used by Scandinavian cross-country skiers. Norwegian champion Bjørn Daehlie was a noted user. There was a hotel in the Alps that was equipped only with rooms of this type. I planned to go there in the first few days of July. That would give me a quick fix.

Even before Antoine had finished what he was saying, Bruno was lapping up his spiel.

And it worked! He had been won over. Well, almost.

'It sounds interesting,' he said. 'But what if it doesn't work?'

'I would take a look at EPO,' I replied.

Bruno took this rather contorted reasoning as a promise. He was both a man of his word and one ready for a challenge. He agreed to draw up a one-year contract with a salary raised to 28,000 francs a month! I couldn't believe it.

I now believe that my mentor wanted to believe in the virtues of hypoxic chambers. This process could perhaps have provided the exit strategy that he so hoped for. I've said this before and I'll repeat it: he was never a committed doper, but a pragmatic one who yielded to the prevailing lore in order to survive. I think he was hoping as much as I was that the experiment would succeed, just as he looked for success by employing a nutritionist, an osteopath and our coach.

My contract was therefore extended until 31 December 1999. I had a little over a year to convince him. Otherwise, it would not be a case of just saying goodbye to the team; I would effectively have no hope at all of remaining at that level. There was no question for me of using EPO, and Bruno never would have forgiven me for what he would have seen as deception.

What I didn't know then was that my directeur sportif would probably not have survived much longer than me. I found out later that he was then already considering quitting the job, worn down by the pressure being applied by his sponsor, annoyed by the behaviour of the diva-like Virenque and sickened by practices that he could see were going to lead to a fatal conclusion. Were the multiple controversies buzzing around the peloton a premonition of the earthquake to come?

My hypoxia camp began on 11 July. I left the house that morning heading for Brides-les-Bains in the Alps, the location of my hotel, the strangely named Auberge du Phoque – the Seal Hotel. I had only been driving for an hour when I heard on the radio that a soigneur had been arrested in a Festina team vehicle that was loaded with doping products. I slowed down and turned up the volume. The reporter gave some details. And then I heard Bruno Roussel: 'We're not missing anyone, all the cars are here.'

I needed to hear that voice to be convinced that I wasn't just having a bad dream. I knew the name of the soigneur: Willy Voet. He was in prison, said the reporter. Everything fitted together and yet, at the same time, it was all wrong. I couldn't make the link between these people I had known for two years and the criminal investigation that was under way.

I was incredulous, as the others must have been out there in Ireland. The scandal had erupted in such an unexpected way. The risk everyone ran was of being caught out by a positive dope control. This just seemed like an extraordinary mishap; but no hypocritical scam, even one that had been so well refined over time, could hope to fend off such an unexpected blow. The Tour de France would make every effort for a week, only to end up well beaten. It would stubbornly deny the evidence, just as Bruno Roussel had done by saying that this Festina car did not belong to him. It was all in vain.

My first reaction was to close ranks, out of feelings of solidarity and fright. Why *my* team, I was asking myself, when I was actually thinking, why me? What was going to happen? And, most importantly, what was going to become of me? Was this the first step towards unemployment? Despite what I had gone through, despite the disgust that EPO still evoked in me, I suddenly felt part of a common destiny. If police inspectors had interrogated me at that moment, perhaps a self-defence reflex would even have led to me deny the reality of what had been going on.

I arrived at the hotel in a daze. As he welcomed me, the owner referred to the news: 'I saw it on the television. It's a strange story.'

I replied: 'Yes, a strange story.' He didn't follow up on his comment. I guess he knew what was going on.

Lionel Laurent had been a biathlon bronze medallist at the Olympic Games in Lillehammer before becoming a hotelier. His experience as an athlete had given him the idea of turning three bedrooms into hypoxic chambers. He led me to one of them, located in the attic. You entered through an airtight door. Installed inside were two motors. One of these rarefied oxygen, reducing its level from 20 to 13 per cent to simulate an altitude of between 2,800 and 3,600 metres, while the other absorbed excess carbon dioxide to prevent the air becoming toxic.

I spent 18 nights shut up in there from eight in the evening till eight the next morning, lulled by the hum of instruments. I followed the developments of the Festina affair in the surreal atmosphere of this machine-run room.

In the mornings, I climbed the surrounding cols. In the afternoons, I watched the Tour stages and all their improbable twists. Festina's tribulations became a summer soap opera that fascinated France. They were headline news in the papers and on the TV.

I was appalled by the amount and diversity of the medical products seized: 234 doses of EPO, 80 vials of growth hormone, 160 capsules of the male hormone testosterone. To this terrifying catalogue should be added two classes of medicine that have received less attention. Also discovered in the car were capsules of a blood thinner and vaccines against hepatitis. These weren't performance-related substances, but actually drugs designed to prevent side-effects, such as thrombosis or viral infection. The dangers, which everyone continued to deny, were clearly demonstrated by these preventive purchases. No one who had ever sung the praises of EPO to me had ever warned me of the risks involved. I was amazed to discover what these good souls were hiding behind their backs to treat me with, just in case …

The public learned a little bit more each day, and I did too. However, I had the advantage over the masses in that I knew the mechanics and the responsibilities of all those involved in the process. So I watched the affair with a knowing eye from a distance of several hundred kilometres, seeing how the relationships between those involved imploded. Bruno Roussel disassociating himself from Willy Voet was a disappointment, even though I had already seen the same phenomenon with Jean Dalibot. Virenque's statements flabbergasted me:

'I want you to know that I am not responsible for the actions of the team's personnel. I've always had confidence in the management. However, when that confidence is betrayed, it is not my fault at all.'

I was gob-smacked at this show of nerve – and even more so by his next performance following the arrest of Bruno Roussel and Eric Ryckaert on 15 July:

'It is normal that Bruno Roussel is helping the police with their enquiries because he is the soigneur's employer. We're in the thick of the action, but our consciences remain clear.'

The guy didn't have a single word of support or even compassion for men with whom he had worked for years and who had been the artisans of his success. I was distressed by what he was saying. Richard even threatened to start a civil action:

'I consider myself as a victim in the first degree of the doping system put in place by our managers.'

On the eve of the French championship, four days before his arrest, we had celebrated Willy Voet's 53rd birthday. Hervé and Virenque kissed their favourite soigneur. They were the kisses of betrayal.

I can understand the resentment that Voet felt towards Virenque and which can be seen exploding from every page of his book. His words are tinged with the bitterness of a man betrayed. I saw how much the soigneur cosseted his protégé. Attentive to his every request, he finally ended up erasing his own personality so that he became little more than the shadow of a boy 25 years his junior. By denying him after his arrest, his master finally cast off his starry-eyed subject and left him to his own devices. The servant finally rebelled.

In the face of all this dishonesty, the arrest of Roussel and Ryckaert seemed a bit unfair to me. These two men had done no more than assume their responsibilities. Bruno's confession, which was passed on by his lawyer, Thibault de Montbrial, on Friday, 17 July 1998, summarised the truth with remarkable concision: 'Bruno Roussel explained to the investigators, who had items in their possession, the conditions under which collaborative management of the supply of doping products to riders was organised between management, the doctors and the riders of the Festina team. The objective was to optimise performance, under strict medical supervision, with the aim of avoiding unchecked personal supply in conditions likely to cause serious harm to their health.'

Virenque's statements had appalled me. The comments, so obviously tinged with relief, that were made by other directeurs sportifs regarding Festina's exclusion from the Tour made me feel sick. All's well that ends well, they said. The race could reassert itself, insisted the event's organisers. How had I been able to deceive myself for two years about the extent of camaraderie, the esprit de corps? What an idiot I was!

The police weren't as naïve as me. They scratched away fiercely at the rottenness. I watched their attempts to disinfect the sport, lulled by the purring of my two mechanical cats.

I forgot I was wearing a Festina jersey. People I came across during my training rides reminded me of that. I was the butt of some invective on these training excursions. 'Dirty doper!' drivers yelled out at me. Pale imitators of mime artist Marcel Marceau mimicked the emptying of a syringe in an arm. I pretended not to see them, lowering my head and pressing a little harder on the pedals. Worst of all was the embarrassed silence of the other guests in the hotel restaurant each evening. These silent accusations were harder to take than the gibes of fools out on the roads.

What were my neighbours thinking, and my friends? How could they believe my denials when others were lying with an effrontery that I would never be able to achieve? I felt as if I was in the body of an innocent man who everyone claims is guilty. I was demoralised. I trained without knowing if it still had any meaning. However, the bike brought me comfort. The effort carried my mind into the misty distance, where I forgot the news. The endorphins secreted by my body under the effort I was producing numbed my brain – or least that was how Antoine Vayer would have described it from his scientific perspective! All I knew was that pedalling was the only thing that prevented me from falling.

Relief came for me from the police HQ in Lyon, where officers had interrogated the members of Festina's Tour team one by one. They drew confessions from most of them, the exceptions being Pascal Hervé and Richard Virenque. In his statement, Christophe Moreau cited the names of his three team-mates who never doped: Patrice Halgand, Laurent Lefèvre and Christophe Bassons. Armin Meier also mentioned my name. The press reported this double exoneration. I was cleared and could breathe easy.

Pascale came to join me in Brides-les-Bains. She explained how she thought the affair was ultimately a good thing for me. There were no Machiavellian ideas in her mind, no mercenary intent, just the feeling that the eruption of the truth could only liberate me from the shackles of my torment. I must admit that each day I felt a little more relieved. Each revelation tossed to the public took some weight off my shoulders.

I felt I'd got a little bit of revenge, but well after the event. I still believed that the cyclone that was lashing my sport was certainly going to carry me away with it as well. My horizon remained completely obscured until Michel Gros appeased my concerns. The ship would steam on, he told me, and I would be on it. He outlined the rescue plan that had been put in place and gave me my programme for the rest of the season.

I left the Alps just as the peloton arrived in a very disorganised manner. The Tour de France had become a tragicomedy, thanks to arrests, strikes and people fleeing into Switzerland. As this unfolded, I felt closest to the position taken by Laurent Jalabert, who affirmed that this Tour was now pointless. I agreed with his frank assessment. His stance was at least coherent, at a time when ridiculous things were being written about the race. As for Bjarne Riis taking on the role of union leader and intermediary between the strikers and the race management, I didn't know whether to laugh or cry.

I returned to the Tarn, where everyone told me that they had never had any doubts about me. After experiencing several days of paranoia, I confess that I wasn't completely convinced by these comments. However, I received an increasing number of sympathic remarks, and these made up for the years I'd been fighting almost on my own.

One of them particularly touched me. Monsieur Bonnet was the father of three young members of my club. In 1997, this man had come to see me and taken me to task.

'Christophe, I'm really disappointed with your results. With your potential, you should be doing a lot better. You have to work harder.'

At the time, I kept my counsel in the face of his reprimand. Why bother trying to explain, to open the eyes of this man, by describing to him the decay within the sport that he loved? Shortly after the affair had surfaced, I saw Monsieur Bonnet again.

'Christophe, I really want to apologise for the comments I made last year. I understand now why you weren't going well. I'm really sorry I criticised you and I want to tell you now that you have my complete admiration. Keep it up.'

I was really moved by what he had said.

I received the support of those who had believed in me when I first started in the sport, but had been disappointed over the previous two years: Claude and Marie Puech, who had sacrificed so much for me; and Robert Vidal, who had told journalists who came to talk to him in 1995 about the exploits of Laurent Jalabert that he was working even harder with a prodigy called Bassons. 'Remember this name: Bassons,' my club president had affirmed.

These enthusiasts and educators, who loved cycling with such passion, were also stunned by the scale of the affair. They were like those old communists who witnessed the other side of the Soviet system and saw their ideals and even their reason for living disappear beneath them. I've since met many others – coaches, the heads of small clubs, parents, teachers, licence-holders and spectators – who have told me about their dismay while at the same time affirming their support. To those who say that doping is an indivisible part of the cycling culture, I say take a look at the faces of these many thousands of honest people. They continue to provide a huge degree of comfort whenever I speak.

The Tour de France was in shreds when it reached the Champs-Elysées. It reached its destination largely thanks to the effects of inertia. By the same mechanical process, the peloton, staggering though it was, continued on with the calendar laid out for it.

I rejoined it in August. It wasn't in great shape, but I was. Eighteen days in the hypoxic room had pushed my haematocrit up from 40 to 43.5 per cent. Two weeks later, however, it had returned to the original figure. In August, I went back to Brides-les-Bains for a week, and this time my level didn't budge. At least it didn't go down as I put myself through a heavy training schedule. Hypoxia had, indirectly, enabled me to get stronger.

As well as having this objective physical data, I also had excellent morale! The affair had perked me up, just as it had demoralised my rivals.

Festina had declared a complete moratorium on doping. Even the use of subcutaneous recuperatives was prohibited. Other teams had announced similar bans. Not all of the dopers had abandoned their habit. Would they ever have done so? But at least they were being careful. The focus was now on restricting use and patching the sport back together.

My rivals were still getting by on the benefits of previous treatments. Steroids were still having an effect. They weren't riding *à l'eau claire*, as the saying goes. But they were at least holding off from recharging themselves. That was just about all I could ask for.

The two most beautiful months of my career were just starting. I finished fifth in the Regio Tour, a German stage race, third in the French time trial championship, third in the Grand Prix Sodimes, fourth in the Grand Prix Eddy Merckx, fourth in the Tour of Poland, fifth in the Grand Prix des Nations. I even claimed the title of best climber in the Grand Prix William Tell in those same Swiss Alps that I'd ridden through at the back of the field just two months before …

Nearly a month after his ejection from the Tour in July, Richard Virenque made his comeback to racing at the Regio Tour. He adopted a low profile. After the time trial, I was the team's best-placed rider. I was nominated the leader. Richard had to ride for me, which he did. On the last day, he was thinking about attacking. No doubt he wanted to draw attention to himself and make a point to those who had already written him off. He ended up sitting in the wheels and abiding by our instructions, which were to preserve my place in the general classification.

The halt that had been called to doping was monitored by the team's management, who had received strict guidelines from the sponsor. The directeurs sportifs were transformed into prison wardens, on the lookout for the slightest infraction of the rules. During the Tour of Poland, which took place on 6–13 September, the team was testing out a new pro from Australia. Every day he used to ask for ice from the hotel owner.

Not long before, this request would only have resulted in a knowing smile. But in the new context of prohibition, an internal investigation was swiftly conducted. The management discovered that this incorrigible rider had crossed the borders to reach Poland carrying a thermos filled with banned substances, including vials of EPO. The offender was severely rebuked for what he had done and ordered to get rid of the package. His team-mates complained bitterly about his foolishness. Among his foremost critics, I seem to remember, was Thierry Laurent – who later returned to amateur status and was sent to prison in 2003 after being convicted of being part of a vast trafficking network that was supplying young riders around Perpignan.

I harboured no illusions, however. I knew that my achievements during my summer romp were the result of fear among other riders. The panic triggered by the Festina affair was now over. The police investigation had moved on, and with it went any feeling of danger. The judiciary was focusing purely on the dealers. The consumers no longer had any reason to fear.

The Tour of Spain reassured them. The peninsula remained a sanctuary. In Italy, France and Belgium, the authorities were hovering over the cycling scene like vultures. But in Spain the Guardia Civil maintained a respectable distance. Having arrived in a manic-depressive state, the peloton rebuilt its morale in the Andalusian sun. Ultimately, what had been cast as the end of the world was no more than a passing episode. They had been silly to get so worried, and now they returned to their old habits. The Vuelta beat all speed records, with one stage run at an average of more than 51 kilometres per hour.

Things had got too close for comfort, though. The previous sense of impunity had led first to carelessness and then to effrontery. For a Tour de France car, decked out with logos as if in a carnival, to be sent across borders when it was packed with EPO and growth hormone underlined to what extent doping had become the norm. The penitents learned their lesson: the networks were reorganised in a more discreet fashion. There was no question of allowing the possibility of anyone stumbling upon a walking pharmacy again.

The routine restarted with just some simple adaptations to accommodate the new constraints.

I noticed this return to normality at the world championships. The good results I'd had in the latter half of the season and the positive image I presented, as well as the enforced desertion of several national celebrities, had earned me selection for the French road team.

Race day, which featured 11 laps of a circuit in the Dutch town of Valkenburg, was enough to convince me that normalisation was well under way. The pace was flat out. I abandoned a little after halfway. My role was to protect Jacky Durand, to constantly ferry him up towards the front of the pack, to keep him out of the wind. There was plenty of wind that day as the weather was bad, and yet the speed of the race was staggering!

My impression was corroborated in the following weeks during my final two races of the season: Milan–Turin and the Tour of Piedmont. My opponents were back at their previous level. That affair? What of it? It had been a fine affair for some!

In the autumn, the police in Lille summonsed me as part of their investigation. They wanted to interview me. It was better for me to come to them, they told me. It was a question of discretion. Seeing vehicles with Lille's 59 registration plate in Labastide-Rouairoux would have got people talking.

I flew up to Lille on the day the police had requested. Two plainclothes officers picked me up at the airport. They took me to the police HQ and told me they were taking me into custody, adding in the same breath that this was an essential formality to ensure the validity of the process. It still gave me quite a shock. I still had in my mind the apocalyptic accounts of those who had been interviewed during the Tour de France: the revolting sandwiches, their shoelaces being confiscated, the stench of the cells, the rectal examinations …

But the officers questioning me immediately put my mind at rest. They told me they knew I hadn't been doping. They simply wanted to know more about how things worked at Festina.

A few days before my meeting, I'd found myself racing with Pascal Hervé and Richard Virenque. The two men had heard that the police had summonsed me, probably from their lawyers. They came to see me in my room. I was surprised by their visit. Since our problems in March, they hadn't spoken to me. We had a long chat. My team-mates advised me to say as little as possible.

'Answer yes or no and do not say that you saw syringes circulating,' one of these charmers warned me.

Their advice was useless. The police knew more about what had been going on than I did. I was seated opposite the officer asking the questions. To one side, the other officer was typing my answers into a machine. He stopped occasionally to go back over a point.

At midday, we went out for lunch in a small restaurant on the corner of the street. A room had been reserved upstairs. I was surprised to find Laurent Lefèvre in there. He was being questioned in another office. The meal took place in a good atmosphere. I insisted on paying my share. These damned principles again! I also didn't want to look like an informer who gets paid off for juicy titbits.

We returned to the police station, and my hosts took me to the science lab. A forensic scientist asked me to urinate into a flask and took samples of my hair. Having got used to very formal behaviour during doping controls, I was surprised by the casual atmosphere in which these tasks were conducted. As I was leaving the lab, I was praying that my flask didn't get confused with another. If there had been a positive result, there was no question of invoking some technicality or of providing a backdated medical certificate!

The officers took me back to their offices. They read me the statement put together during my questioning, and I signed two or three copies of it. They escorted me to the station and even took me to my train. We all shook hands and went our separate ways. I never knew their names. They went back to their world and I returned to mine – two worlds that at one time I would never have imagined would collide.

My world … Was it still mine? My fan club organised another edition of the Fête des Ténors in November 1998. The Jalabert brothers, Christophe Rinero, Gilles Maignan, Didier Rous and Marion Clignet came, but the atmosphere was frosty. Something had broken between them and me. Only Jérôme Chiotti seemed keen to get on with me. He had already commenced an honest dialogue with his conscience. In May 2000, this introspection would lead him to admitting having used EPO during the 1996 world mountain bike championship, which he won while in Festina colours. He sportingly handed over the rainbow jersey to the rider who had finished runner-up and deserved it more than him.

The rest of the cycling family cold-shouldered me. They didn't trust me. Conversations stopped when I approached. The police had had no shortage of stool pigeons. You had to be on your guard. People now viewed me with a good deal of prejudice, and with a touch of superstition too. I was the stranger who had brought ill on the house. The authorities that had been martyring cycling had been making the same noises as me. It was a sign that I was an accomplice, one of the executioners' henchmen.

The press didn't help my relationship with those around me. They described me as a phenomenon, which was bad enough, but worse still they were saying I was the antithesis of all that was wrong. With *Les Misérables* in mind, I was pitched as poor Cosette, with the rest cast as the appalling Thenardiers. This really annoyed me.

However, I wasn't very talkative at that time. 'I think cycling is on the right track,' I dared to say, against all of the evidence. I didn't want to overburden anyone. I was just happy that my solitary battle had paid off to an extent. I had clocked up 35,000 kilometres on the bike over that year. At least I hadn't pedalled for nothing this time.

I wasn't the sole target for suspicion. Relationships had soured within the cycling family. At the world championships in Valkenburg, the atmosphere was less upbeat than it had been two years before in Lugano. We still talked about money, girls and cars as we had done in the good old days. However, these were no longer conversations between mates, slapping their thighs and each other on the back, but just a way to fill the silence.

Solidarity no longer counted for anything due to the weight of common guilt. The peloton now thought of itself as a band of confidants. I was automatically excluded, without even knowing it. But I was made to understand what the situation was. Colleagues called me 'Mr Clean'. This wasn't intended as praise, but to show their contempt.

Chapter 6
Stilled Voices

At the end of 1998, Prosport, the administrative body that oversaw Festina's sporting activities, was dissolved. The watchmaking brand brought the team under its own direct control. It took the opportunity to renegotiate contracts, lowering salaries. The team's millionaires had to accept heartbreaking revisions.

Richard Virenque was asked to accept conditions that he deemed unworthy. The fallen hero announced his retirement. France cried in pain. A few weeks later, France stamped its feet with joy on hearing that he was reconnecting with his public as part of the Italian Polti team. Luc Leblanc, who was already part of this team, paid the price of this resurrection. His inability to get on with Virenque forced the sponsor to make a choice. It was too bad for Leblanc that he was pushed towards retirement without his homeland shedding a tear. The former world champion's palmarès spoke volumes, however.

The cycling economy was heading through a turbulent period. As for me, the beggar and good-for-nothing who had gently been pushed towards the exit, I suddenly became the golden boy, as in some schmaltzy novel. The servant was dubbed the valiant knight, in a parody of those swashbuckling tales.

When it comes to sporting spectacle, the most valuable commodity is being unique, exceptional, original. This is what distinguishes elite sport from mass-participation events. The most highly prized kind of singularity is obviously that of the champion, the winner, the one person seated up high on their stratospheric podium. This allows them to amass fortunes. But within a peloton that had damaged public confidence, my originality, which was no longer hidden, also became a valuable commodity. Moreover, the proof of my probity, which had been sealed by the judiciary, offered excellent references from a marketing perspective for those wanting to restore the image of a brand.

In 1995, several team managers had been weighing up my sporting future. By June 1998, I was no more than a guinea pig on which to test alternatives to doping. In early 1999, I was a brand of washing powder: Bassons, with outstanding cleanliness, washes whiter. Guaranteed without chemicals, it works only with *l'eau claire*.

I had no illusions about the reason for the sudden sporting attraction I had for my new groupies. Antoine Vayer, who had been my guiding angel in June in the contract situation I previously described, was now being courted on all sides. Festina wanted to keep me; Michel Gros had assured me of that. Unlike others on the roster, I could even expect to have my salary reassessed in an upward fashion. Banesto, the team of my idol Indurain, showed some interest, as did Crédit Agricole. Other teams were also making noises.

I must at this point mention Gilles Delion. This French talent was a professional in the early 1990s. He had witnessed the spread of EPO and the dismantling of hierarchies that this contagion brought about. Like me, he had been faced with an obligation. Like me, he had refused to comply. He had left the sport.

Delion had just enough time to win a stage of the Tour de France and a great Classic, the Tour of Lombardy. Then haematocrit levels took off and his hopes of victory went with them. This star performer increasingly struggled to follow the peloton's frenetic rhythm. He went deeper into his reserves each time he raced. He was on the verge of anaemia. Mononucleosis laid him out. It was probably the result of his body's rebellion against the inhuman efforts that these new androids were demanding of it. He was then struck by another misfortune: he spoke out. Offering an insider's perspective, he denounced the cheating that was eroding his sport. This healthy, perhaps even saintly man had become an anomaly in this world of freakish good health. He didn't really leave. He was kicked out for unsavoury conduct. It would be more appropriate to say he went for being too clean.

I think I would have suffered the same fate if the revelatory events of 1998 hadn't happened. I was lucky, but he wasn't. For years, the rebel denounced the excesses of his former world. Nobody listened, because nothing emerged to substantiate his accusations. He seemed a bitter man to all but a small circle of insiders, who viewed him with the respect that is owed to someone perceived as a madman. Today, facts provide an echo for my words. I hope one day that the same will apply to those of one of my forerunners. I'll never be the pioneer. Another man deserves this honorary title more than me: Gilles Delion.

I finally decided to continue my career at La Française des Jeux. I signed a one-year contract in mid-October 1998 that offered me a gross salary of 28,000 francs per month. I had immediately dismissed the idea of staying with Festina. There I had the backing of Michel Gros and the sponsor, but I was the target of hostility from the barons. The atmosphere was deteriorating even further.

The atmosphere at La Française des Jeux on the other hand seemed convivial to me. When the two teams used to stay in the same hotels, I would see their guys laughing, a joyful experience that had been lost to us. Also, hadn't the Madiot brothers been the first to believe in my sporting value and approach me in 1995? By joining their band, I hoped to turn time back and rediscover the naïve enthusiasm that had filled me then.

In late November, we had a training camp at Renazé, the village in Mayenne where Marc Madiot lives. Our host started the first meeting with a speech in which he repeated the instructions of the big boss, Bertrand de Gallé. Esprit de corps and the refusal to dope would be the guiding principles of the season. This credo was in vogue at the time. But it remained intangible. The sponsor has paid dearly for this great show of obstinacy. The team is now on the verge of the second division, owing to a total lack of results.

In Mayenne, I met the man who was the main architect of this policy: Dr Gérard Guillaume. He described his philosophy of medicine to us. It encompassed everything that I had tried vainly to apply over the previous three years. The doctor spoke about diet, alternative medicine and Chinese principles. He referred to the beneficial effects of ginseng, royal jelly, grape juice and non-alcoholic beer. These words flowed into my ears like a fountain of honey.

However, these naturopathic precepts provoked scepticism among my new team-mates. Their conversations were full of anxiety. They behaved like children frightened at the idea of having to face the new year without their habitual security blanket. I was disappointed by their lack of enthusiasm. I had thought they would be relieved to get rid of the medical straitjacket. It was only now that I realised the extent of their psychological dependence on it.

I was even more taken aback by the talk among the young professionals who had just been hired. They were stepping up from the amateur ranks with full knowledge of the latest pharmacopoeia. In the three years since I'd left those ranks, the gangrene had spread right through them as well. Adopting a less than innocent attitude, these lowlifes were asking the older riders how to get around the new prohibitions. The renewal won't happen thanks to them, I said to myself.

However, I still hung on to my hopes, especially as the French regulations now featured a new constraint: longitudinal testing. This threw a new stick in the wheel of the dopers. The cycling fraternity regarded this medical oddity with disbelief. The initiative was studied from every possible angle in order to detect a weakness in it, in the way a cat burglar examines a safe before breaking into it. This was clearly going to be no easy break-in.

Longitudinal testing was inviolable in principle. Athletes had to undergo a detailed medical examination four times a year. Any insufficiency, any abnormal physiological parameter would result in a temporary withdrawal of their licence, and therefore of their ability to work. The various controls that were in place up to that point only established the status of an individual at a particular point and using a single reference – blood, urine, or even breath for PFC. Longitudinal testing enabled comparisons to be made over a long period and it combined various methods of examination. Therefore, it was possible to detect a radical change in metabolism or an abnormal increase in capacity, both signs of possible cheating.

This new weapon, like blood-testing controls, was not a tool in the fight against doping but part of the framework relating to preventive medicine in the workplace. But the development appeared serious enough to encourage a few oldstagers to bring their career to a premature end. Those who were still too young to take advantage of this option had to submit to this analysis whether they liked it or not. Only a few of those opposed to this development resisted it, such as Laurent Jalabert and Richard Virenque, who were protected from any sanction by their exile in foreign teams.

On 19 January I made my way to INSEP, the National Institute for Sport, Expertise and Performance, which is located in the middle of the Bois de Vincennes in Paris. A mobile laboratory had been set up there. The first blood samples were even taken in the presence of journalists.

Another three appointments followed during that same year. From April, the system began to demonstrate its effectiveness and revealed the substantial metabolic imbalance within the French peloton: 67 riders had a significant excess of iron, the probable result of massive use of EPO. In my case, the laboratory had detected another deficiency …

Showing prodigious skill, the wreckers were soon finding chinks in this new means of reinforcement. The rider's union took umbrage at the fact that the results and even some statistics might be revealed. Lawyers made threatening noises, citing the labour law and medical confidentiality, even though no one's name had been mentioned. They won the case without the courts putting up too much resistance. The results were hidden away. The analyses were relayed to team doctors, who were the only ones who could decide whether to stop a rider working… In addition, licence withdrawals were restricted to a fortnight.

A laboratory in Troyes, which had hitherto had little to do with sporting affairs, was the only establishment overseeing this protocol, which had received strong support from the Minister of Youth and Sports. But its monopoly was challenged for legal reasons. It was therefore decided that each rider could choose where to be examined, as long as the lab was entitled to carry out such procedures. The principles of uniqueness and continuity were consequently eroded. The whole process was diluted by a cacophony of conflicting interests.

Already undermined from a legal standpoint, the requirement to undergo this monitoring now simply depended on the sponsor's determination to insist upon it. This undoubtedly reassured those who were recalcitrant, and they soon joined the process with a great deal of fanfare.

However, in the initial months of 1999, the novelty of this process still evoked fear. This new complication and the entreaties of the sponsors had forced the French riders to be cautious. The profession was in crisis. Deviations from the rules were condemned and threats of reprimand were vehement. Justice was working. Heads were falling into the basket, not only in France, but also in Italy where there were several cases involving the cream of that nation's peloton. Elsewhere, things were calmer. Just one question was nagging away at my team-mates: what were our foreign counterparts going to do? Would they play the game?

The first races of the season didn't provide any more insight than those in previous years. The kilometres I'd ground out in training over the winter enabled me to do well. I took enough high finishes to become the provisional leader of the Coupe de France series. The third place I claimed in the Tour du Haut-Var even led some gossip columnists to swoon. Was this not a sign of the renewal that had been promised? I didn't dare disappoint them by saying that I had already figured well in this event in the past. I also liked to fool myself.

The slogan of the moment, which was being done to death, was: 'Let's make a clean sweep of the past.' I believed it. I could have asked for nothing better than to draw a line under what I had just experienced. But there was misunderstanding about the interpretation of this slogan. It should have said: 'We're cleaning the slate from 1998.' The only troubles these two-wheeled revolutionaries wanted to eradicate were the little ones that the police were forcing on them.

My illusions were quickly doused. April came and brought its usual infernal pace. Nothing had changed, least of all the mentality. One incident provided me with the proof of this. During Paris–Roubaix, when the riders were already scattered by the demands of the race, a rider in my group crashed in front of me. A tube fell out of his pocket and came open, spilling its contents onto the cobbles. They were Anémine pills, which were a caffeine-based stimulant. The scene was comical in terms of how it unfolded, tragic in terms of what it demonstrated. The reflex response remained unchanged. The riders were still addicted.

From these Classics, that once again went down as easily as hemlock, I only drew one small bit of consolation. On the third attempt, I finally managed to finish Paris–Roubaix. I finished in 40th place, 13 minutes behind the winner.

As I entered the velodrome in the northern city, a wave of contentment washed over me. It rose to my lips in the form of a laugh that was transformed by sheer fatigue into a rictus grin. I could feel the mask of dried mud cracking on my face as a result of this grimace. The crowd were applauding. I only heard them vaguely, just as one hears a horn far off in the mist. Filled with jubilation still, I wanted to accelerate – but I couldn't. I crossed the line holding my head high with pride. Immediately afterwards my shoulders slumped, as if my head suddenly weighed a ton. I was exhausted, but I had reached the full extent of what the bike could bring me. It was a brutal form of pleasure, patterned with mud and fatigue. 'You don't get anything until you have given everything,' a proverb has it. That day, tossed about on the roughly hewn cobbles of the north, I pushed my body until it revealed unfathomable depths to me. I visited a terra incognita hidden deep within myself.

I dragged myself into the ancient changing rooms, the stone floor worn by the rubbing of shoes. I undressed like a zombie. To stay upright in the shower I hung on to the chain that controlled it while the warm jets of water reinvigorated me. Grime oozed from my every pore. I looked down at my feet in the dirty water, which was draining away into the gutter. I closed my eyes and felt a great void within me. I had touched nirvana.

This feeling of happiness is more private than the winner's, which can be read in all of the media's stories, but is equally intense. This egotistical pleasure redeemed past humiliations and was an advance on those still to come.

My team-mates were right to be worried. The speed of the foreign teams hadn't dropped. Fortunately, they hardly ever raced on French soil, such was the trauma left by the frosty reception that the police had given them the previous year. For them, France had become a place of ugly encounters, a den of cut-throats. Only the Dutch Rabobank team had taken their A team to Paris–Nice in March, while some other notable foreign teams had stayed away. Rabobank had crushed the opposition.

Humiliated at every turn, the French riders fumed. Jean-Cyril Robin, whose pride had been stung, sounded off in the columns of *Ouest-France*. 'We are currently in an impasse, because there are still cheats. Cycling has two speeds,' he said. 'Let the police come back and search the team trucks! I think this is necessary. Riders who are still messing around with doping need to be punished, and this has to be made public. The code of silence – never again.' His comments were very heartfelt. I must point out that none of my criticisms ever reached this virulent level!

I admired this demonstration of courage, just as I deplored the evasiveness that followed it. A letter of reprimand from Hein Verbruggen, president of the International Cycling Union – and an arbiter who was quicker to disapprove of this kind of sincere criticism than of unsporting behaviour – was enough to snuff out the rebellion. Robin hid himself away in a moody silence. He never came out of it.

However, the talk around the La Française des Jeux dinner tables remained bitter. The performances of the Casino team, the only French outfit to remain at the level of the foreigners, provoked questions and jealousy. The guys were surprised to see one Frenchman riding with particular ease. The guy had a dog.

'I went up to stroke it and looked at the animal more closely,' one of our group said one day. 'I swear the pooch is a cool bag. It has a zip on its back. Its master's products are undoubtedly stashed inside.'

We laughed wickedly at the joke. Cycling at two speeds, as mentioned by Jean-Cyril, was the focus of conversations. One day, the discussion of this issue really got to me.

'It makes me laugh to see that you've finally noticed this difference. I've been aware of it for three years. Back then, it didn't bother you.'

You can't deny me this: I have always had a knack for creating a bad atmosphere.

I spent another week in my hypoxic room in May. Once again, I didn't raise my haematocrit by even a single point, but I could at least train intensively for the Dauphiné Libéré, which was just around the corner.

There I was about to savour victory, even though I didn't believe this was still possible. On the final stage on Sunday, 13 June, to Aix-les-Bains, I slipped away after 28 kilometres and stayed clear on my own for 120 kilometres into Aix-les-Bains. It was in typical Babasse fashion, lacking in strategy – a mad dash by a hothead, with everyone behind him and just him alone out front. Pierre Chany would no doubt have liked it. He would have knocked out a glowing report for the next day. Others did so in his place.

My success was immediately interpreted as a message from the gods, as a triumph of virtue over vice. 'Was Bassons' victory one of the most important of the season?' asked Philippe Bouvet in *L'Equipe*. I remember something else this passionate journalist once wrote – that it's the riders we want to admire, not their doctors.

Some people didn't see it this way and were more sceptical. They felt my rivals had let me win to demonstrate the sport's redemption. You will easily understand that I didn't want to subscribe to this interpretation. I was five minutes ahead with 50 kilometres remaining and had just one minute in hand on the line; my rivals had therefore ridden with the intention of catching me. Had they gone flat out? A doubt remained in my mind.

I learned a little more about this episode many years later, in 2012 in fact, when reading through the report put together by Travis Tygart, head of the United States Anti-Doping Agency (USADA). According to the testimony of Jonathan Vaughters, Lance Armstrong's team-mate and winner of the overall classification at the 1999 Dauphiné Libéré, Armstrong had wanted to lead the pursuit behind me that day. 'Lance did not like Bassons' outspokenness about doping, and Lance frequently made fun of him in a very merciless and venomous fashion, much like a playground bully.' Vaughters had managed to dissuade him from expending his energy in this little revenge mission, arguing that I was a long way down in the overall classification. Lance Armstrong did, however, finish second on that stage. But the American was simply warming up before the Tour, a new target that would be far more rewarding. As for his anger towards me, it wouldn't be long before it poured out.

At the time of my victory, I was only sure of one thing for certain: I had stood out because the level of the race was not all that high. Only a handful of foreign teams were on the start line. The others were still avoiding the country of Voltaire and Patrick Keil, the judge in charge of the Festina case.

I quickly slotted this cavalier stage win into my anthology of favourites, alongside the Paris–Roubaix I'd finished and some of the other victories I'd taken. I savoured this success because I felt we were in something of a lull. I could still see people carrying centrifuges around, which didn't augur well in terms of renewal. More than anything, though, I could see that mindsets weren't changing. The guys had had some restrictions imposed on them, but this had only happened under duress. They were saying: we've accepted a lot of changes. But, in fact, these had been imposed on them. The arms race, the eternal combat between artillery and armour, was still going on. The first person to find a new product that was undetectable and improved performance would take a big leap ahead.

The great deception persisted. At the 1999 Tour of Italy, Italian journalists, who are never slow when it comes to creating drama, made the riders swear an oath on the head of the person dearest to them that they were not doping. Marco Pantani took the oath. Towards the end of the Giro, a test revealed that his haematocrit was above 50 and he was excluded from the race, which he was then leading.

In this atmosphere of deception, the public did not know who to trust as the great cycling summit of the year, the Tour de France, came into view. In the midst of the quest for purity, *Le Parisien* had the idea of approaching yours truly. The newspaper proposed that I write a daily column in its pages for 10,000 francs. I was going to describe on a daily basis my first encounter with the race for which I had finally been selected.

The Tour is an event apart. Everything about it is bigger, sometimes to the point of outrageousness. For three weeks, the peloton is under the microscope, magnified like the Gauls' village at the beginning of Asterix's adventures. Finding themselves under this magnifying glass, some are overcome by megalomania. For my part, I felt quite humble when I arrived at Le Puy-du-Fou, in the Vendée, from where the great show was setting out. I found I was part of a mobile town, designed to travel in high style for almost 4,000 kilometres. I felt like just a single atom.

That Saturday, I climbed onto the starting ramp feeling like a novice all over again. I had done a reconnaissance of the prologue course the day before. It was fully protected by metal barriers lining both sides of the road. I was astonished by the extent of this logistical operation. I understood the reason for it the next day soon after I set off. A huge crowd, the likes of which I had never seen in my life, had gathered on the roadsides. I can remember the lines of bodies leaning over the barriers were so constant that they disappeared off into the distance. Fervent fans urged me on. The sound resonated in my helmet to the point where it made me dizzy. I don't know if it was the noise, the effort or the emotion that had my temples throbbing. It was 8' 46" of elation.

I told Lionel Chami, the journalist from *Le Parisien* who was ghosting my column, about this naïve emotion that same evening. The next morning, I was surprised and annoyed when I saw my piece in the paper. The reason for this was the short preamble to my words. 'An important detail: Bassons is racing *"à l'eau claire"*, that is to say without using doping products.' Having eagerly opened the paper that morning, I could only see that one statement: I wasn't doping. I couldn't imagine that the other riders, influenced as they had been by recent events, would read it as anything other than suspicion as far they were concerned.

I soon had another grievance to add to this one. Before the start, some journalists had been asking me about the situation in my sport, and I had told them what I really thought. 'I was optimistic in January. I am less so today. We crossed one hurdle but there are still three or four ahead. Controls are being carried out, but there are no follow-up punishments … If there is business that needs to be clarified, I'd like to see the police doing it, so that they can put this to bed once and for all

… I hope that this Tour will take place in healthy conditions, but I have come here with some doubts … Longitudinal testing? Many things have been discovered, but no penalties have yet been imposed.'

There was nothing that hadn't been said before, nothing that wasn't already known, just a statement of doubt.

I was surprised to note the next day when I was reading through the papers that I was the only one to address an issue that had been in the news for months. Everyone else had decided not to respond to questions on this matter. From the Tour director to the most humble of the race followers, an instruction had gone through the caravan: let's forget everything that's happened and start all over again. An honourable truce had been declared. Every unsavoury concern had been buried as the pedalling fraternity went out preaching renewal on France's roads.

The Tour de France is not only the biggest race. It is an incarnation of this whole *milieu*, which only knew how to speak with one voice. I would have the opportunity to observe this phenomenon repeatedly in the days that followed, often at my own expense. Getting a different stance heard meant dissociation from everyone else on the race. I don't think there was a *deus ex machina* imposing a single way of thinking. Cross-pollination of thinking through the generations had produced clones who all acted and reacted in the same way. When one of their number stood out, the system was immediately threatened. Cycling had invented a perfect world, a benevolent and festive dictatorship that only knew how to survive if every member remained united with the pack.

It reminds me of the old British TV series, *The Prisoner*, where men and women live happily in an idyllic village. They have become no more than characterless beings, identified only by a number. One man rises up, Number Six: he wants to know why he is there and who decided on that. He wants to assert his right to think for himself. As for me, number 152, I wanted to give a sense of my impressions of the Tour de France. Like the hero in the series, I wanted to say: 'I am not a number!' I wanted to assert my personality, to make my voice heard.

So I continued to put my views forward. The statements of the obvious I made were regarded as sacrilegious within the lobotomised race caravan. I had things to say. More and more journalists came to hear what I had to say. I ended up giving as many as eight interviews a day without having the feeling I was repeating myself. During my three years of silence, I had had time to refine my ideas and comments. I kept coming up with new ones. I had transformed into an 'ideas' animal. On the phone my parents told me that they no longer recognised the shy child they had brought up. I could feel my grandfather's influence coursing through me. Pascale's love and unwavering support drove the words out of me.

Meanwhile my standing among my peers was dropping by the hour. My initial columns in *Le Parisien* dealt with rather upbeat aspects of the race. But that infamous preamble was still causing shock. From the opening days of the race, I was given a nickname: 'the columnist'. It reminded me of the previous one: 'the clean rider'. The award of both of these monikers hinted at the sense of ostracism towards me.

My words became bittersweet when the supercharged pack pedalled with silky smoothness at an average of more than 50 kilometres per hour, as if the roads of France were all huge descents. The remarks directed at me on the road were more scathing. Udo Bölts came up alongside me during the stage between Laval and Blois:

'Your views on doping are a good thing,' he said to me. 'It's good that you've got character. But why do you, the French, believe that if a guy hasn't come to the Tour it's because he is afraid of the authorities?'

The Deutsche Telekom rider was referring to the absence of his leader, Jan Ullrich, due to an injury sustained in the weeks before the race that had been interpreted as a diplomatic pretext for him to opt out.

After a week, hardly anyone would talk to me. It was because of this, probably, that I spent a little more time pouring my heart out to journalists and in my column. My Tour de France became well structured: I spent six hours on the bike without saying a word, then became loquacious as soon as I crossed the line.

After the condemnatory silence came open hostility. One day, Pascal Chanteur rode up to me and said: 'Stop your bullshit. You are alone, it's pointless. You're just getting everyone's back up. You're doing real damage. Journalists are bastards.'

My former team-mate Thierry Bourguignon tried to open my eyes: 'The journalists are taking advantage of you.'

'I know that,' I said, 'but I am also taking advantage of them to say what I have to say.'

'Why do you always talk about me in your column?'

'Because you're the only one who is still happy to speak to me.'

One day I received an insulting letter in the post from a Richard Virenque fan after I had criticised the special place he maintained in the hearts of the spectators. For the most part, though, the tone of the letters I received was friendly. Showing a degree of schizophrenia, the public supported me, while at the same time applauding the rest. Theirs was a permanent balancing act between reason and passion.

One morning, on the Maubeuge stage, I agreed to yet another interview inside the start village. Rather than being a village, this is more of a fenced-in fortress, protected by guards, who restrict right of entry to a select and properly badged clientele. Sheltered from the plebs, local dignitaries can eat their fill and mingle with the race's principal actors, who take advantage of the calm surroundings before they have to fly. The Tour is a popular and free spectacle. Nevertheless, the roads of France still comprise first and second classes.

I was talking to the journalist while sitting at a sponsor's table. A man waved at me through the fence. He begged for an autograph. He pressed against the fence, his face flush against the metal barrier, his arm stretched towards me, holding a piece of paper in his fingertips. I went up to him, signed my name and swapped a few words with this fan. But this image stirred something in me. I felt a profound sense of guilt: I was involved in this discrimination. I was holding forth with journalists, speaking to them about injustice, but dispensing it in my own way. I felt uncomfortable about this for a good part of the stage.

I made a resolution and acted on it the following day. I arrived 20 minutes earlier. Instead of barricading myself within the restricted-access cocoon, I mixed with the crowds. I felt some apprehension; I hadn't spared Richard Virenque in some of the things I'd said. His supporters could take me to task. But there was none of that. In fact, few people recognised me. The spectators looked at my number and referred to the list published in the local paper. Having been twisting their necks for hours to catch a glimpse of the top of a rider's head, they were delighted to have one standing right in front of them at long last. They offered me encouragement, wished me '*bonne route*' and asked me for a bottle or an autograph. Some asked me: 'Is it hard?' Others: 'How are you doing?' I preferred to avoid these questions.

Few people knew who I was. I received numerous expressions of sympathy, which supported my belief that the public was not totally blind. Up to the point I abandoned, I regularly had this kind of contact. I wasn't subjected to any kind of hostility. I was not aiming to boost my popularity: for all these people, I was only one actor among many others for whom they had a common admiration. They weren't acknowledging Bassons, but a man who was riding the Tour. I derived huge satisfaction from the warmth that enveloped me, before plunging myself into the icy hostility of the peloton, the more touchy section of my readership.

Undaunted by being shunned in this way, bit by bit I adopted a more hardline approach in my column as the pace of the race increased. It got a little bit faster every day, gathering speed as the first major climbs approached. My commentary was extremely acerbic after the Metz time trial on 10 July. It was entitled: 'What is EPO used for?' With feigned innocence, I wondered about the usefulness of this pick-me-up because, although it had officially disappeared, the train we were on was going as fast as ever. In passing, I also predicted that Lance Armstrong would win in Paris.

Having completed my time trial in the morning, I had gone back to the hotel by the time the favourites set off on their run around the course. I watched their performances on the television in my room. The ease they demonstrated stunned me. They seemed to float weightlessly, like satellites that spin at dizzying speeds without seeming to move. At more than 50 kilometres per hour, these unremarkable riders seemed to breeze effortlessly through the wall of air that I'd just bumped up against with each pedal stroke. Disgusted with what I was seeing, I flicked quite regularly to the Formula One Grand Prix at Silverstone. But I kept coming back to the fascinating images of these two-wheeled bullets. I spotted a difficult section where I had struggled: Lance Armstrong went through it in a gear two teeth bigger than mine without showing the slightest sign of discomfort.

I was dumbfounded. The American and I have the same morphology. We are essentially the same size and exactly the same weight. Like him, I had lost eight kilos before the Tour. Armstrong had suddenly lost that weight due to the cancer that struck him in 1996. In my case, I had lost it progressively, about a kilo a year ever since I had started cycling. We also have the same VO2 max at threshold, calculated at around 85. However, on this time trial course we were like two different species, separated by much more than the few minutes that the yellow jersey gained on me that day. On one side there was a poor wretch in a contest with his own body, while on the other was an evanescent being gliding over the asphalt. The heavy carcass that was a drag on me didn't seem to be any hindrance to him at all. I was envious of the difference that this champion said was a consequence of his victory over his disease. He was no longer the same man, he asserted. But was he still a man, in other words a mere human like me? I wondered to myself about that. His disconcerting ease nourished my own metaphysical questioning and also that of my team-mates, tinged for all of us by both jealousy and concern.

A rest day in Le Grand-Bornand followed. It should have allowed those of us who still knew what fatigue was to recover before the stages in the Alps. For several days, my morale had been in the dumps. The criticism that I thought I had allowed to slide off my outer shell had in fact been chipping away at me. Insinuations were sapping what remained of my spirit. Pascale felt I was slowly cracking up. No doubt she had seen through my banter on the phone and could sense my weariness.

She got in her car that morning and made the eight-hour drive to Le Grand-Bornand. She arrived at four that afternoon and left again at seven to do the return trip … Wasn't that a great show of support? Those too few hours I spent in her company perked me up. They also made the absence of my fiancée harder to take.

The next day we set out again, this time to Sestrières, on one of the toughest stages of the Tour. My columns were a thorn in the side of the caravan. It was bristling. Heads were being shaken all over the place as it was being read. Because of its speed I was trapped in the middle of the pack, and the peloton became my court *in camera*. Several critics yelled at me. That morning, I had to raise my voice to silence the prosecutors who slipped up next to me one after another. On the first count, I was reproached for having written that it was not possible to win a stage *à la pédale*, that is to say simply by being strong and without resorting to doping.

'I hope you don't win a stage,' one of them told me.

'Do you think people will believe you?' another shouted at me.

'Listen to them on the side of the road!' I replied. 'Do you take the public for fools? And, how can you dare to deny the obvious when you know what's going on?'

Those accusing me underestimated my resilience. Even I underestimated it. Anger animated my pen with vengeful verve. I had probably not considered what would happen after the words had provided their therapy, when that flame of vengeance became dimmed.

Far from reining me in, this strong-arming and intimidation only hardened my extremism. It was, I knew, suicide by a thousand cuts, with the pen as my instrument. But I didn't really give a damn any more. My fury had been followed by a kind of profound despair that fuelled my literary angst and produced ironic and venomous insight. My musings were getting up their noses, they were clashing with the huge totem that was renewal, and that was all that mattered.

As we were heading towards Italy, the stage would perfectly illustrate my lament about *cyclisme à deux vitesses*, as set out that morning in *Le Parisien*.

The plan had been for me to assist Jean-Cyril Robin, who was our leader. I had to do so immediately. The first climbs were tackled at a brisk pace. After the Col du Télégraphe, the leading pack numbered no more than 70 riders. The selection at the back was ruthless.

'Are we going fast or is it just me not feeling good?' wondered Thierry Bourguignon.

The climb of the Galibier was gobbled up at an even faster pace. I lost some ground on the final ramps, where the 2,600-metre pass took my breath away. Jean-Cyril was not much better. So I managed to rejoin him on the descent towards Briançon. I once again took on the role of pilot fish and did a lot of work for him on the Montgenèvre climb. At the foot of Sestrières, I had completed my mission. I left my leader to his own devices. I climbed it at my own speed. As I did, I remembered my boastful performance in 1996, with Richard Virenque on my wheel. I had matured since then – and seemingly aged, if I was to believe the difficulty I had in staying with the pace.

The terrain and the weather made this stage exhausting. After the Col du Galibier, a terrible storm broke over us in the final kilometres. Only Lance Armstrong had finished before it came down on us: I saw an injustice in that.

I finished numb with cold. The hotel was a kilometre from the finish line. I arrived there in a daze. When I got into my room, I wanted to fill the bath, but it was going to take too long. I lay in the empty tub and doused myself under the hot shower.

A huge feeling of unease fell on the race after Armstrong's demonstration. The American had ridiculed his main rivals on the final climb. I thought I had suffered a personal defeat. However, in the end I hadn't come out of it so badly, I noticed, when I looked at the standings. I was 66th, and 20 minutes behind the winner.

That evening, the TV images of the lone rider scaling the mountain with his hands off the bars (as he checked his watch) sent dark rumours around the race. No one believed there was any value in this performance. In our hotel and in many others, revolt was simmering. The opposition had been humiliated. French, Italians and Belgians crossed paths and exchanged the same disillusioned phrases. Some even spoke of stopping, of leaving the Tour as a sign of protest.

At the dinner table, everyone cried foul: 'You saw how he spun the gear without even opening his mouth – that's impossible.'

'And how he dropped the others in an instant without straining himself. Can you believe that?'

There was a chorus of lamentation, punctuated by a leitmotif: 'What is the secret?' My piece the next morning, which I had phoned in a few minutes before dinner, seemed quite trifling compared to some of the hard words spouted around the dinner table. I wondered if my denunciation hadn't lacked a bit of punch, and whether I should have called back to beef up the point I was making.

The echoes of this wrath reached the pressroom. Journalists of all nationalities were wandering through the hotel corridors. They were waiting for the revolt to kick off. For once, unusually, I kept a discreet distance. The others would finally take over from me. The words of these champions would have so much more weight than the shrill little voice of this small fry. But the discontent remained shut away behind closed doors.

The next day the weather was back to normal. It was beautiful. I immediately realised that the race's barometer had also risen. The storm had passed. Nothing followed in its wake, not even a whisper. They held everything in behind a wall of silence. Seeing this, I thought to myself that a serious affliction was lying in wait for the riders in the shape of a festering ulcer.

As a result, my column, which I thought had been mild, thundered through the mountain scenery and the unearthly silence. Some of my peers sought me out and loudly reproached me. I looked into their eyes. What had they been saying yesterday? I was saddened by this fickleness, this inconsistency.

On my way to the start I crossed paths with Cyrille Guimard. I refused to look at him. The day before, he had denigrated me once again on Europe 1. Yet, during my time in the *milieu*, I never used to pay much attention to what he would rattle on about in the evenings. In the current climate, when most of us now know what was going on in the peloton at the time, this same commentator likes to believe he's very hard on the cheats. He presents himself as whiter than white, campaigning for root-and-branch reform of cycling. Recently, he even explained that EPO had forced him out of the sport because he couldn't resist against the arms race. I was saying as much in 1999. This only confirms to me that everyone has the right to speak on this subject except those with the greatest interest in doing so, the riders.

I then met Daniel Baal, the president of the French Cycling Federation. He shook my hand warmly.

'Keep saying what you think. Bear in mind that I would not condone attacks on anyone who simply wants to express himself.'

I was delighted to hear his words. I confess I had never really known what to think about this man. After that I was inclined to trust him. I believed he was sincere, but I think he got tangled up in political matters when the only option was to go for it. I would later receive confirmation, at my own expense, of this Byzantine side of French cycling. I fear he did not have the means to implement his ideas in 1999, his attempts hampered by the hypocrisy within the *milieu*.

I also got an insight into this duplicity on the start line. Once again I was verbally abused.

The race got back under way. It was a fearsome day. After descending for 15 kilometres, we started up a 25km pass. The word within the peloton was to start slowly to avoid eliminations. The herd shook itself into action. I went up alongside several French riders, hoping for at least a 'Bonjour' in the absence of a message of support. I didn't get any. I was alone. This common cowardice infuriated me. I just had to express this in one way or another. I could have screamed, 'Fuck you all!' But I reacted in another way.

I eased my way up to the front and made an attack. Right away I could hear whistles piercing the air behind me. If they were expecting the little lapdog to come to heel like that, then they were mistaken. I persisted. After a kilometre, I turned around. The pack was on my heels, led by Armstrong's team-mates, who were receiving collaboration from some French riders. These guys were offering a sign of their allegiance to the race's *patron* and showing their disapproval of my unspeakable behaviour. I then sat up and adopted the detached attitude of a rider out for a Sunday jaunt. The herd absorbed me and peppered me with insults. The invective came in all manner of languages. I had already fixed a wry smile on my face. I maintained it, which added fuel to the uproar.

Lance Armstrong slipped in next to me. Immediately, a safety cordon formed around the pair of us. I found myself in a spot from which I couldn't escape. The yellow jersey stared into my face. I had affronted him and I had that insufferable smile on my face.

'What are you doing?' the boss asked me in English.

I knew that he spoke French. But by choosing to speak in his own language, he was emphasising my inferiority.

I have my degree, I remembered at that moment, and I thank the teachers who patiently taught me the rudiments of the language of Shakespeare.

'I'm making the race, I'm attacking,' I said to him in English. The conversation continued – in English.

'You know, what you are saying to the journalists is not good for cycling.'

'I'm simply saying what I think. I'm saying that there is doping.'

'If you're here to do that, it would be better for you to go home and find another job.'

'I'm not leaving when I've not changed anything; if I have something to say, I will say it.'

'Then get the hell out!'

The yellow jersey accompanied his parting words by sweeping his hand through the air. I made out I was indifferent. Stéphane Heulot then approached me.

'You shouldn't have done that.'

I regarded him with a puzzled look. The night before, he had wanted to pack his bags, but now he had choked back his resentment. He had changed direction loud and clear within this pack of gossipmongers, where each bit of news was transmitted as quickly as a warning about an upcoming roundabout or a tight bend. His very public stance had earned him the right to roam. A few kilometres later, when Lance Armstrong had given permission for the racing to start, Heulot broke clear with Thierry Bourguignon. It was 14 July, Bastille Day, I then recalled. Their long breakaway maintained France's vainglorious pride. It ended on the climb to Alpe d'Huez, when the foreigners decided that the French had done enough celebrating of the storming of the Bastille. The stage was won by an Italian.

As for me, I was raging in the face of such thoughtlessness with regard to the public and my sport. I felt I was not there to race the Tour de France, but only to prevent this bunch of hypocrites from sliding into complacency. I dropped to the back of the peloton and on the next ascent I took the opportunity to ride all alone. With no one around me, I mulled over my dark thoughts, putting my rage into each pedal stroke.

On the climb of Alpe d'Huez, I slipped into a *gruppetto* containing the sprinters, the last group on the road that was going to finish inside the time limit. I received some applause and encouragement, which provided me with some solace. On a banner, I even read: 'The Tour without Bassons is like music without an amp.' At least my fans had a sense of what was going on.

Nevertheless, by now it wasn't a case of me being isolated in the pack, but of me standing alone against everyone else. It was the beginning of the end for the impudent Bassons.

Chapter 7

Emergency Exit

I had a tough day between Bourg d'Oisans and Saint-Étienne on Thursday, 15 July. I had spent the previous night mulling over my troubles. During the stage, nobody spoke to me about the previous day's incidents. The issue had been buried. But I was seething too much to be able to keep myself calm. Rage can bring out warlike virtues. But on this occasion, it blocked my legs as I rode, forcing me to fight against it. The fatigue brought on as the kilometres totted up finally brought me peace of mind. I had calmed down, or at least I thought I had.

At the finish, in the middle of getting changed, I gave a first interview of little note. Then Christian Kalb, the press officer at La Française des Jeux, asked me to speak on the cable news channel LCI. On my way to the television studio, Jean-Cyril Robin shouted across to me:

'Be careful what you say, Babasse.'

This casual remark floored me like a punch to the kidneys. Jean-Cyril was the only one who had never made even the slightest remark to me. His early season comments had made me believe he was thinking the same way as me, even if he had remained in a strained silence. Back at Le Puy-du-Fou, as we prepared for the race, he had said he wanted to see how things were before making a judgement on the extent of the renewal. He would deliver his verdict after the Metz time trial.

The time trial had passed, as well as the stages in the Alps. He had seen what was going on, but had kept his counsel. He had become complicit in the charade. No doubt he wanted to be allowed the right to roam, which he would obtain after the Pyrenees, although it earned him no more success than it had Stéphane Heulot.

Until this warning, I thought I was his spokesman to the press just as I was his watercarrier on the road. To an extent, I was opening up the road for him, I was protecting him. He was going to attack soon. But in Saint-Étienne I realised how much I had deceived myself. You are completely alone, I told myself.

I arrived at LCI's studio. The slant of the interview was unambiguous.

'Do you think you will hang on until the end of the Tour?'

It sounded as if bets were already being placed on this among the race followers.

'I don't know. I'm starting to suffer from nervous fatigue. I've had a bit of a blow to my morale.'

What a euphemism! I was actually on the verge of cracking right there in the TV studio. I tried in vain to stop my voice from breaking, but couldn't do so.

A member of the team staff drove me to the hotel in Saint-Galmier. I remained silent, my nose pressed against the car window, thinking over Jean-Cyril Robin's little comment.

You're all alone, completely and totally, my old Babasse, I kept saying to myself over and over again as I absently watched the countryside roll by.

When we arrived at the hotel I went up to my room, which I was sharing that evening with Stéphane Heulot. He was already having his massage. I threw my things down in a pile and fell on the bed. I felt my strength leave me. I was looking forward to the massage, as I really felt I needed to be revitalised. My turn finally came. I was the last.

I had only just lain down when Marc Madiot came in.

'Christophe, I have to talk to you.'

His tone was serious. I could sense what was coming. Lying on the massage table, I steeled myself and tried to look him in the eye.

'Go on, I'm listening.'

Madiot continued:

'Up to now I've only advised you on the way you manage your relationship with journalists. But now, I'm going to be firm: I don't want you to talk with them about doping any more. If they ask you questions about it, tell them you're here to ride your bike and that you're not going to talk about it.'

I didn't accept this desire to abstract cycling from something to which it was inextricably linked. The ostriches running around during the 1998 Tour had had this same head-in-the-sand attitude. While the race was becoming bogged down in ridicule, with searches taking place and riders abandoning in suspicious circumstances, the riders had insisted they would only talk about cycling, that is to say the actual race. This was a fine example of autosuggestion or denial, but each to their own opinion.

I sat up a little straighter.

'I don't agree. Why should I allow myself to be crushed like the others? For a start, I've not said anything out of turn about anyone. I've been asked questions and I have only replied by saying what I think, and that's all. Up to now, doping has only created hurdles in my career. Now, I am finally getting the opportunity to say what I think. I am not going to feel bad about that.'

'But can't you see that you're turning everyone against you? I told you before the start of the race to wait quietly for the stages after the Alps. You would have been able to play your card in a breakaway. If you keep on talking, nobody will let you go. You're sabotaging yourself and your team.'

Marc had lost his temper. He has always been a fiery man by nature. His thoughts always come out in a blunt manner, sometimes brutally so. I liked his frank tone as I felt it chimed with my own. But I wasn't ruffled.

'We'll see. But if that is the case, it will really reveal the level of intelligence of the rest.'

'Good God! You won't get anywhere by acting alone against everyone else.'

His voice suddenly softened:

'What you say is true, but there are enough problems, enough bad publicity. Don't aggravate the situation. That's all that the press want – scandals, dirty tricks. They are taking advantage of you.'

'I know. But that's OK as I'm the only one who is happy to talk. And I do not intend to be silent. I am less concerned with winning a stage than in having a clear conscience at the end of this Tour. I'm sure that won't be the case for many people.'

Faced with my stubbornness, Marc threw in the towel.

'OK, I understand.'

He left, slamming the door.

The conversation hadn't lasted more than ten minutes, but during the course of it I'd got out everything that had been consuming me during the previous six hours of racing. I had remained stoical. Yet, as soon as the door closed, I felt a cramp in the pit of my stomach and a lump in my throat. Tears came to my eyes.

The physio tried to talk to me. He told me that he agreed with me but that, perhaps for my sake, I should talk less. I listened to these words that were meant to reassure me but only made me dig my heels in a little more. Lying on my stomach, I tried to find something else to focus on. But all there was in front of me was a blank white hotel bedroom wall.

The physio went quiet. He kept rubbing my legs, kneading my flesh. This is a sacred moment in a cyclist's day. It is when, after putting his body through hell during the day, the rider puts back a little of the energy he's taken from it. While the masseur's hands are busy working, an incredible feeling of completeness comes over you, rising from revitalised muscles to the brain.

But that evening my fatigue was not of a corporeal nature. An experienced masseur would have understood that. The best therapists know how to find the right words to provide balm to the soul in the evenings after a bad defeat or when riders are close to abandoning. I urgently required the only ointment that could have restored me: fraternity. A friend like Rik Keyaerts or Laurent Gros would have pummelled a smile out of me. They would have found the right phrase to reassure me and would have taken my side without question. They would have told me: 'Let all these idiots say whatever they want.' Or: 'Don't let them take the piss out of you.' Or even: 'Say, Babasse, have you noticed that if you've got a syringe in your ass, you don't feel the need to sit down any more?' I hope those with delicate ears will forgive me, but in this type of situation crudeness is almost de rigueur.

The physio was a temporary employee hired for the Tour, and he was only there to treat the meat. His vapid words struck me as hard as Marc's rantings.

I was feeling distressed when Lionel Chami called me so that I could give him my impressions of the day. My brain was empty. I didn't know whether to answer 'yes' or 'no' to his questions.

'I'm not feeling very good. I'm sorry, but tonight it's going to be difficult to find something to say.'

Consequently, we agreed that there wouldn't be a column the next day. We arranged to meet on the start line.

When I got off the massage table, I rushed to Dr Guillaume's room. I pretended that I needed something to help me sleep. I had never asked him for even a sleeping pill up to that point. My request surprised him. He knew something was wrong. It did not take long before I burst into tears.

'I've had enough.'

I poured out my feelings. The doctor listened to me.

'Would you like me to give you some tranquillisers?'

'No, no, no.'

I crumpled up in tears again. Guillaume could do nothing for me except give me pills. What an irony! A pharmacy coming to the rescue of poor little Mr Clean.

The doctor knew the human body inside out. He knew how to treat serious wounds and minor injuries. He knew every little muscle, the smallest nerve. During classes at university, he had learned that 70 per cent of the body is composed of water. But sometimes the body can only produce tears. In this situation, the practitioner becomes helpless and their knowledge useless.

I was lost in a thick fog. I felt as fragile as a silk thread. It was past nine o'clock and my stomach, the other sensitive and demanding part of me, made its presence felt once more. I was hungry. I tried to get my wits together and went down to eat.

A foreign television crew was waiting for me at the bottom of the stairs. They were Dutch or German, I'm not sure which. I think they were German. They had come to see me, or perhaps I'd gone looking for them. I needed to talk, again and again, and still more, to turn the torrents of sadness gripping my chest into a river of words. Whether through tears or words, the emotions had to come out in some way.

Marc Madiot ran up. 'He has spoken enough today. It is half past nine. He has to eat and rest.'

He grabbed me roughly by the arm and dragged me into the small room that we were using as a private dining room. He pushed me inside and closed the door – this kidnapping conducted right in front of the dumbfounded journalists. The others were already seated and most had already started to eat. All conversation ended when I went in. Without even thinking, I sat in the first chair that was free.

Paradoxically, the uncomfortable silence cheered me up, although I can't explain why. Perhaps I suddenly felt courageous, despite having cried like a baby just ten minutes earlier. I held my head up. I had a little wry smile fixed in the corner of my mouth, the same impudent rictus grin that I had flourished the day before in Sestrières. I felt like I was turning the corners of my mouth up and that I looked like a malicious gnome.

Marc sat opposite me. Seated around the round table were also Yvon and my fellow riders. A happy little family. We were all in a circle, but I felt that I was in the centre of it. There was a long silence, broken only by the clatter of forks that resonated more than usual because of the abrupt and awkward way in which they were being flourished. The degree of unease was palpable.

Marc finally spoke.

'I have to speak to you. I do not want you to talk any more about doping with journalists. Am I clear?'

The Last Supper was starting. I didn't need to look to know who was taking the role of Judas.

'Are you talking to everyone or are you just directing that at me?'

'I am saying it to everyone, but you are the one it most applies to. The way you are acting, you are turning the rest of the peloton against us.'

And then came his dagger strike: 'The fact that Stéphane didn't win yesterday is probably because of you.'

I was stunned. I turned to Stéphane.

'And is that what you think – that it is because of me that you lost?'

'I don't know. It's possible. We can't be sure of anything,' he mumbled, his nose stuck in his plate.

I looked around and could see only the tops of heads. I should have told them that I despised them for their cowardice, got up from my seat and left the room. Or I should have pleaded my case, explaining that my fight was also their fight, appealing to their dignity as human beings, to their honour as champions, characteristics that had been debased for 12 days. I should have. But, like the rest, I took refuge in my plate, babbling idiotically: 'Ah, that's great! Brilliant!'

I accepted my defeat.

'OK, I understand. I won't say any more.'

The braggart had disappeared. The poseur's smirk had been wiped away. I had been brought down to size. I felt a stinging sensation irritating my eyes. I devoted my last bit of energy, or my final touch of bravado, to not cracking up. Don't do it in front of them, Babasse! Pull yourself together! I gritted my teeth and swallowed the bitter taste that had come into my mouth. I started eating, or rather stuffing myself, with my head down. My fork was moving faster and faster. I dispatched my meal in a frenzy in less than 20 minutes.

I couldn't wait to leave that room, that appalling atmosphere. I tried to call my grandfather into my mind to gain some solace, but couldn't find him. The man who had always sworn he would face up to things now had just one desire: I wanted to escape. You poor fool, did you think you would be able to defy the whole world, that you were really that clever, I said to myself. I hated myself for no longer being able to hold my head up, to tell this jolly gathering it was my honour that made me different. But what was there to say about the feelings I had towards those who were sitting around me?

I was the first to leave the table.

I took refuge in a quiet corner of the hotel. I tried to call Pascale. She was in Pau, where a competition she was involved in was taking place. She had not returned to her hotel. I needed her, just like a kid who is upset and can't find his mother to comfort him.

I called Antoine Vayer – my coach, my adviser and, above all, my confidant.

'I can't take it any longer. I want to go home tonight, to get the hell out of this hotel.'

Five hundred kilometres away, Antoine tried to reason with me, to soothe my pain:

'You don't abandon a Tour de France like that. Think it over. Don't make a decision tonight. Decide what you're going to do tomorrow. Get a good night's sleep.'

A good night's sleep!

I then managed to get hold of Pascale.

'I've had enough of being away from you, Pascale. I want to see you again.'

My fiancée said she would come immediately. I told her right away that was not necessary. She then said that I could call her during the night.

It was 11 o'clock. I returned to my room. Heulot was watching television. He didn't look up from the screen. He turned it off and went to bed.

I also lay down in the dark. I fell asleep immediately. But that was no more than a reflex action on the part of my neurons, which had already kept me awake well beyond the usual hour. I woke up a little after midnight. I tossed in my bed, mulling over my bitterness for more than an hour. I knew that sleep would not come again.

I went out into the corridor. I tried to be as quiet as possible, but the night seemed to amplify the slightest murmur. Even the carpet out in the corridor seemed to resonate like a church's flagstones. I sat down on the metal staircase halfway between the floors to make sure that no one could hear me. I called Pascale.

'I can't get to sleep.'

I started crying again.

'Tomorrow morning I'm stopping.'

We talked for half an hour. I was whispering, but I had the feeling that every word was going to wake people. At Le Grand-Bornand, I remember that Marc had returned drunk in the middle of the night. He was singing at the top of his voice in the corridors, waking everyone up. Jean-Cyril had got up and asked him to shut up.

I had the impression that night that I was screaming in the dark. All the lights were off. Only one marked 'Emergency Exit' shed a dim light.

I called Antoine and then Pascale again. Neither of them was able to ease my torment. I was in a sort of trance that even today I can barely analyse. Only a psychologist could have accurately described my fragility at that moment. Or perhaps even a psychiatrist.

At about half past three I went back to bed. I was exhausted but I couldn't get to sleep.

At five o'clock I got up. My melancholy state suddenly gave way to firm resolution. I had to leave, to flee this shambles. I got dressed. I wanted to pack my suitcase. Then I realised that I hadn't even unpacked it. I was disconcerted by this.

I went down to reception. It was deserted. I sat on a sofa, my bag beside me, and stupidly waited, like a traveller who has missed the last train and doesn't know where to go. A book was lying on the coffee table. I flicked through it mechanically. I think it was to do with the history of the region, but I'm not sure.

I noticed a breakfast tray had been put down on another table. I don't know what it was doing there in the deserted lobby at that early hour. There was a bowl full of hot chocolate. Beside it were two lumps of sugar, a little pot of jam and a piece of dry toast. I put the tray on my knees and gobbled down these leftovers.

These few calories restored my lucidity. Everything had become clear. My perception of things was extremely acute. I had the feeling that I understood everything, that I dominated everything, that I was a superior being. Fatigue had swept away any sense of doubt.

A beautiful day was dawning. The sky was blue. My decision was irrevocable. I woke first Pascale and then Antoine to tell them about my decision.

'I'm leaving,' I said to them.

My tone didn't allow for a reply. Neither of them attempted to dissuade me.

Towards half past six, the receptionist arrived. He was surprised to find me in the lobby.

'What are you doing?'

'I'm an early riser,' I said with a smile.

'So is it going to be a long stage today?'

'Yes, they are going to have a tough day.'

The man didn't react to the 'they'. He got on with preparing breakfast. At about eight o'clock, the others started to come down.

I didn't want to announce my departure. I sensed an element of psychodrama. I went out and sat on a low wall outside. I called Pascale again.

Dr Guillaume saw me first and came up. I told him of my intention. He tried to convince me to stay but ran into solid resolution. He went off. I waited for what was to come next.

I didn't have to wait long. Marc Madiot came out in a hurry, the heels of his cowboy boots hammering along. I was in no way surprised when he started to lecture me.

'You can't abandon the Tour like this. It's not done.'

He was right: this wasn't the done thing. A cyclist doesn't walk out on the Tour de France. The Tour de France walks out on him. It forces him to get off his saddle, his resources completely spent, and continues on its way without a backward glance. 'Abandon of race number such and such,' the race organisation announces soberly. The race followers then delete that name from the list of competitors and don't think about him again.

There are a thousand and one orthodox ways for a rider to finish. At the feed station, the vanquished knight, he tumbles down from his charger and sneaks away to hide his humiliation in a team car. He can also be picked up by the broomwagon: the man in charge of it pulls off his race number, demoting him, and the disgraced soldier is crammed into the back of the van. The ideal is, of course, to finish a stage covered with bruises, with bones broken. The battered warrior crosses the line, collecting murmurs of admiration, and only stops at the nearest hospital. One can sympathise with the discomfort that awaits him that night. The hero will not start again the next day. His sacrifice will not be in vain either. He gets added to the long list of Tour de France martyrs and helps to enrich the legend – of the Tour, that is, not of the martyr himself.

Marc Madiot understood what had caused my iconoclastic departure. But that morning there was no point in talking to me about the conventions of the Tour de France. Was I breaking some unwritten law? Leaving was all I wanted to do. To me the Tour that year was nothing more than a poor farce.

I was relieved to be leaving. This feeling, verging on delight, confirmed that I was exhausted. Yet I still had to face up to the most difficult moment. I pushed back my shoulders, took a deep breath, vowed to remain stoical, and then walked into the room where the others were having breakfast. I realised immediately that everyone knew what my intention was. The prevailing hostility rendered any words unnecessary. My mind was made up, and theirs were as well.

I went around the table, holding my hand out to each of them. Some of them offered a limp handshake without looking up. Damien Nazon ignored my greeting. Jean-Cyril Robin was the first to say anything:

'Are you sure of what you are doing?'

'You're abandoning all of us,' Madiot grumbled.

My courage abandoned me. I was convulsed by tears. I went out, leaving them to tweak the tactics of that day's racing, which no longer concerned me. I went to say goodbye to the mechanics and soigneurs, who were busy around the truck.

A TV crew from France 3 arrived. I had forgotten about this meeting, which we'd agreed the day before.

'Can I speak to you?' asked the reporter.

'I'm sorry, but this is not the time.'

Out of professional instinct, the cameraman started filming.

'Stop, please.' I said to him. 'I've always played the game with you. Can you play it with me.'

The man lowered his camera. I could no longer carry on in the way that I had.

I had not respected the established protocol. Now I aggravated my situation by delivering what must have looked like the ultimate V-sign: I left for the airport in a journalist's car. In other words, I had packed up and gone over to the enemy.

Initially, I had thought about asking one of the soigneurs to take me to the airport. But at eight o'clock I received a call from Lionel Chami, who had been tipped off by Antoine Vayer. He called to tell me he was on his way. I couldn't wait any longer. So I started walking, dragging my suitcase haphazardly. I had only gone 200 metres when my driver arrived. I got into the car. At this moment, Marc Madiot came running up.

'Ah, I see that everything has been worked out,' he said, laughing ironically, when he saw the *Le Parisien* car. 'This is unacceptable.'

The reporter from France 2 came up to me just after.

'Will we see you next year on the Tour?'

'I hope so.'

Lionel took me to Clermont-Ferrand airport. I got a ticket to Toulouse in order to get back to Pascale as quickly as possible. I needed to be with her. At the last moment, I noticed there was a direct flight to Pau that would get me into her arms even faster. I changed my ticket.

I arrived at my destination at about one o'clock, five days ahead of the peloton, which would arrive in the city on the 21st. It was the greatest escape of my career. A magnificent breakaway.

Pascale was waiting for me at the airport. As soon as I got into the car with her, I started to rabbit ceaselessly on. She listened patiently to my chatter.

We arrived at the sports hall. I had only felt condescension towards artistic roller skating up to then, but I got real pleasure from watching these young girls pirouetting. Their graceful spins and turns provided an amazing contrast with the world I had just left. They seemed unreal. I was floating in a dream.

With Antoine's agreement, I had decided not to speak about my abandon to allow myself some time to relax and sort my thoughts out. My last-moment decision to change my ticket had very opportunely covered my tracks. Those curious about my fate were left waiting for me at Toulouse. I had turned off my mobile. However, a special correspondent from *Le Journal du Dimanche* picked up my trail and arrived at the gym. We went to a riverside bistro. Once there, he filled me in on the gossip that was going around the race caravan about me.

That evening I went for a drink with some of Pascale's friends. None of them was interested in the Tour. The conversation zipped around between all kinds of other things, which were delightfully run of the mill. The conversation was peppered with laughter. I listened and laughed too. I felt good.

The Tour caught up with me at 11 that night. A determined journalist from France Télévision managed to get hold of me on a mobile belonging to the daughter of one of the organisers in Pau ... We agreed to meet the next day.

I spent the night snuggled up in Pascale's arms.

I had been lying to myself in thinking that the Tour and what was being said there didn't really matter to me. The next day, I felt the urge to buy the papers. I then received confirmation of what had been reported to me the day before. I had been renounced, even by my own team-mates. I read Stéphane Heulot's words without initially wanting to believe he'd really said them: 'I deplore his attitude. We are a team of 22 riders. Everyone dreams of doing the Tour. Bassons took someone else's place. He acted on impulse and didn't even say goodbye. Even if he has his reasons, I find this a bit cowardly. I can't conceive of abandoning the Tour in any other way than on the bike, assuming you're not very ill.'

I went pale as I let the newspaper drop. So I was a coward. But was it me who was cowardly, or the team-mates who had let me leave without a word and then denigrated me as soon as my back was turned? With what extraordinary bravura did you agree to shake the hand of a coward, Stéphane? What excess of courage prevented you from spitting at me when faced with my cowardice?

The great cycling family hadn't taken long to start building a plot against me. Even before my departure, a degrading mantra had been circulating within the race caravan. I was a mediocre rider, a bitter man who retaliated by disparaging his comrades. 'Bassons is an insignificant rider, a nothing.' The sentence was used whenever my name arose in conversation. It was a leitmotif that had been created spontaneously within the *milieu* as a self-defence mechanism. Its aim was to smother the peloton's miscreant under a pile of filth. In the eyes of those who were suggesting this, my despicable acts deprived me of any right to speak. What kind of palmarès did I have, asked my detractors, that I dared to prod and poke the champions? By that point we had reached the height of absurdity. I was sounding off about the near impossibility of them winning without resorting to medicine, and they hit back at me about my lack of results. It seemed I'd have needed to have taken EPO and won a big race to earn the right to criticise these corrupt methods. What could I do in the face of such lunacy? In terms of propaganda, the bigger the lie, the more chance you have of getting away with it.

I was also saddled with another sin. I was a manipulator. The accusation came from very high up, from Tour director Jean-Marie Leblanc, no less. 'I can't get the idea that there is some marketing stunt behind this out of my head,' was the line peddled by the big boss. I had clumsily fuelled this rumour by leaving the race in a journalist's car.

Thanks to Leblanc, to Heulot and all of the 'camp followers' who had such admiration for them, I was reproached for having left the Tour de France rather than having abandoned it. I could have adopted a pedantic stance and argued that in the dictionary there is hardly any difference between the meanings of the two words. However, I know that in the eyes of those in the *milieu* that difference is fundamental. I had quit and therefore violated the race, which alone has the right to decide who stays and who goes.

However, none of these virtuous souls had ever taken offence when a rider had cleared off because he felt that the only thing left for him in the race was fatigue-induced cramp. Mario Cipollini never contested a mountain stage of the Tour, but he was still marvellous Mario. Nobody in my team criticised Jimmy Casper when he slipped away just before the mountain stages. And I'm not even going to mention the conspirators who flee at dead of night because they have got wind of a drug control the next day …

I hereby solemnly affirm: I was expelled from the Tour. I only left it under duress from those in the *milieu*. Anyone who claims otherwise is a person of bad faith who certainly contributed to my eviction. My dream was to reach Paris and to carry my ideas to that end point without denying any of them en route. I wanted to complete the Tour *à l'eau claire*, as had been stated in the newspaper, clean in my body and clear in my convictions. I would have achieved a great victory by doing so, and, even better, a statement of accomplishment for my career. I already had my column for the final day planned out in my head, including its conclusion. It would have said: 'Doping continues but it is not, as some claim, a requirement of this sport, a vital imperative. In these times of widespread suspicion, I have shown that clean cycling is possible. Tomorrow, I hope it will be the winner.' Bassons on the Champs-Elysées … what a great media coup that would have been, gentlemen, for me, for you, for cycling! But you didn't want it.

I had to react, to explode even. I turned my mobile on and my agenda for the day filled up in just a few minutes. I spent a good part of the morning answering questions from a string of journalists who came to see me. I set out my case again and again. Far from getting bored, this repetition was good for me, as it seemed as if every journalist went away carrying a little bit of the burden that had been weighing down on me.

I could feel the knot that had been gripping me since the previous day slowly unravelling. Suddenly I felt ravenous, which was a clear sign of psychological improvement. There was a barbecue stall in the gymnasium where the competition was taking place. I stuffed down sausages and chips all afternoon. For a man who regards dietetics as one of the cardinal sciences, this underlined how little importance I was then attributing to my professional future.

At about four o'clock, I went to the Pau sports centre. France Télévision had set up a studio for *Vélo Club*, the magazine programme on the Tour that follows the transmission of each day's stage. Gérard Holtz was barely able to ask me any questions. I delivered a five-minute monologue, which is an eternity when it comes to television. I had to make it clear, to those who were still there, that I was not a coward, not a media manipulator. I was simply a man who was demanding the right to be different. I reminded everyone that I'd had no pretensions towards being a spokesman, but was simply an individual who wanted his thoughts to be heard.

I wasn't really expecting to gain the peloton's understanding, and wasn't disappointed when it didn't happen. The *milieu* quickly switched off by refusing to discuss my wretched case any longer. The show must go on, as they say in Lance Armstrong's homeland. Sections of the general public understood me, which was all I was hoping for. In the months that followed, I received hundreds of messages of support and only one insult-filled rant, which was written by a Richard Virenque fan. I didn't respond to any of these letters of support.

Some of them were really beautiful, and some very official. Minister of sport Marie-George Buffet had assured me of her backing. 'Citizenship cannot end at the stadium gates, at the entrance to gyms or on the roadside,' she wrote.

I was indeed just an average citizen who was demanding the democratic right to express himself. I had no vocation to become a standard-bearer for a cause, however noble it might be. Consequently, I refused most of the invitations I received to conferences. I am not an orator, nor am I teacher. I am not a crusader, nor an inquisitor. On the contrary, I feel closer to the Cathars, who lived in my home region during the Middle Ages and were victims of intolerance. These men only wanted to live according to their religious principles. Their moral austerity was unbearable to the Church, which didn't tolerate any divergence. They were massacred.

I would receive further evidence of support over the days that followed. Pascale and I had planned to spend two days walking in the Pyrenees. I was relishing the prospect of savouring the mountain scenery that I barely had the opportunity to enjoy when racing. But we had to cut the trip short. Every time we stopped, people would point at me and want to talk to me. Cyclotourists recognised me. But I didn't witness a single instance of hostility.

They supported me – and they were also probably going to applaud those who had repudiated me when they came past a few days later. After noticing this inconsistency, I came to the conclusion that cycling aficionados are essentially people who are incapable of hatred. A sense of festival spirit and fun is indelibly linked to the bike. One of the things I am most proud of is that my sport has been spared the ravages of hooliganism.

When walking incognito proved impossible, we returned to the Tarn. We arrived back home at night and sneaked into our new house in Saint-Amans-Valtoret like thieves. We spent two days there with the shutters closed, not daring to poke our noses outside. This clandestine existence amused us. Playing hide and seek helped to cheer me up. I got my bike out again at the end of the third day. I needed it. I went out on the road and my mind started to roam freely once more. I came back from training feeling reassured: I still felt the same pleasure. The rest didn't matter. Focused entirely on these joyful rides, I scarcely followed the end of the Tour de France. All I knew was that they had managed to finish without me.

I also found out that my fan club had organised a protest. They had taken over a climb, as the race was passing close to our home region. The demonstrators had planted a series of black flags and drawn syringes on the road. They had watched my tormentors pass without a murmur, arms crossed. I wished I'd been there to see it.

Coward … The word continued to spin in my head and made me boil. A coward? Me? And what about the organisers of the post-Tour criteriums who disowned me? How should they be described? Another bit of slander spread about me made out that I had taken advantage of my sudden notoriety to renegotiate my terms upwards with these organising committees. But I had only signed three contracts before the Tour. All three were terminated, not because of my requirements, but as a result of pressure from other riders. At Hyères, one criterium director, who was a little embarrassed, told me it was either me or Virenque. With his perspective very much on spectator numbers, his choice was an easy one to make. I, the Machiavellian media manipulator, didn't have any weight. This lack of backbone didn't surprise me. Criteriums are all about making money, not creating trouble. I told myself, however, that come what may, these speculators on glory would have made a packet without any help from me. I could have demanded payment of the contracts that had been signed. But I let them keep the money and hoped they'd choke on their petits fours.

According to my team-mates too I was a coward. I needed some explanations. So I sent a letter to each of them asking them to enlighten me. None of them replied. I met them the following month, at the Tour of the Limousin. They were almost all there. I wanted a frank conversation, but all I got was evasion and a tangle of words.

Rage made me more ironic. All through the race I put in a huge amount of work for Stéphane Heulot. Every day I was at the coalface, working myself to death for my leader. He won the race and was obliged to thank me. I then told him that I was simply doing my job, nothing more. He's an intelligent man: he understood.

Marc Madiot was the only one who agreed to talk. A bullish character, he is not the type to run away from confrontation. It was a 'frank and constructive' discussion, as they say in diplomatic circles. In other words, we yelled at each other a lot. We had hardened in the positions we'd taken, but this row removed the bile that had poisoned our relationship. Since then, we say hello to each other when our paths cross. We even exchange a few pleasantries.

I spent a week in the Limousin with people who had dragged my name through the dirt just a short time before. The atmosphere was surreal. At dinner in the evenings, they were all still grumbling about the humiliation they had suffered the month before. The French riders hadn't come away with a single stage victory during that edition of the Tour. My partners raged against the iniquity of the race. In private, they touched again on my comments. I didn't go to the trouble of pointing out their inconsistency.

In fact, everyone was worried about their future after that clobbering. Would contracts be revised downwards? Lots of big names had obtained big salaries when they had been winning without anyone caring about how they had done it. Their prime concern was to guarantee their pay packet. 'You talk about money and you don't even worry about your health!' I shouted one day. The others all looked at the troublemaker. I had missed another opportunity to keep quiet.

I finished my season in early September, or rather it dragged on until then. A blood test revealed I was anaemic again. In fact, I was in a deep depression. I had been too quick to draw a line under what had happened at the Tour. I thought I had got rid of all the frustration I had accumulated there. But I had simply buried it somewhere. It emerged later and left me utterly exhausted. I spent a month convalescing.

I couldn't get by without the bike, though. I went mountain biking on the trails around my home. Pascale and I also did lots of long walks. We decided to get married the following year. I focused on developing projects that I took real pleasure in and that helped cure me of painful memories. I gently turned the page, regretting none of what I had written. I cured myself of exposure to the Tour.

I had decided that my links with the *milieu* were going simply to be limited to the activity we shared.

On 27 October, Laurent Jalabert's fan club organised the first of its two annual celebrations in Mazamet. After I had taken part in that day's race, I went along to the event in the evening, accompanied by Pascale. We hadn't been invited, and at the door I insisted on paying the entry fee just like any other average punter. It was almost an act of defiance, my way of saying that this wasn't my world. In the end, though, the organisers refused to take my money.

The pros were already sitting down at a table with their wives. Stéphane Barthe, Didier Rous, Gilles Maignan, the Jalabert brothers, Laurent Roux and Pascal Chanteur were there. They had gone off to have an apéritif after the race without inviting us. When we entered the room, they ignored us. We went to sit at a table on one side with some friends from the club.

During the course of the meal, Laurent Jalabert's father-in-law, who is also a cycling official, came to ask me if I was coming to the other evening being organised for 'Jaja', which was being held the following week in Carcassonne. I told him that I hadn't been invited. The man blushed and told me that there must have been an error and offered to correct it. I pretended I couldn't come. The following week, I read the report in the newspaper about the second party. Richard Virenque had been invited, and I understood.

At the end of the year, my fan club organised another edition of the Fête des Ténors, on 7 November. Five hundred amateurs took part in a mountain bike ride, built on the ancient ideal of 'A healthy mind in a healthy body.' The ride consisted of three laps around a 10km course with a refuelling stop at the end of each. There was a meat course at the end of the first lap, beef stew on the second, and cheese and dessert at the end of the third. Water-bottles had been filled with pastis. The bit of toast scrounged from that plate in Saint-Galmier was very much a thing of the past …

Four hundred people attended the dinner that evening. Several professionals had been invited. They all came, with the exception of Didier Rous. But they all slipped away quickly, one after another, each of them offering an excuse. I found out later that they had gone to Rous's house, as he had thrown together an event on the same night. Only Patrice Halgand stayed.

* * *

I thought my adventures at the Tour de France were behind me. I was wrong. In February 2000, I finally received a response to the letters I had sent to my team-mates. The letter informed me that I had been excluded from having a share of the prizes from the Tour de France, which amounted to around 350,000 francs. I would only receive the 500 francs I had won off my own back by finishing well up on one of the stages. I had damaged the image of the team, said my eight colleagues in justification. They had all signed the letter.

I read and reread the letter, unwilling to believe it. Less than a week before, I had seen all of the signatories at the Tour of the Mediterranean. I had moved house and it was the first time we had met each other since September. My former colleagues had shaken my hand. Frédéric Guesdon had spoken in a very friendly way with me, and I had started to think that the wounds had healed over the winter. And then came this letter with its hideous sentiments. It had even been signed by young Jimmy Casper, who in fact was no longer there when it had all happened. I wasn't going to cry over a few thousand lost francs, but I did over the disgraceful behaviour of those who had dared to sign this despicable missive.

Over the months that followed, I tried to get an explanation. But all I got was evasiveness. 'You didn't do your job,' argued Marc Madiot. And what about when I had ridden myself into the ground for Jean-Cyril Robin on the stage to Sestrières? 'It isn't that you didn't do your job, it's the fact that you left the Tour for personal reasons,' said Robin, in an attempt to explain this messy reasoning. Casper had left before the mountains without anyone picking him up on it. These charges just didn't stick.

In fact, my crime remained the same: I hadn't followed the example of the others. I had stepped out of line. I had spoken out, uttered a truth that no one wanted to hear. These petty-minded souls thought they could hurt me by hitting me in the wallet. Instead they just showed that the only thing of value in their eyes was money.

During the off-season, I was going to get another fine example of the *milieu*'s rectitude. The saga began on 28 July, just after the Tour had ended, when Tour director Jean-Marie Leblanc sent me the following letter:

Dear Christophe,

I think, thanks to the media's interference – again! – a kind of misunderstanding has occurred between us since you abandoned the Tour de France. If your case didn't matter to me greatly, I would have let things take their course, but that's not how I see it: after last year, I'm not indifferent to a young French rider standing up against doping. So what has happened?

At Saint-Gaudens, I think, I was asked, with a hint of aggression, if I had to take some responsibility for your abandon.

When speaking to all journalists, I took care to point out my conviction that you were acting in line with your words, you were indeed a healthy athlete. This was scarcely reported, it was too mundane.

I also added that in my opinion you became a victim in the role of spokesman that they wanted you to play each day; *Le Parisien*'s catchline was simplistic and seemed to present you as an exclusive case, and I can understand that it might have upset other riders. In reality, my friends from *Le Parisien*, unintentionally I think, did you a disservice by giving the impression they were offering some kind of scoop, especially on the day you left the Tour. I'm an old media hand and, even the day before, I had guessed their headline would be: 'Bassons: why I left theTour'.

No doubt I was wrong to use the word 'marketing', instead of the expression 'media circus', which is most clearly seen in their treatment of celebrities. And, naturally, there was no lack of emphasis on this! This also resulted in me receiving some overly excessive criticism from your coach and agent, some of which even strayed into the private domain, but I'm not worried about that any longer, knowing that – and you will be able to verify this over time – 'all that is excessive is insignificant'.

In yesterday's *L'Equipe*, where there are still some scrupulous journalists, I was able to say again that you are speaking justly, you are speaking truthfully, but that you have simply been encouraged to talk too much, which has done you a disservice. I hope these explanations will dispel any misunderstanding. And I hope you come back as quickly as possible as the upright and generous rider that you are. But keep a cool head! Perhaps I will see you in one or the other of our end-of-season events: the Tour de l'Avenir or the Grand Prix des Nations.

In the meantime, I ask you to accept, dear Christophe, the assurance of my most cordial greetings.

Jean-Marie Leblanc.

This letter sums up quite well the picture that I have of him. Jean-Marie Leblanc is the head of a business. He directs the race like someone managing a canning factory, with the sole intention of making it thrive and enabling him to avoid bankruptcy. He will do anything to save his business, which is the Tour de France. Caught in a storm, he hedges his bets. He denounces the weak stance of Hein Verbruggen and then goes jogging with him the next day. His race director's car is a model of consensus, as anyone and everyone is invited to join him in it.

The same day, he might perhaps have sent another florid letter to Richard Virenque, who he had tried to exclude from his race. This fanatical desire to stand for nothing and his ability to dodge blows are admirable. Jean-Marie Leblanc is the Talleyrand of cycling. But will established habits be changed by such a man? Wouldn't it be better to have someone with more determination? The revival of cycling will undoubtedly depend on the Tour de France as its iconic event, the place where my sport reaches an extra and extreme dimension, which includes the quantity of doping products.

'Maybe we will see each other again at one of our events,' wrote the head of the Société du Tour de France. Two months later, the same man didn't invite me to the Grand Prix des Nations, a time trial where I had finished fifth the previous year. And my team was excluded from the list of participants in the Tour de France 2000: I honestly don't think that he wanted me there.

The logo of the Tour de France is a notched circle. It looks like a wheel, like a speed indicator or a timing clock. It very neatly evokes the exclusive cult of performance that exists on the race today. All it really lacks is that human being we know as the cyclist. This infernal wheel reminds me of the cogs that crush Charlie Chaplin in *Modern Times*.

What humanity can be found in the race today? Where is its dramatic or comic depth, for brilliant wordsmiths to illuminate while in a state of post-stage, drink-fuelled euphoria? They used to dramatise the stories, of course, embellishing them in order to tease the reader. But they used to retain enough decency despite their euphoric state not to dupe the readers by passing off cheats as heroes and cheap trash as legends.

Dutchman Hein Verbruggen, who was then president of the UCI, also asked to meet with me after the 1999 Tour.

'We need to talk in a quiet spot about all this,' he said to me.

To this day, I am still waiting to hear from him.

The best tribute I received came from the most unexpected direction. At the start of a race, as the peloton was still rolling along quite steadily, some goon tapped me on the shoulder. I turned around, immediately on the defensive, and recognised Philippe Gaumont.

'I just want to congratulate you. You've got balls,' he said.

Erwann Menthéour also offered me some words of encouragement. In *Secret Défonce*, he was open about the extent of his addiction to evil concoctions. We didn't share the same ideas, but we have a common hatred of the prevailing hypocrisy.

These two men sometimes make me think that prohibition has led to free speech being curbed. If a debate had been started, the duplicity would perhaps have disappeared. That would have been something. I am deluding myself, of course. Never, not even in 1998, would the 'penitents' have agreed to even an overview of this debate. It would have required the unearthing of buried secrets, an explanation of certain premature deaths among athletes, and an admission that the majority of victories were tainted. It would have created an infinite number of Ben Johnson-like scandals. It would have suggested the death of a sporting spectacle.

Chapter 8
Free Wheel

A new season. A new team. The fourth in my five-year career. This could only reinforce the idea among my peers that I was unreliable.

My wardrobe gained another set of colours. When I'm not on official duty for my brand, I randomly pick clothes out of my closet. So I end up wearing one sponsor's trousers, the jacket from another, and the polo shirt from a third. I end up looking like some odd harlequin. I am the peloton's bohemian.

Just as I had done every year since 1992, I renewed my licence with the Union Vélocipédique de Mazamet. I have never changed my club affiliation since my debut in the sport. Everyone has their loyalties.

I signed a two-year contract with Jean Delatour. The sponsor was a Lyon-based jeweller, Jean-Pierre Fréty. A bold man. In the 1980s, he had opened his first shop at the foot of one of the Minguettes tower blocks that are part of a housing project in the suburbs of Lyon. His boldness paid off. He is now the head of a large chain known all across France. Driven by a youthful passion for cycling, he has taken on another daunting challenge. He aims to play a role in the restoration of cycling.

Any makeover means Bassons. I was a priority signing, he assured me. I already knew this refrain. I was suspicious – but I was wrong. His intentions were sincere. Michel Gros was appointed directeur sportif of the new structure. In my eyes, he was a fine guarantee of integrity.

All he wanted me to do from the off was to dispel a misunderstanding. Michel told me he would never stop me from saying what I thought, nor from exercising my right to be critical. What he wanted was for me to declare that I didn't have a monopoly on honesty. Once again, I was going to have to present myself as Lady Bountiful, the guardian of morality.

'If others refuse to dope, let them say so themselves,' I replied. 'As for me, the only thing I'm sure of is that I am not going to do it.'

'There are others, you know that.'

'Let's hear them speak up.'

'Some people can't, because they took stuff before and they are afraid or have a guilty conscience.'

'It's not my job to say, "This guy, that guy and that one aren't taking anything any longer." This is primarily because, as I've said to you before, I don't know exactly what others are up to. They simply have to grasp the opportunity to speak out as I did.'

Michel didn't insist. He wouldn't find in me the St Bernard he was hoping for. I had suffered too much because of the actions of people within our *milieu* to want to help him.

At Jean Delatour, I still managed to piece together some scraps of friendship that had withstood three years of tribulation. In addition to Michel, I was working once again with his son Laurent. I had even insisted on the team hiring Rik Keyaerts. The mere presence of these two soigneurs was hugely revitalising to me.

Patrice Halgand was also one of ours. He had always been the rider I had felt closest to. After a year apart, I was delighted that our paths had crossed again. We had the same story, or almost. We had an odd kind of complicity, bound up by things that weren't said. Although we regularly shared the same room, we had never mentioned what had happened to us. We had both been called in by the judicial authorities, but the two of us had never discussed the issue of doping. Patrice refused to do so. At the same time, he never reproached me for unburdening myself, never passed judgement on my behaviour. A *modus vivendi* had consequently been established between us. The subject was taboo. I just wanted to believe his friendship offered tacit support. The man was a great athlete. He had everything to gain from a change in established habits, as that would have allowed him to finally demonstrate his ability.

My new leader was also on the comeback trail: Laurent Brochard. He had been one of the elite circle of barons at Festina. Our reunion was hardly warm, and for a time we kept some distance between us. However, the promiscuity of life in a close-knit group and the narrowness of hotel corridors rendered our attempts to avoid each other ridiculous. The situation couldn't continue.

One day I asked if we could have a conversation. I confronted him head on:

'You don't like me, I know. But what do you reproach me for exactly?'

'We don't like the way you talk. We can't stand your way of presenting yourself as Mr Clean.'

'Who is "we"?' I asked.

Even today, I can't bear this impersonal and generic usage. It is a sign of weakness, an admission of an inability to forge your own opinion. The cyclist says 'we' and thinks 'we' as if he needs to believe there is someone behind him, someone who is ready to support him. However, in doing so he is fading into a mass that will do his thinking for him. He is giving up his personality. Instead of the celebrated 'I think, therefore I am', he prefers 'We are, so we follow'.

'We' is the cycling *milieu*, a rather hazy concept, or the peloton, a moving entity rather than a concept. Because it is indefinable, this 'we' becomes an object of fear. What will 'they' think of me? 'They' may blame me if I don't show solidarity. The timid then become enclosed in a Kafkaesque world where an involuntary desire may, at any time, force their hand. Who decides? 'We don't know. We've simply been given our orders, that's how it is.'

That 'we' becomes a verbal tic, their sole way of defining themselves. The mere idea of having to go back to using 'I' causes terror. The prospect of their career reaching its end becomes a matter of great anxiety. The retiree may have earned hundreds of thousands of euros a month, and even have amassed a fortune, but suddenly he feels helpless, naked as a baby, at the idea of having to find the way ahead all alone. Only one thing retains importance then: staying in the cocoon in order to be able to keep thinking 'we'. The helpless being then hopes that the 'we' will place him behind a steering wheel as a VIP driver or even in a subordinate position within the sport's organisation or a team. He will then have a sense of existing for a little longer. He will be able to continue to say 'we' with aplomb.

At the beginning of the season, two members of my team, Frédéric Bessy and Christophe Oriol, attempted to goad me with that formless 'we'. They picked me up on some things that I hadn't said, but which were flying around like Chinese whispers. Such slanders and rumours were intended to discredit me once again.

'We don't care for what you are saying about doping.'

'OK! Let's talk about it.'

We discussed the issue vigorously, but in a good spirit, setting our arguments against each other. We were completely opposed to each other – I don't think I managed to convince them – but by the end of our conversation they were at least saying 'I'. This sorted out our relationship. Lacking friends, I did manage to establish sincere relationships with these men with whom I shared my life for half the year. I was satisfied with that.

I didn't have the same success with Brochard. I think the 'we' behind which he took refuge exerted too strong a grip on him. That was down to one man: Virenque. His charisma always provoked fascination among his former lieutenants. Caught somewhere between fear and admiration, they remained under his influence. Even though the clan had been scattered, it remained welded together by invisible links. They continued to collude, both in everyday life and also when racing. These acolytes always rode together, despite the different colours of the jerseys they wore. It was like a reconstitution of a body that had been dissolved. They always viewed things from the perspective of one man, their leader, whose rule they respected, whose cause they espoused and whose hatreds they shared. I continued to be one of those subjected to this stubborn enmity, having refused to bend under their yoke. I knew I would pay to the very end for this presumption. I also had to deal with Didier Rous's hostility towards me. It was particularly vehement and could only be explained by his desire to make Virenque forget that he and I had been friends. For Virenque's sake Didier Rous was trying to make amends for this error.

Laurent Brochard and I never managed to get on. He remained distant with me, especially in races and even more so when Virenque was in the vicinity. He was afraid of being seen with the pariah, the renegade, the leper.

In the midst of one extremely hot day of racing, I dropped back to our team car to pick up bottles for my team-mates. I had one for everyone. I started handing them out, but Laurent refused my offer. So I gave two bottles to a team-mate who, a few minutes later, offered one of them to our leader. This time it was accepted.

I resumed training on 15 November in order to be ready for the off. The 2000 season would be one of renewal, a very real renewal this time, according to those in the know. Hmm! I remained sceptical. In 1999, I had been overly convinced that speeds would follow a very different curve. They did, in a way: the riders were climbing faster than they descended!

I had some good finishes in wintry weather. I came third in the Grand Prix d'Ouverture La Marseillaise.

Médéric Clain, who was riding for a small team, Besson Chaussures, came up to me at the start of the year.

'I have to shake your hand. It's thanks to people like you that I am still riding a bike.'

He was probably sincere, but his good intentions weren't enough. He later tested positive, was suspended and even ended up receiving a suspended prison sentence.

I also received another show of support, from the government this time. On 31 March, I went to Paris to take up an invitation from the minister of youth and sport. Marie-George Buffet spent an hour and a half with me. The conversation focused on my sport, which she clearly knew very well. Since her first visit to the Tour in 1997, the minister had obviously learned a lot.

I barely had the time to make small talk. I needed to get on with my season, the way fruit farmers have to get busy in that crucial period before the weather becomes less clement and their crop starts to rot. I finished 16th in the Critérium International, behind a bunch of Spaniards, who were looking more and more like the new conquistadors of cycling. I also figured well in Paris–Nice, where Laurent Brochard finished second overall. But my knee flared up and forced me to rest at the worst possible moment. With a heavy heart, I had to pull out of Paris–Roubaix, my favourite race. I was denied a visit to 'Hell'. Just my luck!

The season continued. The pace picked up. I wasn't even disappointed any more. I'd seen guys starting in the mornings with the insides of their arms covered with blue dots left by syringes.

I returned meekly to my role of team-mate. I went to the front of the bunch and set the pace without a second thought, without the slightest inclination to escape. I brought to this role of spear-carrier a fury founded on resentment and even a slightly suicidal attitude. I gave every little bit of my strength. When the pace quickened, on the approach to the finish, I fell back sombrely. I had done my share of work. This dedication had Antoine in despair. 'You should take care of yourself and try to play your own card,' he said reproachfully. I tried, sometimes. I was messing around with my gearing, discreetly using a bigger gear, dancing on the pedals and attacking like never before. I would gain a few metres, turn around and wasn't surprised to find Pascal Chanteur or some other French rider pursuing me. They would join me and turn their heads away to avoid meeting my eye.

I constantly received such blows. The amazing thing is that they didn't toughen my skin. I still couldn't manage to become immune to them. I constantly wavered between hope and despair. I went from one extreme to the other. Sometimes I felt so good at Jean Delatour that I was ready to stay there for ten years. At other times, the *milieu* upset me so much that I wanted to leave on the spot. The thought occurred to me that it would be wonderful to experience the crazy rush of quitting the race at the first crossroads and setting off randomly into the countryside.

I regularly discussed this with Gaumont. An odd friendship developed between us, underlining how true it is that opposites attract. We shared the same aversion to the falseness around us and a taste for straight talking. After testing positive once again, Philippe should have been sacked by Cofidis, but they kept him on the roster. In the end, however, he was considered a liability and thrown on the scrapheap, not so much because of his faults as his determination to accept them. Driven on by spite, he then returned to track racing. He became the French pursuit champion. This title earned the ugly duckling automatic selection for the Sydney Olympics, to the chagrin of the governing bodies.

During races, we talked at length.

'You can't imagine, Babasse. All these two-faced bastards keep congratulating me on my title and selection. The only thing that pleases me is knowing how much it annoys them. What a bunch of hypocrites!'

I would have liked to have his self-assurance, his ability to tell people how things were. At other times, I wanted to be like my accusers, cold monsters motivated solely by greed and insensitive to the genuine reputation of cycling, to its future. I would have liked to be blasé, cynical. But I couldn't manage it. I remained passionate about the sport, a utopian. I was well aware that when my sport was hit by jolts I felt them too intensely. The sport was stronger than I was. On these occasions, Pascale had to call on all her ingenuity and patience to ease my moods.

I vowed to watch the Tour de France with Zen-like detachment. But I couldn't stop myself boiling with indignation. Leblanc was right not to select us: my team, and me more than anyone, didn't belong in this freakshow. Most of the other French riders didn't either. They proved insubstantial again. Only Richard Virenque, Christophe Moreau, Pascal Hervé and Didier Rous showed they were at the same level as the foreign riders. I knew them well. The ghosts of Festina, which had been banished in 1998, were reappearing. They were taking their revenge while receiving the applause of the organisers who had recently repudiated them.

Christophe Moreau's fourth place didn't surprise me. In 1996, we were producing more or less the same performances in time trials. The seconds that separated us then had become minutes.

The 2000 Tour began with three exclusions following blood tests that were considered abnormal. Several stage winners had already undergone suspensions for the same reason. Marco Pantani was in the midst of a judicial investigation in Italy. He was sluggish on the 2000 Tour of Italy and, guess what, was suddenly prancing over the French passes a month later. Nobody was surprised. The Tour was indeed the new Court of Miracles.

A good third of stage winners had been involved in doping affairs in the past. Corticosteroids were discovered in nearly half of the urine tests conducted. But all of these results had been declared negative by the International Cycling Union because in each case the rider had a therapeutic justification for the product's use.

Steroids had only recently become detectable and were a good example of the masquerade being enacted. The peloton had learned quickly from the difficulties that Ludo Dierckxsens had experienced in 1999. The Belgian had won the stage from Saint-Étienne, coincidentally the day I abandoned. In a state of panic when he was about to undergo the post-stage control, he admitted that he had taken steroids without a medical certificate. But his urine test proved negative … 'A fault confessed is half redressed,' the proverb has it. But that doesn't apply in our tribe. The Belgian had to leave the race in secret the next day.

Dierckxsens had been punished for speaking too soon. Lance Armstrong was well protected from a similar fate. Despite several positive tests for steroids during the year of his first Tour victory, he managed to keep on racing, thanks to backdated certificates, and ended up with the yellow jersey on the Champs-Elysées. (Armstrong would later claim that the president of the ICU, Hein Verbruggen, encouraged him to produce a prescription to avoid another doping scandal, although Verbruggen denies being involved in a cover-up and says he has never "acted inappropriately".) To an extent, Dierckxsens took the rap for Armstrong. The petty conman, the grifter, had been punished, while the big cheat pressed on with the blessing of the cycling authorities. What a beautiful tale of sporting morals.

In 2000, the riders had been warned about Dierckxsens' misfortunes and told how Armstrong gained salvation. So now they were riding with certificates of convenience in their jersey pockets. Was anyone shocked by these hypochondriacs? Was anyone indignant? No one took the baton up from me. In all honesty, I would have been shocked if they had. Things were going better without me around.

During the 2000 Tour, another positive test was marked out for public condemnation, that of Emmanuel Magnien, my former team-mate at Festina and La Française des Jeux. Dr Guillaume had given him an intramuscular injection of corticosteroids before the Tour so that he could take his place in the starting line-up. The doctor had honestly recorded this in his patient's medical record. But this wasn't enough. The rider and his doctor were denounced in the public arena.

In my opinion, it was no coincidence that this, the most contentious of the 49 positive tests for corticosteroids recorded on the 2000 Tour, was picked out and tossed to the public. The aim was twofold. It was to discredit the anti-doping battle by demonstrating the absurdity of such a contentious case, and to attack a doctor who had dared to speak out against doping.

There is no question that, in the eyes of the rules and perhaps from an ethical standpoint too, Gérard Guillaume should not have given this injection. He wanted to help an injured rider to take part in the Tour. It's my belief that injury and illness are among our profession's imponderables: they must be respected. But I think the crime the doctor was effectively charged with was one of failing to tow the line not long before. Consequently, his imprudent actions with Magnien benefited his opponents. It enabled them to cover their tracks and to back up the claim of 'all rotten, all doped', which is the best protection for the real cheats.

A similar mishap befell my soigneur, Rik Keyaerts, in 1999, when he was still working for Festina. He was arrested during a routine traffic stop. Some medical products were seized. One was on the banned list – a vaccine against wasp stings, to which Rik is allergic. He was upset by what was a very insignificant matter, when he was one of the few to have kept his distance from the enormous increase in the trafficking of growth hormone, anabolic steroids and EPO then taking place.

At the time, my entrenched position made me well aware of these deliberate attempts to confuse everyone. In an interview with *L'Equipe*, Bruno Roussel affirmed that Hein Verbruggen had assured him that he could bring about anyone's downfall if he wanted. This threat worried me: I knew I was not in the UCI's president's good books. That was why I was afraid of being nabbed during a drug control. I was obviously not immune to the possibility of there being some questionable metabolites in my urine. I could imagine the sad effect this would have on fans and, above all, the smirks with which Mr Clean would be greeted.

I had already been taken to task about my stays in hypoxic rooms. To my detractors, this technique could be likened to a form of doping. I didn't know how to respond to such quibbling. Could the same argument not be employed to suggest that riders who decades before had replaced their bottles with lead weights in order to gain extra momentum were doped? Did it mean that those riders who became acclimatised to altitude before making an attempt on the hour record in Mexico were cheats? Was training also a felony, since it tends to develop an athlete's faculties?

This was all part of the same nauseating claim that all methods were a fiddle, that camomile is as dangerous as EPO. This disingenuousness was introduced deliberately, even scientifically I should point out. The goal was to create such a bewildering tangle over this inextricable point that the only solution would have been fatalism. Since everything was doping, since all of the riders were doping, even Bassons in hypoxic chambers, you just had to let them get on with it.

What was doping, and what wasn't? During my four-year career, I had kept on asking myself that question. Subjected to constant stress, I was often asked what definition I could give. But how can you draw a straight line between legal and illegal in this no man's land where reason gets lost?

Even today, I can only outline my own conviction. Doping is any exogenous aid that leads to the artificial development of physical faculties. I don't think that every means of assistance that helps improve the body naturally is doping. In my opinion, hypoxia shouldn't be prohibited. However, if I had kept blood bags when my haematocrit was at its maximum level in order to reinject before a race, I would then have been doping. These red blood cells would no longer be mine, but a means of exogenous aid.

I'm not some kind of mystic who would refuse any other than a celestial intervention on my body. I regularly undergo blood tests as part of a complete inventory on my body. When I'm sick, I look after myself and I have injections like everyone else. I then wait until the effects of the medication wear off before resuming competition. I want it to be me propelling my bike, not my doctor. If a medical intervention were to have had a long-lasting and fundamental effect on me, like Obélix and his magic potion, my sporting career would have ended there and then. I think I would have stopped competing because it would no longer have held any interest for me.

I'm no longer a caveman when it comes to sport either. I think science can be beneficial by optimising training and lifestyle. It can underpin knowledge of physical capacity with empirical methods and prevent athletes floundering in the dark, as was long the case. But it has no right to distort equity.

My fundamentalist stance has been heavily criticised. However, experience makes me think it is indispensable. I disagree with the proponents of hormonal rebalancing, who argue that high levels are an illness and that athletes should get treatment accordingly. To those people, I would say that their analysis, which advocates to a certain extent the use of medical products, reflects ignorance or even blindness about the motive for competition, which can be summarised by the short but very pertinent Olympic motto: 'higher, stronger, faster'. Authorising the use of drugs in sport would automatically open the door to the stakes being raised to murderous levels. Only prohibition can ensure that the best athlete wins. This apparent cliché is a cardinal truth of sport, and without it sport will certainly die in disgrace.

'It is safer to have a haematocrit of 50 than a level of 36 like yours,' Eric Ryckaert used to say to me. He was perhaps right from a medical point of view, but wrong from a sporting perspective. Taking EPO in these conditions wouldn't have cured me, but would have added my contribution to a scam. If I finished some of the longer stage races tests anaemic, sick in fact, it was because I was having to ride with cheats. I wanted to be able to look people in the eye and not feel I was duping them when I was riding. I was prepared to give all of myself, but only myself.

I can see all too well that, as a result of these quirky explanations, I am getting embroiled in a debate that I want no part of. My only judge is my conscience. If I disapprove of a practice, I don't use it. I'm not concerned with what the regulations lay down. My goal through sport is to find the best of myself, not to live in someone else's skin. I worship the body. But I see it as an essential and indivisible part of my being, not as a mere disguise for Superman, into whose character I would disappear in order to make an impression. I thought that when I raced, and I still think that today.

Doping is less of a threat to health than it is to sport. EPO has already enabled athletes of average means to become Tour de France winners. Steroids have already turned a mediocre sprinter, Ben Johnson, into a world record holder. In the future, gene therapy will be able to turn out supermen capable of beating the world 100 metres record one day and winning the Tour de France the next. What will become of sport and, more significantly, humanity then? As it is already possible to make people faster and faster, will it soon be possible to design people who are more intelligent? Sport is a good place for ethical reflection about science. Just how far do we have the right to go?

Medicine has an ethical imperative to help the fight. It is vital that it makes its know-how available to sport.

Professor Albert Jacquard had understood the risk to sport. In the wake of the Festina affair, he signed a manifesto against doping that had been initiated by Antoine and was called '100 for 2000'. He wrote:

> When I saw this manifesto, I thought, 'Finally there are some people who are thinking differently about sport.' But I would go further still. The reason for doping is competition. Sport is all about getting the best from yourself, not being better than anyone else. And the reason for this competition is our Darwinist concept of society, which leads us to believe that the next man is an enemy, when he is actually an inspiration. Balzac drugged himself with caffeine to ensure he couldn't sleep and thus boost his imagination, not to be a better writer than Stendhal. Therefore, this was not doping. Besides, the simple fact of wanting to overtake someone

else, even if done with artificial assistance, is a form of doping. The idea of competition seems shabby to me. There is a rugby team in Dakar called 'The score, who cares!' Personally, I prefer them to PSG.

This geneticist was a world leader in his field. I would have liked to have him as my personal doctor, me who was undoubtedly the only one in the business not to have one. I would have confided unreservedly in a man blessed with such principles. The great man died in September 2013.

Back in pre-war Chicago, Eliot Ness only succeeded in convicting Al Capone on charges of tax evasion, despite all of the crimes the gangster had committed. When I was racing, incorruptible members of the anti-doping campaign were beset by the same ignominious helplessness when faced with the assassins of the sport. It was not an equal contest, because they were fighting it with inadequate weapons. Many products remained undetectable, such as growth hormone. When a test for EPO was finally established, the use of synthetic blood compounds began to replace it. Typically, cheats don't wait until the end of the validation process that can last several years before using a product. They are immediately on the backs of the lab assistants, grabbing hold of the molecules as soon as they come out of the test-tube. If necessary, they steal them and get copies made in mafia-run pharmacies. It is absolutely necessary to be first, whatever the cost. The fact that the new product may have a beneficial effect on performance is all that matters to them. Their horizons only stretch as far as the finish line. Never mind the long-term side-effects. When any new drug appears, athletes die as a result of using it inappropriately and recklessly. This irresponsibility still amazes me. Even in my era, the peloton was already talking with evident glee about the benefits of gene therapy …

When a swindler happened to get collared, he benefited from protection in high places. He would only incur a paltry sentence, from two weeks to a few months. Some teams did announce the sacking of miscreants, but they would be discreetly reintegrated into the circuit, often in another part of the same team! Leaving a malcontent on the side of the road was too risky. As a result of this laxity, the balance between risk run and benefit obtained became skewed. Consequently, monitoring not only failed in its role within the penalisation process, but also in that of preventing drug usage among young riders.

In my opinion, speaking out remained the best deterrent. This alone could blow apart the hypocritical silence. It is what drives me to tell my story here, at the risk of reinforcing this image that I hate of me being the destroyer of doping. It is what made me so unpopular among those who intuitively sensed the danger of words. Affirming 'I don't dope', a phrase of the utmost banality, was still being portrayed as some kind of message from the Antichrist.

'Cycling can only be rebuilt on the truth,' insisted Bruno Roussel. I shared his opinion and still do. For this reason, I am in favour of lifting patient confidentiality for athletes. I know this principle is as sacred to a patient as the presumption of innocence is to a defendant. However, in sport this laudable protection has become the basis of a great lie. All the results of longitudinal testing must be made public and the anomalies made known. Would this be an affront to human dignity? Do you think those honest athletes who for decades have found themselves excluded from podiums in so many disciplines and regularly humiliated by thieves care about this?

And what did the peloton think of this in 2000? An incident that occurred during a race offers eloquent insight. A funny guy was messing around with an empty tube of salbutamol, which is a banned substance. Ostensibly, as my neighbours sat around laughing, he was pretending to breathe in deeply and feel better instantly. Then he put the angled nozzle upside down in his mouth and went around the group mimicking a diver swimming with a snorkel. He probably had a prescription for it in his pocket to fall back on in the unlikely event of an official daring to offer a reprimand. While I was mulling this over, the peloton was having a giggle.

Chapter 9

End of the Road

I was 26, the age of maturity and achievement in cycling, the age when you take the most beautiful victories and put together the palmarès that will ensure you remain in people's memories, or at the very least in the annals of the sport. I was 26 but I knew my career was nearing its end, that my days in cycling were numbered. My only real achievements were one or two thankyous offered here and there by a grateful leader. My comparative lack of bouquets provided a feeling of something that was incomplete, such is the way that this mixed-up *milieu* impacts on even the simplest pleasures.

In terms of competitive spirit, the only urge that I had left was to beat the records I'd set in training. I loved this internal battle with myself on the roads of the Tarn. It seemed to me that I got a better taste there of the core of what my sport could offer than I did in races. I was battling against an opponent of my own stature, one I was sure was not doping. I had so often felt completely fulfilled when racing, but I was now seeing this pleasure marred by the humiliations dealt out to me by other competitors who were better prepared.

Despite everything, I still secretly dreamed of winning a race and crossing the finish line without raising my arms, just to show others and to prove to myself that victory was not all-important. I also aspired to finishing a grand tour *à l'eau claire*, believing it could be done, but not really believing it.

A new opportunity presented itself with the 2000 Tour of Spain. My team was selected to ride there. Michel announced my selection for that race.

During the Tour du Limousin that preceded it, we were racing when the peloton heard the news of my participation in the Spanish event. There was widespread laughter. Pascal Lino began to bawl:

'Hey, guys! Do you hear that? Babasse is going to the Vuelta! That's brilliant!'

Pascal Chanteur raised the stakes:

'You won't last a week, man, with the little green men and the DDE.'

The 'little green men' referred to the Kelme team, and the 'DDE' are the Euskaltel riders in their bright orange jerseys, which resemble those worn by the DDE workmen who maintain French roads. The performances of these two Spanish teams provoked smirks on the international scene.

They were right to mock. I was not all that reassured when I flew to Malaga, where the event was starting. The Vuelta was one of the fastest races in the world and one of the least monitored. A week before leaving, an analysis had revealed that my haematocrit was 36 as a result of having done two stage races back to back. Pascale filled me with black pudding, lentils and chocolate, and as many other iron-rich foods as possible. This regime, some vitamins and plenty of rest enabled me to line up in good shape.

During the first week, I couldn't understand the prejudices of the race's detractors. It seemed no worse than any other. Every day reassured me a little more. Wisely shut away in the midst of the peloton initially, I began to creep slowly up towards the front. I even started to feel a bit antsy. On the seventh stage, on Saturday, 2 September, a rider escaped after 25 kilometres. On a reflex, I jumped on his wheel. We rode for 30 kilometres together before being joined by four other fugitives. Our 'pedalling party' lasted for a total of 150 kilometres. We were five minutes ahead and 40 kilometres from the finish when the peloton launched itself fully in pursuit. It mercilessly swallowed us up with two kilometres to go. Nevertheless, I was happy that I'd been able to unleash the 'cannon'.

It wasn't long before alarm bells were ringing, though. On the Monday, the first mountain stage gave me plenty of warning that another race was kicking off. Apocalypse arrived the next day. The stage between Alp and Arcalis, in Andorra, only covered 135 kilometres, but featured three passes. Over the first hour, we gobbled up 52 kilometres. On the early ramps, the peloton blew apart. At the front, the 'little green men' and the 'DDE' set a fearsome pace. Soon there were just six Spaniards at the front ... At the back, it was every man for himself. The *gruppetto* was slow to take shape, such was the suddenness and intensity of the attack.

A big group then formed two minutes ahead of me. I tried to get up to it. It was my only chance to avoid finishing outside the time limit, given the speed of the guys in front. As I made my effort, I went past four riders from an Italian team. Three kilometres later, the same riders went past me at 50 kilometres an hour, clinging to their team car. After the descent, there was a flat section. I still hadn't got up to the group. Other riders went past me, sucked along in the air pocket behind their respective team cars. One of my team cars then came up alongside me and the driver told me to do the same. I refused.

'But can't you see that everyone is doing it!' he ranted.

Everyone is doing it. Despite my fatigue, those words stirred up memories within me. The same argument had been made so often to me about doping.

As I rumbled along, I could see the same pitiful farce all around me. Some riders were clinging to cars, others were drafting behind them. I overtook a man struggling badly, and then he suddenly shot away from right under my nose, catapulted forwards by some obscure process. I was equipped with an earpiece that day, which allowed me to follow developments in the race. Through this I could hear that these cheats had all got up to the *gruppetto*, while I remained in desperation just a few metres behind this pack.

The race commissaires were coming and going, and were either blind or accomplices to all this. This spectacle made me sick. At the end of the second pass, I realised that I had no chance of getting back to the group if everyone was behaving like this. I stopped and got off the bike.

I climbed into my team car, from which I followed the end of the stage and watched the continuation of the masquerade. A rider who had been 12 minutes behind the *gruppetto* at the foot of the last climb rejoined a kilometre from the finish. A rider from my former Festina team was hanging on to one of the police escort motorbikes ... A commissaire adjudged that this rider was breaking the rules. He went up alongside his directeur sportif and advised him to get his young buck to stop voluntarily if he did not want to experience the infamy of exclusion from the race.

'That's the Tour of Spain,' concluded Michel Gros at the finish. Half of the Jean Delatour team had abandoned.

'Our team can't do anything on a grand tour,' grumbled Laurent Brochard, who had nevertheless been able to limit his losses.

He was right. My colleagues had the option of using recuperatives, but the help these provided was not enough for us to haul up alongside the Spanish riders. Our moral standards prevented us from doing well in such a race. It was impossible to finish the Vuelta without recuperatives at the very least. As for winning it ...

The day after my withdrawal I was comforted to hear that Jan Ullrich had also abandoned. The German hadn't managed to stay with the pace either. The Spaniards completely dominated the Vuelta. As we have found out since, most notably thanks to the Puerto affair, Spain's doctors had dethroned their Italian counterparts. Even the likes of Lance Armstrong had called on their services. By a kind of cycling-style eugenics, they had managed to create a race of rider superior to the rest.

After my latest abandon, my umpteenth defeat, Rik drove me to the Spanish border, where Pascale came to pick me up. I returned home with my morale at rock bottom. In the car I brooded silently.

I spent some long days moodily mulling my situation. Fortunately, Pascale was there at my side. She endured all those months when I was not a pleasant companion. This was much more than a consolation. It was a testimony, proven confirmation of the force that binds us. The peloton may have loathed me, but it had played a key role in some beautiful news. We had decided to go ahead and get married. The ceremony was set for 28 October.

The preparations for the big day distracted me from my worries. Alas, not for long! I received a letter informing me that I was going to be called as a witness in the Festina trial. The hearing was to open on Monday, 23 October in Lille, in northern France. The judges wanted to hear what I had to say, but what could I tell them that they didn't already know? I felt that I would once again be out on a limb, playing the role of accuser, antagonising former team-mates, and this time not in the peloton or the media, but in a courtroom. I so wanted to be just left in peace. And this was happening a few days before my wedding! Just my luck!

I had to take the stand on the afternoon of Tuesday, 24 October. I arrived at the hotel the night before. In the restaurant, I bumped into Bruno Roussel, who was staying in the same place. We exchanged a friendly little wave from a distance, but without daring to approach each other for fear of people suspecting witness tampering. We sat down at tables a long way apart. The atmosphere was surreal. I felt uncomfortable.

There was feverish excitement on the Tuesday morning, which was the second day of the trial. In court Richard Virenque finally admitted that he had doped. Responding to the presiding judge's question, 'Did you know that you were taking doping products?' he reluctantly murmured a simple 'yes'.

When I was called to testify in the late afternoon, the riders who were accused had left the chamber. I didn't know whether this was because of me. After this confession, my testimony had become secondary, I thought, and that suited me well. But I was wrong.

The presiding judge and the prosecutor were perfectly courteous, but their questions put me in a quandary. They clearly wanted me to tell them that through doping and forcing me to follow their infernal pace, the other riders had undermined my physical integrity. I was asked to relate how my team-mates and management had encouraged me to dope. In short, I had to substantiate the criminal charge of 'endangering the life of another person'. For 45 minutes, I tried to tell the truth, the whole truth and nothing but the truth without playing the victim. It was a bizarre game. My questioners wanted me to give names, for me to personally incriminate such and such a person. But I was trying to explain that it was the whole system that was pernicious.

I could sense Bruno Roussel, Willy Voet and Eric Ryckaert behind me, and that made me uncomfortable. They were going to pay (even if the penalties were ultimately suspended prison sentences), although they were not the worst offenders. Because they assumed their responsibilities publicly, I also knew they were bringing another sentence on themselves: banishment from the peloton. At the time I didn't know that Eric Ryckaert was already suffering from widespread cancer, which struck him down just a few months later in January 2001. His death affected me deeply. On hearing about it, I could only think that the opprobrium he had suffered since 1998 had eaten away at him from the inside. The practitioner had faced a terrible dilemma: to accompany the riders on their lethal escapade or to leave. Clearly, he hadn't made the right choice. But he had never shown the cynicism demonstrated by many of his colleagues in the peloton. He had never forced me to dope either; ultimately he had respected my choice, as Bruno and Willy had done.

The saddest, or most laughable, aspect of all this was that the UCI was a civil party in the trial … Their lawyer even dared to ask me questions that were intended to undermine the defendants. All this made me want to vomit. I wanted to escape the atmosphere of hypocrisy.

But when the proceedings were suspended for the day, the court asked me to return the next morning. I could not escape. That evening, I found myself in a bar in Lille with Antoine Vayer and Erwann Menthéour, who had transformed himself into a singer. He had adopted the look of an artist, wearing a long black leather raincoat. He got me to listen to a demo of his song 'God is Dead'. After a few drinks in that crazy atmosphere I felt good.

After testifying again the next day, I raced back to the Tarn and Pascale. I had only two days left in which to complete the wedding preparations. The frantic bout of activity that followed prevented me from brooding. Our wedding day completed the therapy. It began solemnly at the town hall and finished in the middle of the night with plenty of bawdy songs, of which my home region in the south-west has an infinite repertoire. All my friends were there. There was only one rider, Patrice Halgand, and my directeur sportif, Michel Gros. They slipped away at one point during the day to sign a contract extension.

We spent three days on honeymoon in Corsica. Then we returned home and buried ourselves in our books. Pascale had decided to take a course to become a sports teacher. Passing the exam would allow her to apply for a post as a technical director. She convinced me to do the same. 'What if we could pass it together?' she suggested with a hint of a challenge in her eyes. My pride forced me to take up the gauntlet. So I spent the winter going through the preparation modules at a training facility in Talence, outside Bordeaux, and swotting up on specialised books. The project brought me relief. It felt like a sign that I had mentally turned the page on cycling.

For now, however, I was still a professional rider under contract. I resumed training reluctantly, thinking of my bike as an instrument of torture, as something I'd been condemned to do. But as soon as I started to turn the cranks, this depression lifted. I rediscovered the pleasure of riding, of feeling the countryside rolling by, of pushing my body to its human limits, while my brain felt released and went soaring away from my problems. I revelled in this solitary effort that sent me home exhausted but happy.

I tried not to think about the moment when I would meet the other riders again and pedal amidst people who had already decided to excommunicate me. The first edition of my book, *Positif*, had been published over the winter. I had recounted my woes in the peloton from when I started in the sport to my encounter with Lance Armstrong. I wasn't at all sure that this insight into the *milieu* would be welcomed. In fact, I was quite sure it would be received very badly.

I was a worried man when, in January 2001, I rejoined the Jean Delatour team in Hyères in southern France, where a week-long training camp was taking place. Unsurprisingly, everyone gave me the cold shoulder, to say the least. Even Patrice Halgand, who had been at my wedding, was avoiding me. I didn't hold it against him. He had been forced to make a choice. He had to think of his career. Having a friendship with Bassons would have been like dragging a dead horse behind his bike. The handicap was too great.

In an attempt to lance the abscess, Michel Gros convened a meeting. It turned into a real drama. The other riders accused me of not respecting them in my book. It didn't take me long to realise that they had not read it. But others had, or perhaps they were simply responding to rumours about what it contained. Whatever the case, it was obvious the reviews were not favourable. Once again, my team-mates asked me to state publicly that other riders were clean. Once again, I refused. My argument was very familiar by now: everyone must have the courage to shout from the rooftops if they weren't prepared to accept the rules of the *milieu*. I didn't want to act as a warning voice for a collective, as I had already been asked to do so many times before. Later I had reason to be glad I'd shown caution: several of the team-mates who were asking me to put them in the clear tested positive in the seasons that followed.

After that my fate was sealed. I was even more of an outcast. Laurent Brochard no longer spoke to me. He let Gilles Bouvard lead the campaign, and he came out biting. He spoke about me in a loud voice, so that I could hear his unkind comments. In the mornings, the riders who came for breakfast shook hands with each other, but not with me.

I was relegated to the table for the new pros. They didn't know how to deal with my awkward presence. At first, they spoke to me, but were quickly pulled into line by the older riders. Gradually they turned away from me, embarrassed. They didn't speak to me any more, or only did so when they were sure that we were alone. Fraternising with me risked reprimand, even exclusion. In order to get a new contract, it was better to be friends with Brochard than with Bassons.

Braver than the average guy, a Bulgarian called Ivaïlo Grabovski did sympathise with me in spite of everything. We shared a room for a while, but then he too was brought into line. He turned away from me and then moved into the next room. I think the presence at his side of 'Mr Clean', this troublemaker who was preventing everyone from injecting themselves in peace, also began to weigh on him. The newcomer understood that he needed to *faire le métier* if he wanted to survive. A few years later, he tested positive for EPO.

I must confess that I was doing nothing to resolve my situation, as had always been the case. Instead of keeping a low profile I responded to hostility with provocation. I let it be known that I had bought my new Mercedes with money earned from the sale of the rights for my book. I could have used the great line uttered at the Cannes Film Festival by Maurice Pialat, the director of *Under the Sun of Satan*. On being booed as he received his award he said to the audience: 'You don't like me? Don't worry: I don't like you either!'

At the end of the training camp, the team decided on everyone's calendar for the season. Michel Gros told me that I had been slated to take part in Paris–Nice, but that Brochard had vetoed that. I suspected he would also do the same for the other races he was riding, including the Tour. So I was dropped down to what was effectively the reserve team and confined to second-level races with the new pros. At the end of our conversation, my directeur sportif told me it would be a good idea for me to look for another team for the following year …

In late April, I was registered to start the Circuit des Mines, a good-level stage race that took place in Lorraine. At the end of the first day, I was the best-placed rider on the team. Consequently, I should have been the leader, the rider protected by the other Jean Delatour men. But they clearly refused to support me. They sat comfortably at the back rather than controlling the race at the front. One day when the race was particularly nervous, a team-mate, Eddy Seigneur, got himself into a breakaway that included one of my rivals for the overall title. According to the rules of racing, Seigneur should have stayed at the back of the breakaway group. He didn't bother about that and instead started to ride with my rival. I eventually caught up with them. My team-mate then slipped away to the back, giving himself time to recover. Then he came back up alongside me, laughed in my face and made another attack. On the final day, I finished ninth overall in the standings, just ahead of a young British rider, an unknown who had just arrived in the professional peloton, Bradley Wiggins.

At every race start I had to put up with mockery from the peloton's loudmouths. Didier Rous, Pascal Chanteur and Christophe Moreau were particularly strident. 'So, Babasse, have you had your jab today?' 'What product have you taken today?' 'Did you forget to take your EPO?' Then came the laughter. I let it slide off me. The former Festina riders came back one by one from suspension. In the dock in Lille, they had promised to make amends, to reform themselves, and presented themselves as nice boys who were just unfortunate victims of the system.

But I soon realised that their contrition was not sincere. They had regained their haughtiness, and I was going to pay for the humiliations they had endured. When I think that I had refused to rebuke them before the judges in Lille …

In a hotel where several teams were dining in among other clients, Jean-René Bernaudeau, who headed another squad, shouted at me and gave me a dressing down in public. Didier Rous interrupted him: 'Leave it, he's just a bastard. There's no need to speak to him.' People from my own team laughed, others lowered their heads, focusing on the plate in front of them in a sign of submission. After the finish of another race in Rennes, a team-mate kicked down my shower door to retrieve his shampoo, which I had taken by mistake.

I realised that I wasn't simply detested. I was the scapegoat, that is to say the one person who had everyone on his back. Insulting me and railing against my name became a sign of belonging. Several riders told me: 'We don't want you any more.' Always that 'we', heard time after time … Manifestly, nothing, not a single thing had changed since the Festina trial.

In May we came to the Four Days of Dunkirk. It was raining, the roads were slippery, and keeping your balance was a dangerous game. In the middle of a peloton flying along at 50 kilometres an hour, Didier Rous and Christophe Moreau were amusing themselves by elbowing and cutting in front of me. I almost fell off several times, almost finished in the verge. This time, the intimidation was going too far. During the third stage, I let myself drop to the back in order to abandon. I had just enough time to see Pascal Chanteur and others celebrating my withdrawal and heading back up to the peloton waving their arms in the air as a sign of victory. They had finished me off! I handed over my number. My directeur sportif asked me why I was abandoning. I pretended to be sick.

The only advantage to the isolation I am describing here was that I was able to prepare quietly for my exams. After dinner, alone in a bedroom that no one wanted to share, I swotted hard. I was motivated by the desire to leave the *milieu* as quickly as possible. The peloton's ostracism was a good spur for my desire to learn. I passed the written and then the oral exams. I was one of the quota selected to progress to a teaching position, which guaranteed my career conversion.

I then had to select my future specialisation. Naïvely perhaps, I wanted to stay in cycling. I wanted to work with young people, to talk to them about prevention and ethics. Reforming the cycling *milieu* could only be achieved through educating the younger generation. I set up a meeting with Patrick Cluzaud, the national technical director of the French cycling federation (FFC), who I thought had always seemed to have an honest attitude. I offered him my services, explaining my project to him. From the outset, he laid down a prerequisite: 'Don't talk about doping without warning me beforehand.' He also set some other conditions. 'From this point on, I am asking you not to have any contact with your coach, Antoine Vayer.' I sensed his unease. He didn't want to get on the wrong side of the rest of the riders. I realised that I wasn't welcome.

I was feeling down, my morale was right in my boots. I really had to make a clean break from this *milieu*. More than that, I had to change my life and, first of all, move house. At home in Mazamet, I was too well known. There I would always be the ex-rider, the guy who had been a rebel. I would constantly cross paths with people who liked me, but also with others who hated me. I had to find anonymity in a bigger place.

Fortunately, I could count on the support of the minister of sport, Marie-George Buffet. She received me in Paris and was very understanding about my situation. Shortly afterwards, I was offered a position in Bordeaux in the Regional Directorate of Youth and Sports of Aquitaine. My focus would be on triathlon. Another city, another sport – deliverance! The salary was only one fifth of what I had been earning as a cyclist. But I grabbed it with both hands.

But first I had to bring an end to my racing career, which had reached an impasse in any case. It had been a long time since I'd really had a sporting presence. I was finished as a rider at the age of 27. I decided not to wait until the end of the season before taking a new turn. I drew a line under my contract with Jean Delatour, indifferent to the money I was losing by doing so.

I had informed the team's management and some journalists a few days before the French championships that took place in Argenton-sur-Creuse. On the morning of the race, I was given the opportunity to write an ironic article in *L'Equipe*, basically saying 'good riddance!' It ended up undermining my morale. On the start line, some riders made it clear in no uncertain terms that they were pleased to see me go. There were only a few spectators to offer a touch of sympathy.

The Tour du Doubs on 8 July was my last professional race. I rode it in almost complete anonymity, on roads that were almost deserted, while, on that same weekend, the 2001 Tour de France started in Dunkirk in the midst of a huge throng. I went home and put my bike in the basement (I quickly sold it). I packed my jerseys and my trophies into large suitcases that I took down to the cellar. One tiny detail raised my spirits: I could now let the hair on my legs and arms grow. There was no longer any need to shave them as all riders do …

I went into 'exile' in Bordeaux and started a happy life there.

Chapter 10

Armstrong and Me

I had a house in the suburbs with a big garden, with an oak tree at the end of it from which mushrooms sprouted in abundance in the autumn. There was nothing to recall my former career, no cup on a shelf, no picture on a wall. My two children, Coline and Thibault, weren't aware of my past for a long time, until a staff member at a local leisure centre talked to them about it one day. I didn't want to hide anything from them. I had just moved on.

I viewed my early retirement as both a defeat and a victory. I had been soundly beaten in my crusade against doping. The cheats were still imposing their law. They had turfed me out of the peloton. Everything could continue as before. I hadn't helped in any way.

And yet I had no regrets and even felt a certain pride. I had resisted – I had not given in. Looking back, I could see the reasons for this. I had been protected by some idea of morality and, of course, of good and evil. It had been instilled in me by my family history, stemming from my grandfather's flight from Franco's Spain, by my parents who placed hard work and honesty above all else, by the education that my teachers had lavished on me, and by my analytical mind, which has enabled me to reflect on issues that some people would just go along with. It was also down to the fact that I wasn't the son of a racer, and therefore not someone who had been immersed in that environment to the point where you find normality in things that are far from it.

All that was important. But perhaps the best defence against temptation came from another feeling that I hardly dare to admit to – self-esteem. I have already spoken at length about it: doping is a rite of passage that allows those who yield to it to be accepted into the cycling 'family'. Even adulterated victories forged admiration. Laurent Brochard summarised it perfectly during the proceedings of the Festina affair: 'If I had stopped the EPO, would I have still been welcome in the *milieu*? Would I have continued to produce good performances?' Anxiety about being accepted by the peloton, anxiety about being recognised by the public – I never felt either of these. Doping would have enabled me to gain the admiration of the guy next to me, but I would have hated myself. In a sense, I opted for narcissism …

My pride, or at least the urgent need to be able to look at myself in the mirror, had enabled me to refuse what they wanted to impose on me at any cost. I had never been in an all-consuming quest for popularity. Unlike Richard Virenque, I never sought to sustain myself on the basis of recognition by others, applause or the encouragement of the spectators at the side of the road. Beyond his ferocious greed and Machiavellian spirit of competition, I think Lance Armstrong, because of his personal history, also needed to feel loved, hated, envied. In short, he needed to feel he existed in the eyes of others.

Lance Armstrong. Like an emperor, he continued to crush everyone at the Tour, stamping on the pedals when the moment seemed right to knock out his opponents. I was not greatly interested in the 2001 Tour, which finished, after 3,454.2 kilometres, with a third victory for the American, who was almost seven minutes ahead of Germany's Jan Ullrich. A few stage round-ups on television at night and a glance at the results in the morning paper provided me with all I wanted to know. Half of the top ten finishers on the Champs-Elysées and three-quarters of the stage winners were convicted of doping offences in the years that followed. Business as usual.

The *milieu* continued in its bad habits. It would not reform itself. I got confirmation of that a few months later, in October at Paris–Tours, one of the final Classics of the season. Richard Virenque, who had received a one-year suspension after a confession had been forced out of him, had returned to competition. It was a winning return: the climber, the king of the mountains, came out on top in a race across the plains, as flat as a pancake, a race reputed to be the domain of *rouleurs* and sprinters. The press spoke of his 'panache', his 'redemption'. Who knows whether Virenque was riding clean in that race, but my general feeling about the sport was: what a farce! Far from mending itself, cycling seemed to be sinking a little deeper into the absurd. If, in football, a goalkeeper had become an irresistible attacker at the end of his career, this conversion would have been a surprise. If, in athletics, a marathon runner had won a 100-metre race after a year out of competition, it would have been questioned. But not in cycling, where unrestrained applause was *de rigueur*.

I was disgusted. Was this really sport? Fortunately, I very quickly found a response and an antidote to the doubts that were plaguing me. I was invited to Millau to take part in a symposium on doping organised by Gilles Bertrand and Odile Baudier, two trail-racing enthusiasts. I didn't know anything about this endurance sport, but an event took place the following Sunday. It was a 67km yomp in the mountains, with cramps guaranteed and suffering expected. I was tempted to give it a go. I bought a pair of trainers and a headtorch, and found myself on the start line at five in the morning.

The race did indeed veer towards torture and I had to abandon after 37 kilometres due to pain in my left knee. But a vocation was born. I found myself feeling reinvigorated by being among 3,000 competitors whose objective was simply to test their limits. This was sport as I conceived it: a fight against, or rather with, yourself, in the midst of a crowd of others doing the same thing. A solitary effort among thousands of other solitary efforts, side by side, stride by stride, with shared pain, everything and everyone mixed together – all accomplices, not adversaries. Feet black and blue, my body in agony, I was as happy as I'd ever been. I was living again.

I vowed to come back and finish the race (I've managed to do so once in six attempts). I signed up for other trail races, week after week. I've improved and learned to manage my effort, with the sole objective of arriving at the finish completely drained, having given everything. I've won several races but have only considered this classification as one measure among many of my performance.

Performance. When I was trail racing I did feel a bit like a mechanic working to get the best performance out of a car engine. I was calibrating my body. I was fine-tuning it, improving it. Consequently, winning in a poor time without giving the best of myself disappointed me. Finishing in the depths of the classification having improved my performance delighted me.

Trail racing washed the disappointments out of my head, by offering me all that I had missed in the professional peloton. It also became a lifestyle. I trained diligently every day; I watched my diet, checking on my body fat (even today, it remains the same as it was 15 years ago when I was a professional athlete). How to describe this pleasure in running, in seeing the countryside roll by while the brain is in endorphin deficit? The mountains become more beautiful, the forests even deeper. Even towns take on another aspect. I well remember the Paris that I crossed in the early hours of the morning, when the city of lights was still sleeping. From the Eiffel Tower to the slopes of Sacré Cœur, taking in the banks of the Seine and Notre-Dame … That was a magical moment.

I also got into skyrunning. The idea is simple and crazy. A three-kilometre course with more than 1,000 metres of climbing, the slope getting steeper near the top, to the point where it reaches 65 per cent. These races are run either as time trials or massed start events, and you have to manage your effort in order to achieve optimal performance. I loved the feeling of having given everything when I crossed the line, where I collapsed to the ground or ended up bent double by the effort, my breath ragged, my heart on the verge of exploding. Once again, where I finished mattered to me less than the physical sensation.

Unfortunately a groin hernia forced me to abandon trail racing in 2010. Because life without sport seems insipid to me, I returned to my first love, mountain biking. Since the end of my career, my only connection with the bike had been the 28km round trip I did every day to get to and from work.

I bought a good bike and went out into the mountains just to see how I got on. I soon found myself frantically pedalling up the climbs, hurtling like a daredevil down the most slippery slopes, tackling them with the recklessness and rage of a kid. I'd rediscovered the bug I'd had when I first went out on a bike.

In February 2011, I ended up breaking a promise I had made ten years earlier: a perjurer and renegade, I took out a cycling licence.

I signed up for mass participation events. Almost 20 years after first riding it, I lined up in the Roc d'Azur. The race takes place in October between Fréjus and Roquebrune, in the hills overlooking the Mediterranean. Every year it brings together 17,000 competitors, who are divided into different categories. Finding myself in the midst of other competitors seeking chiefly to test themselves, I immediately rediscovered the spirit that had won me over in trail racing. The rider next to you is not someone to beat, but a fellow competitor who is pushing you to surpass yourself.

That year, I finished 25th out of 2,300 entrants, 40 minutes behind the winner. In 2012, I was 30th but 30 minutes behind the winner. In 2013, I finished 40th, but 26 minutes down on the winner. I've been losing ground in the classification each year, but improving my time. Consequently, the way I see it is that I'm progressing.

Since then, 40 weekends a year, I go and compete in races all across France. I receive peerless assistance in the shape of Pascale, Coline and Thibault. My family is happy to indulge my whim, and if that changed

I would give it up. All four of us climb into my old estate that has 250,000 kilometres on the clock and we head off to the Pyrenees, the Alps, the Jura. I take great pleasure in sharing these moments with my family. Pascale supports me 100 per cent in what I love to do, and I do the same for her. This desire to indulge each other surprises a lot of people, who cannot believe it when I tell them that we have never raised our voices at each other. Once again, I consider myself a lucky man.

I'm not naïve. I know that doping exists in mountain biking, just as it does in trail racing. In both disciplines, I also came across former professional cyclists. Although they were no longer in the peloton, I had no illusions about their performances. They would stop at nothing to get a sponsor or claim a prize for victory. But I also know the opinion that the other competitors had of them. Doping remains the exception rather than the rule, contrary to the established practice in the pro peloton.

The temptation is there, of course. A drug can enable someone to finish a race, or to deaden a recurring pain, just like the one that regularly takes a pincer-like grip on my knee. It can allow someone to boast about their achievement, to hold forth to all and sundry about an impressive result, bragging, for example: 'I finished 1,500th out of 10,000.' Big deal! In the end, you are only cheating yourself. It is just about the most ridiculous thing you could do, like something from a Molière play, where the false pretences of the characters only serve to make the audience laugh.

Consequently, trail racing and mountain biking have appeased me and reaffirmed my philosophy of what sport should be. Hardened by that, I went back to watching the Tour. But I watched it for what it is: a spectacle rather than a sporting event. Like most spectators, I have admired the countryside traversed by the peloton and watched the events of the race unfold as if they were pre-set choreography, like an action film shot in the midst of beautiful panoramas, with countless extras and a storyline that captivates but which you know is ultimately nothing but fiction.

As one year followed another, I watched Lance Armstrong's fourth, fifth, sixth and seventh victories. The American was toying with his opponents. On the climbs of Alpe d'Huez, Le Grand-Bornand, Plateau de Beille and Luz-Ardiden, he put the other favourites in their place, overtaking riders who had escaped earlier, as if they were nothing more than additional spectators who had been dumped in his path. Sometimes he gave signs of being a man in trouble, playing it for laughs, grimacing – before delivering the final blow in the next kilometre. The rest of the peloton were reduced to swilling the dregs from the chalice, and little by little a bad feeling came over me. I have to admit to it reluctantly: the American was taking his revenge on me.

I have related the hard time he gave me on 14 July 1999 on the descent from Sestrières, as we were heading towards the finish at Alpe d'Huez. Of course, I didn't forget his moral lesson. The irony, the salt in the wound, came a few years later, when the blood samples taken from him that day were analysed. They showed up as positive for erythropoietin. Lance Armstrong had been pumped up with EPO while he was accusing me of sullying cycling.

He had referred to this when questioned by reporters in St Galmier on 16 July after I had abandoned the Tour. Asked about my withdrawal, he first pretended to have no memory of me, before striking out at me with a new complaint, as reported by the British journalist Jeremy Whittle in *The Times*. 'If it's the rider that I think it is, the one who's always speaking about problems in cycling and doping, then I told him during the stage to Sestrières that I respected what he was saying but that I thought there was a professional and a correct way to do it. What he's said is not good for him or his team, his sponsor and cycling. I understand his position, but if that's what he thinks, maybe he's better to go home. I don't think declarations in newspapers are in his best interests. If he wants to ride professionally, he can't speak like that, because sponsors will walk away from the sport.'

But Lance Armstrong had at least criticised me face to face. That underlined his status as the peloton's *patron*. I had refused to bend to its will and I had been dispatched. The rest had lain down and suffered the consequences for that. They accepted his humiliating domination. They paid for their cowardice, which seemed to me as despicable as the yellow jersey's lies. In the end I thought Lance Armstrong wasn't a bad guy, that he wasn't any more dishonest than the rest. He was just smarter, more intelligent, more cynical perhaps. Consequently, seeing him ridicule people who had ridiculed me wasn't something I was unhappy with.

In fact I was close to rejoicing every time he stood on the pedals and left the rest for dead. I used to enjoy listening to the defeated riders who, with their heads down and their mouths still skewed by the effort they had just made, praised the man who had just made them look like idiots. I could imagine their outbursts of anger and cries of helplessness when they were back behind closed doors in their hotels. Sometimes I thought it was all going to explode out into the open, that another rider would speak out just as I had done. But there was nothing beyond that humiliated silence.

The most amusing thing was to listen to the tangles the commentators got themselves into as they attempted to give it all a veneer of legitimacy. They tried to maintain a degree of suspense when the script had already been written and agreed, and the spoils carved up. Sitting alongside them, former riders talked only about race tactics and strategy, when the weather and road conditions had little bearing on the American's superiority. They knew that the secret lay elsewhere. In his role as an expert on France Télévisions, Laurent Jalabert even reproached Armstrong's rivals for lacking panache. He knew from experience that that wasn't the secret.

In the course of his confession in 2013, Lance Armstrong gave details of the products he had used. I was surprised to discover that it was quite conventional. It included the classic products that his main rivals were also using. Most of the riders who stood on the podium with him during those years were convinced of the need to dope, using the same ingredients. There was nothing that could explain his sudden superiority.

I therefore remain convinced that the repentant rider hasn't delivered the full truth yet.

During all of those years, the peloton accepted the hellish pace set by the US Postal team. The superiority of Armstrong's team, even more than his own achievements, removed any doubt that I had about the origins of that performance. I could see George Hincapie, whom I had known as a pure *rouleur*, climbing passes full on. I had also known many of his team-mates: Frankie Andreu, Tyler Hamilton, Floyd Landis, Levi Lepheimer, Roberto Heras, etc. They had ridden with me in anonymity within the peloton. But now I saw them performing in a very different way, riding proudly at the front under their new banner.

It reminded me of Festina's heyday. Clearly, US Postal, who later became Discovery Channel, weren't the only ones who dared to resort to organised, methodical and carefully controlled doping at that time. I would smile as I listened to the official explanation of the American team's superiority, as provided by Johan Bruyneel, their directeur sportif, and the rest of the management: the kilometres they'd clocked up, ruthless training regimes, reconnaissance of the passes in all weathers, including freezing rain and sometimes even snow, the incessant toil. I knew some of these arguments perfectly: they were the same ones that Festina had used to explain their control.

Lance Armstrong added another explanation to all this: resilience. The cancer survivor had tapped into new psychological resources during the race. He gave hope to all those suffering from the disease. Criticising him consequently became a moral crime. It was a novel and unstoppable justification, except there was nothing at the heart of it.

In 2004, the noble herald of the fight against cancer showed a less pleasant side. On a Tour stage without any importance, a breakaway was starting to come together. It included one Filippo Simeoni. The Italian rider had testified against Michele Ferrari, Lance Armstrong's doctor. Right in front of the cameras, the American chased down the breakaway and intimated to Simeoni that he had to drop back into the peloton, even putting a hand on his shoulder. 'I can destroy you,' Armstrong told him. Then he made a gesture of zipping his lips closed as a sign of remaining silent. It was an incredible scene of intimidation captured on live television. It brought a bad memory to my mind. It highlighted Armstrong's insolence, his sense of impunity, the spinelessness of the peloton in which nobody dared to protest (some even spat in Simeoni's face), as well as the complicity of the commentators and organisers who only offered up feeble objections to this unsportsmanlike behaviour.

The seven-time yellow jersey announced his retirement in 2005. A few weeks later, *L'Equipe* revealed on its front page, under the headline 'The Armstrong Lie', that he had been doped with EPO. Tongues were now loosened, but only because he was no longer around. Criticism erupted from a peloton that had hitherto been mute: 'This is outrageous'… 'We suspected this was going on.' The false looks of bewilderment on the faces of riders and directeurs sportifs amused me hugely. Some of them showed real comedic talent.

I too was contacted by the media, who wanted my comments. I no doubt disappointed them. Without defending him, I tried to explain that Armstrong didn't have a monopoly when it came to hypocrisy and sporting and moral fraud.

Then the American was exonerated thanks to an accommodating report from the UCI. He came out of retirement in 2009 and returned to the peloton. I could imagine the embarrassment of those who had raved on about him. I wished I could have been an invisible man and slipped into the peloton to hear their groans. I secretly hoped he would win another Tour, so that all the cowards would end up swallowing hemlock!

I have no grudge against Armstrong. His team-mates have since revealed the hardness of the man. I can testify to it, having spent a minute with him that was among the most painful of my life. But, at the risk of repeating myself, he was not the worst. For me, he isn't the demon of the peloton that many want him to be, much less the reason for all of cycling's ills. That's too easy.

The Tours that followed demonstrated that. Average speeds did not fall. Just as in the Armstrong era, riders did not flag. During a Tour their performances and haematocrit levels would remain constant from start to finish. Not an ounce of fatigue, not a single physical weakness could be detected after three weeks of racing over thousands of kilometres.

All that changed was that the team-wide doping of the Armstrong era was replaced by individuals acting alone. Riders tinkered behind closed doors, multiplying the risk of being caught. Their clumsiness was demonstrated by absolute carnage in terms of positive cases. I'm not going to reel out the long list of dozens and dozens of riders found guilty of doping over the years that followed. Like all fans, I was caught between amusement and disgust as I watched this farce.

In 2006, nine riders, including three of the favourites, were prevented from starting the Tour de France because of their involvement in a doping scandal in Spain, the Puerto affair. One of Lance Armstrong's former team-mates, Floyd Landis, won that year's race. His form had collapsed one day in the Alps, but the very next day, after a marathon breakaway, he almost completely regained the ten minutes he had lost. Enthused by this turnaround in fortunes, the commentators shouted themselves hoarse, calling it the return of cycling from yesteryear with its twists, turns and resurrections. I knew very well that this wasn't the case. The body is incapable of recovering so fast, in scarcely more than one night, from such a sudden bout of fatigue. A few days after the race finished, it was announced that Landis had been doping with testosterone. I was surprised the American had committed such a basic mistake. It was a rookie's error, because the riders have long mastered the use of testosterone. But Floyd Landis had drunk some alcohol, which had changed his parameters. I understood all too well what had been going on.

In 2007, it was the turn of Michael Rasmussen to be caught out by the authorities – when he was wearing the yellow jersey. He had an anaemic pallor and was frighteningly thin. The fact that he looked like a walking corpse didn't prevent him from sailing through the race. He was my age, born just ten days before me. Like me, he came from mountain biking. I hadn't noticed him. He had hardly shone. Suddenly he emerged at the age of 31.

It is always surprising when average riders suddenly explode into prominence. The 2013 Vuelta produced another example of late blooming, this one even more spectacular. American Chris Horner won it at almost 42 years of age. I had known him when we were both in the La Française des Jeux team in 1999. He was almost three years older than me. I had only ever regarded him as a very ordinary rider, unlike the Australian Bradley McGee, who had also joined us at that time. Horner had then become an unremarkable domestique. Fourteen years later, he won a grand tour. Unsurprisingly, rumours abounded regarding this performance – rumours Horner denies and which have not been substantiated.

As they toyed with the rules, some riders were caught and sanctioned. But, once the suspension was completed, they came back as strong as before. In which case doping must be nothing more than a placebo … Alexandre Vinokourov became Olympic champion in London in 2012 after a two-year suspension. Rui Costa became world champion in 2013 after a disciplinary exile. Other riders announced their retirement suddenly, after which they could no longer be tested. Then they reversed their decision and became irresistible, like Mario Cipollini, the Italian sprinter, who was crowned world champion six months after announcing he was leaving cycling.

I had to take a renewed interest in all this funny business. In the middle of the 2000s, I ended up getting involved in the anti-doping campaign. The ministry had asked me to work on prevention among young people, as I had always wanted. But it had also asked me to be a regional correspondent of the French Anti-Doping Agency (AFLD). Consequently, I also became responsible for repressing doping and, whether I liked it or not, I was plunged back into the peloton's pharmacopoeia. I started to find out about new methods and new molecules that were circulating in the bunch. I needed to get up to speed fast!

In 2004, I was invited to the office of the minister at the time, Jean-François Lamour, who was preparing a new law against doping. I was received along with my former team-mate Jean-Cyril Robin, the Olympic track champion Florian Rousseau and a young French rider called Sylvain Chavanel. The latter distrusted me even though I had never raced with him. Clearly my bad reputation lived on in the peloton.

One avenue that the minister was exploring was to suppress the use of soigneurs, those characters without any special training who had long served as suppliers. For my part, I insisted on a focus on the role of team doctors. I said I couldn't understand why they were needed. There are race doctors who can deal with the effects of crashes and other ailments. They should suffice. Even if they are not necessarily providing banned products, team physicians are playing a role in the system. They are the keystone when it comes to ensuring that riders don't test positive, or in administering recuperative products. They also sign the 'therapeutic use' exemptions (TUE). These medical certificates allow a rider to use a drug that is on the banned list. During drug controls, the rider presents the certificate. He cannot then be prosecuted if traces of the drug are found in his urine. The use of TUEs has reached almost epidemic proportions in the peloton. With the UCI's complicity, these certificates have sometimes even been backdated, as was the case with the one provided by Lance Armstrong in 1999 after testing positive for corticosteroids.

Thus the Tour, doping and Armstrong made their back into my life. In the late 2000s, I received a phone call from an American detective. He was working for the insurance company SCA Promotions. It had paid millions of dollars to Lance Armstrong in the form of bonuses for his victories. They were extremely interested in suspicions that he was doping. The company hoped to recoup its funds by proving that these victories were the result of cheating. I couldn't offer the detective any help, however, as I was only an innocent party in this story.

Later, in 2011, I received another email from the United States. It had been sent by Travis Tygart, director of the US Anti-Doping Agency (USADA). He was investigating Lance Armstrong's performances. He wanted to know more about what had happened on the descent from Sestrières in 1999. Thank goodness for automatic translators! Thanks to them, I managed to talk with him about my experience. He wanted us to meet up in Paris, but this couldn't be arranged. Once again, I don't think I told him anything that he didn't already know.

I wondered why so many investigations into Lance Armstrong had failed to go the distance. Even the one overseen by Jeff Novitzky, the Food and Drug Administration (FDA) agent who had brought down sprinter Marion Jones and baseball player Barry Bonds in the Balco doping scandal, had failed to achieve a result. Nevertheless, I still wanted to believe that the truth would emerge in the end. From this Travis Tygart, perhaps? He made me a strong impression on me. He seemed to have sharp teeth and appeared not to want to let go.

In fact, just a few months later in October 2012, his report was presented to the UCI. It comprised one thousand overwhelming pages, based principally on the testimony of Armstrong's former team-mates. I was honoured with a passage describing the bullying that I had been subjected to during the 1999 Tour.

The day the report was released to the public, I racked up 16 interviews with French and also English-speaking journalists who wanted my opinion. I had no other choice but to respond, despite being a rider who had been out of the sport for years. This depressed me. I was still the only one who dared to speak out. What happened in the wake of the report didn't reassure me much either: *omertà* remained the rule within the peloton. The mentality was not changing.

Travis Tygart's impressive work strengthened one of my beliefs: the fight against doping can no longer rely solely on controls. These are necessary, but no longer sufficient. What is required is exactly this kind of investigative focus, tenacious detective work that includes collecting clues, physical evidence and testimony of repentant riders such as that provided by Frankie Andreu, Floyd Landis and Tyler Hamilton. The cheats also need to run a financial risk equivalent to the extent of the money they have fraudulently won. Otherwise, the temptation will remain too strong.

My media revival didn't stop there. In the autumn of 2012, I was contacted by a photographer from *Sports Illustrated*. He told me I had been nominated by the American magazine for their Sportsman of the Year award. The unknown, the 'little rider' who had been mocked in 1999 by the peloton and the organisers of the Tour de France, found himself in the midst of stars like Lebron James and Michael Phelps. My photo deliberately made me look like Mr Nobody. In fact, I wondered what I was doing there in this gathering of stellar names. Ten years earlier, Lance Armstrong had been elected Sportsman of the Year by the editorial team at *Sports Illustrated*. On this occasion, he was among those being considered in the category of Antisportsman of the Year. What an irony!

My nomination was backed within their editorial team by Alexander Wolff, whom I did not know. In November 2012, he wrote:

> It has become almost a mantra, a way to dismiss pro cycling's entire dope-saturated era in one disgusted swoop: Everyone did it. Tour de France organisers said as much last month, when they declined to redistribute the seven Tour titles stripped from Lance Armstrong for what the US Anti-Doping Agency called 'one of the most sordid chapters in sports history'.
>
> Every podium finisher but one during Armstrong's seven tainted Tours has been implicated in doping. So to write off the era bookended by the Festina Affair of 1998 and Operation Puerto in

2006 seems at first blush like a worthy way to bring closure to a shameful period.

There's only one problem. Not everyone did it.

Who is The Unknown Rider, the most deserving cyclist who stuck it out clean?

There's no way of determining how far down those results tables we'd have to go to find him. But we do have the example of a Frenchman named Christophe Bassons. And for his courage, principle and symbolism, he's my Sportsman of the Year – the year we'll remember as the one in which we finally lanced, as it were, cycling's boil.

Blocked for 15 years, the truth was finally coming out. Cornered by USADA, Lance Armstrong decided to confess in January 2013 in an interview with Oprah Winfrey. I have never felt the need to get up in the middle of the night to watch TV. In fact I felt indifferent to this worldwide mea culpa. I was content to watch excerpts the next morning in case I was asked to give a reaction, which obviously I was.

That he admitted to doping, that he asked for forgiveness from those he had clashed with, that it had been shown that what I was saying in 1999 was true brought me no comfort. At that time, I could only think about his children. How was he going to explain to them that he had cheated and lied? How were his kids going to be able to live with that shame? How were his kids going to respond to their father, who will remain as one of the greatest frauds in sporting history? So, yes, my first impulse was to feel sorry for Armstrong.

What *do* their children think? This question nags at me every time that a rider decides he can't keep on lying any longer and admits to having doped. The list of them has kept on growing recently. Denmark's Bjarne Riis, who won the Tour in 1996, Germany's Jan Ullrich, the yellow jersey the following year, Belgium's Johan Museeuw, German sprinter Erik Zabel – all have confessed. Erik Zabel … another of those who had collared me when I was still in the peloton and accused me of giving cycling a bad image.

Recently, a French Senate commission released yet more names, of both French and foreign riders who had tested positive for EPO in 1998: Laurent Jalabert, Jacky Durand, Mario Cipollini, Laurent Desbiens … All bar Laurent Jalabert have admitted that they cheated. They confessed with a smile playing on their lips, without remorse. In order to clear themselves to an extent, they explained that this practice was necessary at the time.

At that time, some of them swore, on the heads of their children sometimes, that they weren't doping. Therein lies the most pitiful consequence of doping, its worst corollary: it envelops the athlete in a lie.

I don't believe in either the sincerity or the usefulness of all these confessions forced out under duress, under the pressure of facts and evidence. I don't believe in the requests for forgiveness, which come in little more than a whisper. Once absolution has been obtained, the sinners return to the big family of cycling. They become directeurs sportifs or coaches, like Bjarne Riis, Jeroen Blijlevens, Steven De Jongh, Bobby Julich and Erik Zabel. They become commentators on television, like Laurent Jalabert, Richard Virenque, Jacky Durand and Christophe Moreau. They dive back into the system or defend it in public. For them, it is unthinkable that cycling can be done any other way. It is and always has been like this. Nothing could change it.

For the same reason, I am opposed to the reconciliation commission that the UCI is trying to put in place. In exchange for confessions or information, the offending riders would receive an amnesty. But what would we learn that we don't already know? Thanks to the Festina trial, thanks to Travis Tygart's report, thanks to investigative works like *L.A. Confidentiel* by David Walsh and Pierre Ballester, thanks to the courageous testimony of members of riders' entourages such as Lance Armstrong's soigneur, Emma O'Reilly, or Betsy Andreu, wife of

Frankie, and thanks to very precise accounts of penitents such as Willy Voet and Tyler Hamilton, we know almost everything about what happened. Stunned spectators have been taken into the privacy of hotel rooms where blood bags were put up on coathangers, where syringes circulated freely in the corridors, wrapped up in napkins, where drugs were hidden in cans, where threats and retaliation were common currency. They even know about what was at least the passive complicity of the UCI.

The work in uncovering all this has already been done by others outside the UCI. Rather than pushing doors open, I would prefer to see the international federation focus on its own means of functioning. How much proof did it need to accumulate before finally deciding to suspend Lance Armstrong and strip him of his Tour de France victories? How many modest riders were thrown to the mercy of the press in order to protect the big guns?

I am well placed to understand the system of 'double standards' that still reigns in cycling tribunals that are meant to promote sporting equity. I experienced it in a humiliating manner.

It was on 1 September 2012, and I was taking part in the French mountain bike marathon championships at Langon in Brittany. In line with my incorrigible habit, my tendency to ride like a mad dog, I attacked without any concern for tactics. I ended up leading the race as one of a group of six escapees. But, with 25 kilometres remaining, I was struck by hypoglycemia. I found myself adrift, without any strength, and was forced to retire.

A little annoyed with myself, I dismounted in a quiet location. There was an official, known as a 'signaller', at that point on the route, and I told her what I was doing. She took my race number, 017, and my name, and she transmitted the announcement of my retirement to the organisers at the finish line. I then went back to the changing room without passing through the finish. I showered and got dressed while the other riders were finishing. I even bought some souvenirs for my children and then set off in all serenity for Bordeaux, about 500 kilometres away.

Two and a half hours after the end of the race, when I was halfway home, I received a phone call. The guy responsible for the dope control was demanding to see me within half an hour. So I called him to explain my situation.

I thought the file on this had been closed, but then I received a summons from the FFC. The French federation wanted to hear what I had to say. I went to Paris on 18 October 2012 and found myself in front of a disciplinary committee. Three weeks later, the news came by registered letter. I had been punished for what is known in the jargon as 'a refusal to submit to a drug control'. I, the amateur rider who was pedalling purely for his own pleasure, had ended up as a victim of procedural confusion. I was handed a one-year suspension. A year! Ironically, it was the same length as the ban given to Richard Virenque, who had charged himself up with EPO and other hardcore products. It was even six months longer than most other doped riders got in the Festina affair. What impressive sporting justice! Cycling's tribunals apply La Fontaine's fable to the letter: 'Depending on your social height / The law will see your crime as black – or else as white.'

I didn't need to succumb to paranoia to work out the set-up. This was soon after the Tygart report came out, when the Armstrong affair was in full swing. Then, as I have said, I was asked by the media to give my opinion on cycling and I did it my way, bluntly. As in 1999, they wanted me to pay for my frankness. I conducted a quick investigation of my critics. I discovered that many of those involved in my case were either former riders or long-standing administrators who weren't exactly fond of me.

At that time, I was also guilty of another crime, that of lèse-majesté. I was contacted by the organisers of Cycling Change Now. This movement had published an article of faith that appealed to me: 'We are convinced that the world of cycling must fundamentally shift how the sport is managed, including the implementation of an independent anti-doping system.'

Australian entrepreneur Jamie Fuller had gathered doctors and former riders like Greg LeMond, Jörg Jaksche and Eric Boyer around him. I met but quickly distanced myself from this group of rebels. I encountered some really good souls there, but also some pushy individuals who were ready for anything. I also realised that there were too many people there trying to re-establish an unblemished image or simply trying to get by.

Invited to a meeting held in London in late November, I felt once again that someone was attempting to take advantage of my image. That wasn't the last of the surprises in store for me. At the end of the conference, a British reporter stopped me. He asked me if it was true that I was set to join the management at the British Sky team. I was stunned. I had never been contacted by this team, which, since 2012, had been attracting questions and even criticism about its performance. I was furious that this rumour was going around. Again and again, people wanted to get their hands on me as a moral guarantee.

While some people were trying to take over my reputation, the French Cycling Federation was attempting to destroy it with this iniquitous suspension. I knew I was in the crosshairs. Ever since I had taken out a licence again, I had regularly been tested. In 15 months, I had been tested more often than during my entire professional career. That perhaps explains why I felt so bitter …

They had been waiting for me to make a mistake that they could use against me, and here was a good opportunity. The suspension came into force ten days later when I was organising a major conference on doping in Bordeaux! At the request of my boss, who was understandably embarrassed by this affair, I had to cancel this meeting.

What to do? Rather than appeal and by doing so shamefully cover up my suspension, I decided to make it public. I wanted to prove the total absurdity of the system by outlining my own situation. While over in Switzerland the UCI was still defending Lance Armstrong despite 1,000 pages of evidence accumulated in the Tygart report, the French Cycling Federation was not hesitating to hammer me. By a supremely ironic quirk of fate, I had been punished just before Lance Armstrong, as if our lives were to remain linked to the end.

I decided to use this nonsense as an opportunity to demonstrate the lack of justice in cycling's tribunals.

Once I had cried foul, French television and the mainstream media pointed their cameras my way and opened their columns up to me. They enabled me both to defend myself and go on the attack. I also took on a lawyer, Thibault de Montbrial, who had defended Bruno Roussel during the Festina affair.

On 11 December 2012, I appeared in front of the Disciplinary Appeal Committee. Embarrassed by the hype, it partly absolved me by stating: 'Christophe Bassons has shown evidence of his good faith' and referring to 'an absence of fraudulent intent on his part'. But it upheld the suspension, cutting it back to just one month. This judgement of Solomon was not enough for me. I also couldn't understand the lack of response from both the Ministry of Sport, which I was depending on, and from the AFLD, at whose disposal I had put myself.

Wanting to make each of these bodies face up to its responsibilities, I then publicly announced that I wanted to appeal to the Administrative Tribunal and possibly sue both of these organisations for defaulting on their duties. Indeed, the proceedings brought against me demonstrated that the FFC was applying rules that weren't compliant with the sporting code and that the ministry was tolerating this abuse. For its part, the AFLD had not bothered to take a decision, as required by the same sporting code. All of these bodies had therefore failed in their duty.

Four days after this announcement, the AFLD took up my case and I was finally acquitted.

My anger has not dissipated, however. I will continue with the judicial process against those who tried to smear me or did nothing to defend me. I want to know what happened, if only for the sake of all the underlings who have been wrongfully condemned in this way while the authentic dopers have been continuing to ride with complete impunity.

These recent misadventures confirm to me that the system in which doping blossomed is still in place. They also demonstrate that I am still the black sheep of the cycling *milieu*. I had further confirmation of that a few months later. Having finished in the top ten in a race counting towards the Mountain Bike Marathon World Cup, I found that I had been automatically selected for the French team that was taking part in the world championships on 29 June in Austria. That was what the UCI regulations stipulated. This was a wonderful surprise for me, but less so for my federation, and in a final act of pettiness they refused to provide me with the national team jersey. Consequently, I had to buy one for 100 euros.

Chapter 11

When the Song Remains the Same

Sometimes people ask me if I'm happy with what has happened to Lance Armstrong. This question really annoys me. Why should I be happy? What has changed that would satisfy me? Lance Armstrong has good reason to see the irony in the status of scapegoat that has been conferred on him. Over the winter of 2012–13, it seems I hardly stopped speaking about this man with whom I had only talked after all for just a minute of my life, even if that minute did seem particularly long. Several intermediaries proposed the setting up of a meeting between the two of us. I was not against this kind of meeting as long as it was not simply a short-lived media show.

I also knew that Tyler Hamilton wanted to meet me. In his book, he returned to the Sestrières incident. He admitted he was ashamed at not having supported me in 1999. 'I feel awful about the way he was treated. I always knew the peloton would not talk to Christophe after Lance singled him out – but shame on me for doing the same. We succumbed to the pressure that Lance exerted.'

That Sestrières altercation must also be figuring in the film that Stephen Frears is putting together on the American's life. This amuses me. I was contacted by the person who is who going to play my role. It's a strange feeling. Here I am facing the prospect of an appearance on the big screen, me whose only desire is to live peacefully with Pascale and my children.

Did my agreement to meet Lance Armstrong again in December 2013 fit in with this goal? Via intermediaries, I learned that the American wanted to meet me. My first impulse was to say no. I was afraid of being manipulated, trapped. Was he intending to get me involved in his complicated judicial affairs, to use our tête à tête as a way of appeasing the American courts? I am fully aware of the importance of redemption in American culture.

And then I said yes. I realised that even though his request might have been self-serving, I also needed to have this meeting. I had questions, lots of questions, to ask him. I had personal issues that I wanted to settle before moving on to other things. The conversation we had started on the descent from Sestrières had only lasted a few seconds. It needed to be completed.

In addition, I could see a good reason for having such a meeting with regard to the prevention of doping. What could be better than showing that choices made in the short term do not always turn out to be the best in the long term? It was to be me, the little outcast within the pro peloton in the years between 1998 and 2001, against Lance Armstrong. As they say in tennis, we would be at love-all with Bassons to serve!

The meeting took place in a room at Fouquet's, a renowned restaurant on the Champs-Elysées. Lance Arsmtrong had finished seven Tours de France with the yellow jersey on his shoulders on this avenue. I saw him arrive with a cap pulled tight down on his head. His features were drawn. The week before, he had met his former masseur Emma O'Reilly and asked her to forgive him for dragging her name through the mud after she had called his performances into question. I also knew he had just met with Filippo Simeoni in Italy.

Lance ordered a drink and fiddled with embarrassment with the glass throughout our conversation. He immediately returned to what he had told me during the 1999 Tour. He tried to explain that he hadn't wanted to wound me, and then stated, 'If that was how you felt at the time, I really have to apologise. I'm sorry.'

'There is no need to apologise,' I replied. 'At least you said what you had to say to my face.' I explained how French riders had done as much he had in terms of my eviction from the race thanks to their hypocrisy, insults and intimidation.

He told me that he had plenty to say about cowards and hypocrites too. 'My life today is full of personalities of this kind. When you live through the kind of period that I experienced, you learn all kinds of things. You don't only learn lessons about cycling, but about life too. You learn who your real friends are. There are people who I could have sworn were on my side. I would have trusted them 100 per cent. I thought that they would stick with me. But, hey presto! They disappeared! At least I know who I'm dealing with. It's great when you walk about in the yellow jersey, everyone is having a good time and wants to pat you on the back, saying: "What a great guy!" But then I discovered what people are really like. I've found that out for myself. Suddenly, there were far fewer people around me. But I'll tell you this: last year's events, which started with USADA, and all the problems that resulted from that both for me, my family and those around me, no longer have any value.'

He continued, his bitterness evident: 'I was demonised. But the former leaders of the UCI are as evil as me.' He added: 'Unfortunately, cycling is not a better sport today than it was 12 months ago.'

I couldn't agree more. I found myself taking to his defence. 'I don't agree with you taking the blame for the whole *milieu*. I don't think you're responsible for everything that's happened. The UCI, the federations, the organisers also have to take some of the blame. We have to put an end to this hypocrisy.'

I added: 'I'm happy with my life now. I am a father to two children. I have a job that I enjoy. I don't have any regrets. I am proud of what I've done and I've got plans for the future.'

He smiled and replied: 'I've got children too and I'm very proud, but I've got no plans. My life is complicated. It always has been, but it is particularly complicated at the moment. I am stuck in legal quicksand.'

He told me how he had decided to start doping when his team managers began to get impatient at his lack of performance and were talking about sending him back to Texas. 'That was in 1994. They really had a go at me, but I said, "No, no, I'm not taking this lying down." I told them: "Fuck you ... I'm staying." This is a cultural problem. The riders are fighters, we're there to fight. I said: "I'm carrying on. I'm not going home. I'm staying here to fight."'

I knew everything that he was talking about so well from personal experience. I had also experienced that same pressure for results. I had just made a different choice. He had drawn on his determination, his strength of character and his obstinacy to remain in the peloton come what may. I had called on these same qualities to resist. I've never regretted it, and that night, as I sat face to face with him, I was even prouder of what I had done, even more convinced that I had made the right choice.

He still tried to justify himself, though. I felt he was trying to convince himself more than he was trying to convince me: 'There was a general feeling in the 1990s that Lance Armstrong and his team-mates, those riders who made the decision [to dope] were animals. But they were human beings confronted with a choice: I wasn't from anywhere special, I didn't do any studying, and if I'd gone home, I would have had nothing. However, there were things within my reach that could do me good, an awful lot of good, and they weren't detectable. I said to myself: "Yes, I am going to play the game." And almost everyone said "yes". Apart from you, I only know of two people who made a different decision: Scott Mercier and Darren Baker.'

These two riders quit Lance Armstrong's US Postal team rather than accepting its doping programme. 'You three, you are educated people. You have degrees. But,' Armstrong continued, 'in the future, perhaps tomorrow, perhaps in ten years or in 20 years, there will be something that won't be called EPO but XYZ, which will improve performance and is undetectable. For the next generation, there will always be that moment when a decision or choice has to be made.'

Lance went on to describe the spiral of lies and denials. The obvious question comes: 'Are you doped?' And the subsquent answer takes on a meaning of its own. 'When you can say no once, four times, you can say no a million times.' It is impossible to retreat from this position. 'I wish I had not been put in this position, but that's the way it goes. I did all I could to succeed, I did the training, selected my team, drew on motivation, anger and the desire to win. Doping was the end point, the final piece.'

I explained that I would like to get him involved in the anti-doping campaign. In essence, everything that he was saying was less valuable to me or to him than it was to all of the young people who could be subjected to temptation in the future. He looked at me, laughing: 'I'm not sure I'm the right person. I am probably even the worst person. I think you'll be much more credible if you do the talking. Your opinion is much more credible than anyone else's.' He laughed again and added that the only value he could be credited with in the fight against doping was as an example. 'It has been said that the hounding of me serves as an example for others.'

We continued to talk about these issues and then went to dinner at a great Italian restaurant next to the Arc de Triomphe. We talked until one in the morning about his life, about mine, all over a bottle of wine. We also discussed his experiences and his perspective on the current state of the sport in more detail. As I suspected, Lance Armstrong has got a lot of very interesting stories that could put some great riders from the past and some still active now in a very delicate position. As the evening progressed, I became more depressed. While I was thinking about contributions to the fight against doping, Lance kept saying that he was tired with all these stories, that he was tired of fighting, but that he didn't want to do what Floyd Landis had done and denounce others in order to save his skin. There's a ridiculous aspect to that situation. If Lance were to lose all of his money, it seems that Floyd Landis will end up recovering a good deal of it, allowing him a bigger nest-egg than he had before being suspended and sanctioned for doping.

I returned to my hotel with a feeling of relief as if a weight had been lifted off me. I was right to agree to this meeting. As for Armstrong, I understand he went on to have a few more drinks as a way of digesting everything he had just heard.

To be honest, I'm tired of talking constantly about the past, about my problems with Lance Armstrong and Richard Virenque. What I would like now is for people to listen to my position on what is currently happening, because what I perceive is familiar.

When I look at cycling today, I get the impression that history is repeating itself: riders who are supposed to be *rouleurs* are climbing passes at the front of the race, and those who are supposed to be climbers are riding time trials at more than 50 kilometres per hour.

But what strikes me more than anything is the morphology of the riders. To win the Tour, it now seems you have to be very slender and have little muscle. These riders don't look like they could do anything on a bike, but they produce the same power as those in previous generations. All notions about the power-to-weight ratio seem to have been overturned.

As I mentioned above, my current position as regional anti-doping representative, with responsibility for implementing anti-doping controls on behalf of the AFLD, enables me to keep abreast of the latest news about substances that can be used by athletes for doping purposes.

Currently, questions are being asked about the extent to which products such as AICAR, GW501516, TP500 and GAS6 are being used. Some of them have already been found during searches of vehicles and have been used by some athletes, doctors and soigneurs. These substances provide an equivalent effect to EPO, because they improve the performance of the athlete by boosting the transport and utilisation of oxygen by the body.

Their effect is very well known. The combination of AICAR and TP500, for example, increases the number of mitochondria in the muscles. These cells are in a way little energy plants, which transform substrates (carbohydrates, lipids, proteins) into energy through the use of oxygen. These two products also bring about an increase in lipolysis (the breakdown of 'fat' to provide energy). They maintain lipolysis during intense efforts.

To be more specific, when an athlete is riding at 80 per cent of his maximum, in principle he stops burning fat and only burns carbohydrate. By using these products, he can continue to burn fat as well as carbohydrate, even at 95 per cent of his maximum. This additional power, which stems from the use of fat reserves, offers a huge advantage. It is absolutely impossible to achieve naturally. Meanwhile the public can see another effect of the products in the physical transformation of competitors into athletes who don't seem very muscular and are very lean. They have a very low fat percentage because they are able to burn all their fats, including those in muscle fibres, and benefit from an increase in energy.

With regard to growth factor GAS6, this allows the secretion of endogenous EPO. It is completely undetectable.

Meanwhile, directeurs sportifs attempt to put forward rational explanations for the performances of their riders as if chanting a mantra. They talk about intense training, reconnaissance of mountain passes in the rain and the fog, about improvements in equipment ... These arguments have been heard a thousand times before. The story is beginning again, just as it did 14 years ago with Lance Armstrong and his US Postal team, just as it did with the Festina team.

The media and spectators seem more cautious now, even sceptical, but I fear that their desire to dream might end up anaesthetising their critical senses. Like a movie buff entering a dark auditorium, the public wants to believe the spectacle being served up. It wants to be gripped by suspense, by the magic of the images, even if the finale has already been written. We are 'sentimental crowds with a thirst for the ideal', as a French song has it.

When he first said farewell to the Tour on the Champs-Elysées in 2005, Lance Armstrong knew how to play on this sentiment perfectly. 'Finally, the last thing I'll say to the people who don't believe in cycling, the cynics and the sceptics: I'm sorry for you. I'm sorry that you can't dream big. I'm sorry you don't believe in miracles. But this is one hell of a race. This is a great sporting event and you should stand around and believe it. You should believe in these athletes, and you should believe in these people. I'll be a fan of the Tour de France for as long as I live. And there are no secrets – this is a hard sporting event and hard work wins it. So Vive le Tour forever!' In short, not believing in him meant not believing in the Tour. To disparage him meant disparaging *La Grande Boucle*.

He touched a sensitive nerve. The French have a visceral attachment to their Tour. They fear nothing so much as a July without it. 'The Big Buckle' provides them with a flattering image of themselves, a France full of colour and joy, a happy-go-lucky country. So, despite the doubts, they come out onto the roadsides and become vital extras in the spectacle.

So why spoil this pleasure with stories of adulterated urine? It can't be ignored, but you've got to see reason. Doping is part of the sport. It has always existed in the Tour. You cannot cover 250 kilometres, crossing three passes, without chemical assistance. And too bad for Bassons and his peers, those birds of ill omen, who are trying to say that this is not inevitable.

Are the French really that bothered by doping? I don't know. They are the world's biggest consumers of drugs, after all.

So much the worse for those who die prematurely, such as Marco Pantani, the winner of the 1998 Tour, who was found in a squalid bedroom in 2004 after an overdose. I don't think this rider I rubbed shoulders with in the peloton died as a result of doping, as some claim; I think he fell into drug-taking as a substitute for the sporting pharmacopoeia. If there was an addiction on his part, it was to glory. Having been acclaimed on the roadsides, he no longer existed from one day to the next. In my opinion, drugs did nothing more than fill this gap. His dramatic end only adds to the legend of 'The Pirate', some insist. But did these free thinkers ever ask him if death was the fate that he wanted?

My six years within professional cycling's inner circle weren't enough to upset my judgement on the value of things. I have never measured myself in terms of the glory I've had, by making a comparison with the rest of the cycling tribe. I remained one of my sport's small fry, but I was privileged in terms of my insight into Mr Everyman. This enabled me to switch back to the 'civilian world' without feeling any bitterness.

I became a cyclist because I loved the bike. I gained a childish pleasure from pedalling on my machine. I found this same satisfaction within the professional fold, despite the snubs I suffered. When this was no longer the case, I stopped. As an amateur now, I'm even happier that I can identify exactly what I expect of my sport and of my body. I have retained just one certainty from my years of struggle: pedalling is as essential to me as eating and drinking.

Will cycling be able to reassess the effect of previous bad practices one day? Reform requires a change in the governing bodies that oversee the system. In September 2013, the UCI elected a new president, Britain's Brian Cookson. 'My first priority will be to make the anti-doping process fully independent,' he said.

Is this the beginning of a new era, or the continuation of the great carnival? The president is British, while the best team of the moment is also British. After all its Olympic medals on the track, Britain is increasing its grip on cycling. In 2014 the Tour de France will start in England. What is Brian Cookson going to do? Will he promote spectacle or favour sporting integrity? Let's wait and see, as the British say.

Sometimes I get the feeling that defences are being lowered. Use of caffeine is now authorised, as are a certain number of prescriptions outside competition, etc. I am particularly concerned by the Anglo-Saxon attitude towards corticosteroids. They sometimes display laxity with regard to their use, considering them as benign. Permitting their use would be a mistake. 'Corticos' aren't obsolete, a relic of a distant doping past, as some would have us believe. French teams, for example, still use them extensively.

Governments must also take their share of the responsibility and not simply cover themselves in the reflected glory of their athletes as a means of raising national prestige.

I believe it is a mistake for doping prevention to have its focus on the risk to health. In my opinion, this argument is ineffective. Basically, raising an athlete's blood cell count with an injection of EPO if they have become anaemic on a race may be considered a good thing. After all, iron injections are already allowed. This theory of rebalancing is one that some sports doctors are promoting. In their view, they are not doping but treating their riders.

The argument is defensible from a medical viewpoint, but not from an ethical and sporting perspective. I'm not a masochist, but what would sport be without fatigue and pain? They are an indispensable part of it, as much so as performance. Throughout the generations, moments of weakness have added to the grandeur, to the nobility of cycling, certainly as much as breakaways have. The public and the watching fans are as moved by suffering and injury as they are by victories.

What is the best way to foster prevention among young people? Once again, the argument about danger to physical wellbeing cannot work. At the age of 20 who is afraid of dying?

The first step should be for sports educators to stop telling children: 'On Saturday, you must win at all costs.' This is the first incentive to dope. They should say instead: 'Win, but without forgetting who you are.' As I mentioned earlier, it is also vital to instil self-esteem. A great French psychiatrist, Christophe André, explained to me the importance of this characteristic for young people who will soon be adults. I then launched two campaigns on this theme in my region. One shows a teenager with a Post-It note stuck to his forehead that reads 'cheat'. The slogan says: 'A label is sometimes impossible to remove'. The other shows a kid in front of a mirror. The slogan: 'It is sometimes difficult to look yourself in the face'.

As one of those involved in prevention, I play on the need everyone has to be recognised, to be seen to exist as a human being. This does, of course, include public recognition, but also being recognised within a certain group or *milieu* that might encourage individuals to bend their principles to fit the common discourse by, for instance, insisting that they 'do the job the right way', even if they don't feel comfortable doing so. It's a bit like the teenager who smokes cannabis to be part of a group; in the end, this youngster exists as part of the group, but not as an individual.

As for the arguments put forward by the peloton in cycling's defence, there is one that seems perfectly acceptable to me: when it comes to doping, fingers are always pointed at cycling, but the sport doesn't have a monopoly on it. In my position, I can clearly see what is happening in other sports. I have noticed, for example, the routine use of dietary supplements in rugby. Of course, football isn't affected by this scourge … 'There is none of that around here' is the clarion call of its top brass. This blindness is laughable.

Cyclists should be proud of being so highly scrutinised. Cycling is popular. It is the perfect vehicle to bring about the overhaul of sport, because the other disciplines will have to follow it or die. How long did the ancient Olympics survive with all its excesses? If sports are not scrutinised and overhauled, athletes could become like those men in Ridley Scott's film *Gladiator* who had to 'win or die'.

Sports cannot be simply contests without any restraints where the strongest crush the weakest. They must also have a rulebook. Are these ideas outdated or avant garde? I still don't know whether my discourse will end up sounding like the ramblings of an old codger or the words of a slightly deranged prophet. Frankly, I don't care. I know that, for me, this ideal is the only way I can conceive for living my life. And the only way to guarantee my happiness on a bike.

Christophe Bassons is a former professional road racing cyclist. Born in 1974 in Mazamet, France, he turned professional at the age of 22 before leaving the sport just six years later. Today he works for the French Ministry of Sport and Culture to prevent doping. He lives near Bordeaux.

Benoît Hopquin is a French journalist and author. He is a senior reporter for *Le Monde* and is based in Paris.